EARLY SCHOOLING IN THE UNITED STATES

John I. Goodlad
M. Frances Klein
Jerrold M. Novotney

and Associates:
Alice Burnett
Lillian K. Drag
Esther P. Edwards
David Elkind
Judith S. Golub
Else W. Hjertholm
R. Bernice McLaren
Edna Mitchell
Frances Prindle
Judith Ramirez
Lois Sauer
Joanna Williams
Robert Williams

Foreword By
Samuel G. Sava
Executive Director |I|D|E|A|

A CHARLES F. KETTERING FOUNDATION PROGRAM

McGRAW-HILL BOOK COMPANY
New York   St. Louis   San Francisco   Düsseldorf
London   Mexico   Sydney   Toronto

Library of Congress Cataloging in Publication Data

Goodlad, John I
    Early schooling in the United States.

    (|I|D|E|A| reports on schooling. Early schooling series)
    Bibliography: p.
    1. Nursery schools—United States. 2. Education, Preschool—1965–   I. Klein, M. Frances, joint author. II. Novotney, Jerrold M., joint author. III. Title. IV. Series: Institute for the Development of Educational Activities. Early schooling series.
LB1140.2.G577   371.21'0973   73–12311
ISBN 0–07–023763–8

|I|D|E|A| is the service mark for the Institute for Development of Educational Activities, Inc., an incorporated affiliate of the Charles F. Kettering Foundation.

|I|D|E|A| was established in 1965 to encourage constructive change in elementary and secondary schools. It serves as the primary operant for the Foundation's missions and programs in education.

As an institution committed to stimulating constructive changes for the benefit of mankind, the Kettering Foundation believes strongly in the potential of education to help bring about such changes.

Robert G. Chollar

President and
Chief Executive Officer
Charles F. Kettering Foundation

ACKNOWLEDGMENTS

Acknowledgments for permission to use excerpts from copyrighted material include:

Benjamin S. Bloom, *Stability and Change in Human Characteristics*. Copyright 1964 by Benjamin S. Bloom. Used by permission of John Wiley & Sons, Inc.

Jerome S. Bruner, *The Process of Education*. Copyright 1960 by Jerome S. Bruner. Used by permission of Harvard University Press.

Annie L. Butler, *Current Research in Early Childhood Education: A Compilation and Analysis for Program Planners*. Copyright 1970 by D. Dwain Hearn. Used by permission of the American Association of Elementary/Kindergarten/Nursery Educators.

Milly Cowles, "Four Views of Learning and Development." Copyright 1971 by Milly Cowles. Used by permission of the National Education Association.

Martin Deutsch, *The Disadvantaged Child: Selected Papers of Martin Deutsch and Associates*. Copyright 1967 by Martin Deutsch. Used by permission of Basic Books, Inc.

Ellis D. Evans, *Contemporary Influences in Early Childhood Education*. Copyright 1971 by Ellis D. Evans. Used by permission of Holt, Rinehart and Winston, Inc.

Ira J. Gordon, "Parent Involvement in Early Childhood Education." Copyright 1971 by Ira J. Gordon. Used by permission of the National Association of Elementary School Principals.

Robert D. Hess and Roberta Meyer Bear, *Early Education*. Copyright 1968 by Robert D. Hess and Roberta Meyer Bear. Used by permission of Aldine-Atherton, Inc.

J. McVicker Hunt, "How Children Develop Intellectually." Copyright 1969 by J. McVicker Hunt. Used by permission of the author.

Gordon E. Hurd, *Preprimary Enrollment Trends of Children under Six*. Copyright 1970 by Gordon E. Hurd. Used by permission of the U.S. Office of Education.

Lawrence Kohlberg, "Early Education: A Cognitive-developmental View." Copyright 1968 by the Society for Research in Child Development. Used by permission of the Society for Research in Child Development.

Alice Lake, "The Day-Care Business: Which Comes First, the Child or the Dollar?" Copyright 1970 by Alice Lake. Used by permission of The McCall Publishing Company.

Maya Pines, *Revolution in Learning: The Years from Birth to Six*. Copyright 1967 by Maya Pines. Used by permission of Harper & Row, Publishers, Incorporated.

Evelyn Weber, *Early Childhood Education: Perspective on Change*. Copyright 1970 by Evelyn Weber. Used by permission of Charles A. Jones Publishing Company.

CONTENTS

FOREWORD

EARLY SCHOOLING IN THE UNITED STATES

This volume reports on one of several studies of early schooling conducted by the Institute for Development of Educational Activities, Inc. (|I|D|E|A|), an affiliate of the Charles F. Kettering Foundation.

Dr. John I. Goodlad, director of |I|D|E|A|'s research efforts, places the need for this study in context when he refers to "the recent educational discovery of the young child." To those who know something of the history of early childhood education, the adjective "recent" may seem puzzling, but the key term is *educational discovery*.

Until about fifteen years ago, efforts at preschool education were motivated mainly by humanitarian concern for lower-class children left unsupervised for long periods, or by a belief among the upper class that, as Dr. Goodlad phrases it, early education was "not harmful and perhaps useful" for their children. Thus, preschool education was on the one hand a form of welfare and on the other a loosely defined privilege to be ranked with going to the seashore in summer and associating with the "right" families. In neither case did schooling have serious educational significance.

That concept of early schooling has changed. In our time, the work of developmental specialists such as Bruno Bettelheim, Martin Deutsch, J. McVicker Hunt, Benjamin Bloom, Jerome Bruner, and Jean Piaget has won broad assent for the proposition that the early years—those between birth and six—are crucial to the child's development. We have seen a new national interest in preschool education, as evidenced by the federal government's initiation of Headstart, by the opening of many new preschools (some of them profit-making ventures), and by increasing enrollment in private and public school programs below the kindergarten level.

Despite these encouraging signs that we are beginning to take the early years seriously, the mixed results from preschool efforts and the findings from this |I|D|E|A| study indicate that we have far to go before we match our new educational *interest* with a commensurate educational *skill*. We have come to recognize the importance of the early years in human development—but we do not yet know how to design educational programs appropriate for those years.

This lack of knowledge—in addition to the importance of capitalizing on developmental research and translating it into practice—places the study of early schooling in an institutional perspective. In considering possible preschool program directions for |I|D|E|A|, we thought it only sensible to find out what *is* being done—not only in the United States, but in a country with a long history of preschool practice (England) as well as a country with a short history but an urgent national concern (Israel). We inquired into Asian preschool practices because relatively little is known about them and we thought that some interesting variations on western viewpoints and practices might be identified.

Finally, a thorough study of early schooling practices aimed at improving education in elementary schools was considered important to |I|D|E|A|'s Change Program for Individually Guided Education (IGE). This program tries to recognize and accommodate such differences among children as age, emotional maturity, intellectual aptitude, learning style, and all the other factors that distinguish students even in their earliest years. Clearly, the quantity and quality of a child's preschool experience (or lack of it) also required consideration; this study has helped us make judgments that have been incorporated into our elementary school program.

These are reasons for supporting this three-year inquiry—but they are not the reasons for its formal publication. We feel that the study is important on its own merits, beyond its utility to |I|D|E|A|, and that its facts, conclusions, and speculations will reward any educator interested in those crucial years of human development.

Samuel G. Sava
Executive Director
|I|D|E|A|

INTRODUCTION

Among educational researchers and administrative planners, at school board sessions and teachers' meetings, one frequently hears the question, "How should children be educated?" This inquiry becomes almost plaintive as more and more evidence accumulates that what we are doing is not successful and that new ways must be found. Too often, we educators go in search of solutions to our educational enigmas without knowing what we already are doing. In many cases, we do not know what is actually going on in the schools, what the day-to-day practices are, and exactly how our children are being taught. Before coming up with ideas for improvement, it might be useful to find out, first, what is being done now and, perhaps, what seems most to need attention.

Suggestions made about how things ought to be which are not backed up by information about the way things are frequently are doomed to failure or oblivion when implemented in the schools. The first question we must ask if we are to change our schools is, "How are children being educated now?"

The problem is especially significant with respect to the early childhood years. The past decade has witnessed an enormous increase in interest in these years because of our expanding awareness of their importance to the child's later development and achievement in school and society. We are on the verge of a substantial expansion of early schooling which soon may reach and affect almost every child in the United States. Educators ask, "How should these children be educated?" and they are coming up increasingly with ideas for what *ought* to be done. But there is already an extensive array of preschools in this country. Just what are these schools like? How are young children currently being educated in these schools? Here is the base from which we must work. To provide some answers to queries about the realities of early schooling in the United States today is an essential purpose of this volume.

Perhaps an anecdote will serve to sharpen for the reader our conception of bases needed for rational educational improvement. We solicited a position paper to assist us in our portrayal of the state of the art in early schooling. The resulting glowing picture of enlightened schools for the young across the United States clashed incongruously with the picture beginning to emerge from our data about what actually was going on. I drew this to the author's attention, inquiring as to whether she was drawing her conclusions from observations of those experimental, often college-associated centers to which she served as a consultant or from the general run of nursery schools in her city. A chagrined reply came back some weeks later. Spurred by my letter, she reported subsequent visits to local nursery schools in her vicinity, admitting that her work normally did not take her to such schools. What she observed was sobering indeed—a far cry from the exemplar models on which her position paper had originally been based.

Her pre-observation view of the field probably is not unique. There are educators at all levels in the educational hierarchy who should take a look at the grapes before they expound on what would be good for the vineyard.

As Samuel G. Sava points out in the Preface, the Institute for Development of Educational Activities, Inc. has sought insights into realities of practice for nursery schools in England, Israel, and eight countries of Asia. Our intent, however, is not merely to describe existing practices, important as this is. Rather, we seek to present an image of reality from which to project needed reforms. We believe a delineation of the state of the art to be essential if, first, the necessary drive for needed changes is to be created (there must be, in other words, an awareness of need) and, second, specific purpose and substance for expression of this drive are to be found.

Our goals and methods were fashioned roughly after those of policy studies. First, there is identification of a problem area; in this case, the rapid growth of interest in early childhood education and the desire to manifest that interest in some kind of schooling experience for children on a large scale. The development of a few good experimental centers does not begin to meet that demand. Second, we offer an analysis of funded knowledge with respect to the problem area and of practices seeking to reflect that knowledge and, therefore, to be exemplary. This analysis, attempted in Part One, provides a desideratum against which to judge or through which to screen existing practices. Third, there is an effort to get a fix on existing practice, a research activity for which there are few guidelines. Somewhat inexplicably, few such efforts have been undertaken and consequently, little work of a cumulative nature exists. Our sample, procedures, and findings are described in the chapters of Part Two.

Fourth, we present an analysis of the fit between guiding ideas and exemplar practices and observed practices—in this case, in 201 nursery schools in nine American cities. The results of such an analysis reveal strengths and weaknesses and give direction and substance to the fifth stage—recommendations for improvement. Part Three, then, is devoted to this analysis, the identification of needs, and the formulation of recommendations for early schooling. Any sixth step—taking action on recommendations—falls outside the scope of a written report.

To ease for the reader the problem of going through page after page of data, we have summarized most of our findings in a series of tables grouped in Appendix A. Only those tables deemed essential to the reader's understanding are included in the narrative of Part Two, in which the sample of nursery schools is described. The instruments used to gather the data appear as Appendix B. Appendix C is an annotated bibliography of the field of early childhood education in the United States.

In the process of conducting surveys of early schooling in England, Israel, Asia, and the United States, the instruments were developed and subsequently refined. The |I|D|E|A| Nursery School Survey Form which resulted is included in Volume 2 of this series* and may also be requested directly from the |I|D|E|A| offices in Dayton, Ohio.

Many persons involved with early childhood development and education will object to the use of "schooling" rather than "education" in the title of this volume and throughout subsequent pages. Choice of the word "schooling" is quite deliberate. We want to make clear that our concern is with the narrower concept of schools as institutions and the education children receive there, not with the whole of the educational process and the many other agencies and media shaping the young child. We do inescapably become involved with this larger process in discussing at various times what constitutes good

---

* Norma D. Feshbach, John I. Goodlad, and Avima Lombard, Early Schooling in England and Israel, McGraw-Hill, New York, 1973.

education for children, but schools and schooling remain our central foci.

"Early schooling" is defined for our purposes as formal, institutionalized education in schools below the level of the primary or elementary school which begins with kindergarten or first grade. However, this definition encompasses a fuzzy age range. We looked at nursery schools, an institution usually considered to precede kindergarten in the United States. But kindergarten is not uniformly available, so the nursery schools of our sample sometimes included children of five years or older. Likewise, on the lower end of the age scale were to be found some infants and toddlers. We had hoped to be more precise and definitive, but the ambiguities of the field itself prevented us from being so. Nonetheless, when we address ourselves to the data, we are speaking of nursery schools.

Parts of this manuscript were written by the late Esther P. Edwards and also by Judith S. Golub, who in addition contributed significantly to editing the whole. With the exception of Lillian K. Drag, who prepared the annotated bibliography, the others listed as associates collected data on the nine cities, as described in Part Two, and contributed to preparation of the forms used for this purpose. They cannot in any way be held responsible for the manuscript itself and especially not for the conclusions and recommendations, for which I take sole responsibility.

To the many nursery school directors and teachers who assisted us so generously, and to Paula deFusco, Carol Mason, Joan Rydbeck, and Patricia Webber who typed the manuscripts at various stages of preparation, my colleagues and I express sincere thanks. A special note of thanks goes to the Center for Advanced Study in the Behavioral Sciences where I was a Fellow during the year immediately following completion of the research reported here. The Center provided a unique opportunity for reading widely in the field, for reflecting on the data, drawing conclusions, and finally, writing a substantial portion of the manuscript.

John I. Goodlad
Principal Investigator

ONE

SCHOOLING FOR THE YOUNG CHILD

CHAPTER 1

THE YOUNG DISCOVERED

There is evident today in the United States an upsurge of concern for the education of young children. During the past dozen years or so, this concern, with its emphasis on the crucial importance of the child's earliest experiences for the whole of his later life, has come to the forefront in our social, educational, and political thinking to a degree that only recently would have seemed unlikely. Even in the late fifties, when national concern with the processes and products of education began to make themselves felt in new programs and new pressures on the elementary school, preschool pupils and their teachers still formed an enclave apart. A relatively small and often select group, they busied themselves comfortably with finger paints and rhythm bands, juice and crackers, and jungle gyms, well out of the mainstream of educational controversy.

Preschool had been conceived of by all except a handful of perceptive individuals as actually *ante*-education—something before *real* education begins—as the very term *preschool* implies. It was still the era when play was considered the prime medium for the preschool experience. The notion of play as the context of preschool life was not a trivial one for students of early development and education. Parents and teachers were anxious about the integral development of young children but, following the lead of Gesell and others, they believed that formal instruction must await increased maturity. It would benefit a child little to push him too soon into structured learning. Without the essential attainment of necessary maturational levels, what he was taught would in any case not stay with him and might, in the future, even interfere with later learning. What could help him was the chance to unfold—physically, emotionally, socially—in an environment that was warm, secure, and responsive. The young child coming to his first school needed space to play in, large equipment to develop muscular strength and coordination, aesthetic and dramatic experiences, and the chance to find himself as an individual among peers. From these things he could benefit, and within the context of more or less supervised and structured play he would find them. These children did indeed learn and grow. Usually, they successfully made the transition to "real" school when they turned six. They soon began to read and count, to accomplish the expected academic tasks with considerable success. Their preschool experience apparently "worked."

What few people failed to realize in those days, however, was that most of these children came from a background of comfortable homes where literate parents had talked and read to them since babyhood; where music was played and the visual world was observed and discussed; where children were escorted beyond the confines of the home, whether to a nearby supermarket, playground, or zoo or long distances via boat and train. In a very real but then largely unrecognized fashion, these homes supplied palpable cognitive elements in the children's total educational experience. The youngsters needed little additional intellectual stimulation when they arrived at nursery school, for they already were experiencing considerable stimulation at home. Home and school collaborated more, and to better purpose, than generally was recognized.

Most preschools in the fifties were privately run. Inevitably, they drew to them children whose parents could afford to pay their fees. Only a handful of public school systems offered classes below the kindergarten level, and even kindergartens generally were provided only by school systems in the affluent suburbs. Where public kindergartens existed in big-city systems, there were not enough places for all the eligible children. Those who actually had the opportunity to attend kindergarten were those whose parents registered them first: by definition, they were the children of the alert, the aware—those who could read notices and act upon them. The children of the very poor, the disoriented, the non-English-speaking or illiterate, the immigrants from rural areas, were inevitably left out. Yet these were the children who most needed the preschool experience.

Ironically, in the 1950s, one of the screens sometimes used in allocating the limited number of places in kindergarten was tests of readiness. If a child showed up well on these tests, measuring or predicting certain skills presumably related to early success in school, he was more likely to be selected. The tests tended to corroborate family advantage. Only a decade later, thinking had so altered that federal funds were made available to provide preschool learning activities to the very children who would have been excluded by the tests of the fifties.

Before the 1960s in this country, then, educational experience prior to the first grade was largely restricted to the upper- and middle-class child. In this respect, the United States differed from many European countries where early schooling had begun as a response to the pressures and needs brought into existence by the Industrial Revolution. Froebel in Germany in the eighteen-thirties and forties, Montessori in Italy in the first years of the twentieth century, the McMillan sisters in England during and after World War I—all had concerned themselves with the children of factory workers, dispossessed peasants coming to the cities, slum dwellers, the depressed and deprived. The thrust of preschool education had been to meet the needs of these groups. Crèches for babies and toddlers whose mothers must work, health and immunization programs for young children who suffered from rickets and malnutrition, attempts to educate little boys and girls who received no education at home—these had been the strong concerns of preschool educators in Germany, Italy, England, France, and Scandinavia. In Russia after the Revolution, preschool classes had been seen as a means for building the new society, even as they freed mothers to work in field or factory, but in the United States the opportunity to attend nursery school was the prerogative of the relatively well-to-do. Geographical setting played a role as well. For the child on ranch or farm, in the country village or the small city, as well as for the poor child, school began with the first grade.

Of course, there were some nursery classes run by settlement houses, church groups, or other philanthropic organizations in the central areas of the big cities. Some limited preschool education for children of the poor has had a long and honorable history in the United States. It was on the early schooling of poor children, during the era of intense influx of immigrants in the seventies and eighties of the past century, that Froebel's ideas had their greatest impact. Education of the young child had been seen as a vehicle for reaching and influencing immigrant families isolated by language and cultural barriers who were clustering in what were rapidly becoming big-city ghettos. Hull House in Chicago and Henry Street Settlement in New York City were typical of those neighborhood houses in urban centers which offered classes for young children as part of their family services. The teachers were young idealists who taught children in the mornings and in the afternoons visited their charges' homes, where they supplied clothes and shoes, food and advice, and even job counseling and access to medical and psychological assistance. It was their example which was gradually to move the public schools into offering such ancillary services. The public schools had conceived of their role at first as a narrowly academic one and only slowly came to realize that the child who was cold, hungry, ill, or abused was hardly in a position to learn effectively.

But even eighty years later, nursery classes or day care centers of this type were still few in number. They could enroll only a small fraction of the thousands of children who lived in the major urban centers and whose families could spare no money for preschool fees. Very often the basic emphasis of these centers was on the child's physical well-being: they fed him, scrubbed him, rested him, checked his immunization and his nutrition, taught him some table manners and hopefully some improved ways of getting along with his peers. The educational component, as in the middle-class nursery school of the same period, was negligible. Some of the philanthropic operations were excellent, insofar as they went; but some were mere baby-sitting establishments for which the word "school," even in the hyphenated form, "nursery-school," was a misnomer.

During World War II, nursery school classes and child care centers were made available to many children located near war-related industries. Most of these were true learning centers, staffed by experienced teachers and well-supported by federal funds under the Lanham Act. It was clear that "Rosie the Riveter" was not going to get much riveting done unless someone looked after her kids, and since ships and planes were top priorities, funds quickly were allocated and nursery schools were set up. Outstanding among the centers operated in connection with wartime industry were those in two Kaiser shipyards, Swan Island and Oregonship. They were models of comprehensiveness and imaginative concern, meeting most needs of the shipbuilding families. They ran twenty-four hours a day; whatever shift Mom or Dad worked, the children were looked after. For the tired mother coming off work at the end of the day, they provided hot meals which could be picked up with the children and taken home. When new families arrived in Portland, tired and bewildered in a strange city, the centers often looked after the children for several days until the parents could find housing and become settled. Medical care for the sick child, counseling for the troubled parent, a sense of community for the out-of-state family homesick in an intimidating industrial world

—all these were supplied, and more. James L. Hymes, Jr., director of the Kaiser centers, wrote:

> But perhaps the concept most basic to the Kaiser answer is indicated by the name. These are good nursery schools, but they are more: they are Child *Service* Centers. The premise is that if a shipyard family needs help involving children, the Centers should provide that help. No peacetime precept, no *a priori* rule must stand in the way of service to children, to families.[1]

When the war came to an end, the Lanham Act funds soon came to an end, too (1946), and the buildings that had served as nursery schools or day care centers were turned to other uses or stood shuttered and empty. The notion that early schooling should be available as a right to a broad range of children and their families, rather than as a special program for the few (be these the suburban well-to-do or very small groups of the urban not-at-all-well-to-do), had just begun to take hold when it faded to a memory.

A DECADE OF TRANSITION

The late 1950s ushered in one of the most tumultuous decades in American educational history, a period that profoundly influenced views about educating the young child. The testing programs of World War II had revealed academic deficiencies in high school graduates for which the assumed permissive theories of "progressive education" took a large share of the blame. Reform emphasizing the role of academic disciplines, particularly mathematics, the natural sciences, and foreign languages, already was underway when Sputnik (1957) alarmed the American people. Educational change and innovation moved to the forefront of national policy for the ensuing decade.

Curricular Reform and the Bruner Hypothesis

Curricular overhaul, beginning at the secondary school level in selected subjects, spread horizontally to most fields and downward to the elementary school. The aim almost uniformly was to replace accumulations of content, often lacking order and a clear sense of priorities, with a few central ideas and processes affording structure for a field of knowledge.[2] To figure out how to teach children and youth well became exciting, intellectually challenging, and important in a way that it had not been since the heyday of progressive education. Teachers and academic specialists in all the disciplines, who were so often worlds apart, began working actively together, observing what worked in selected classrooms, revising material, throwing ideas away, and starting in again.

Bruner's concise summary of a conference of specialists, meeting at Wood's Hole, Massachusetts, provided some of the rallying rhetoric for curriculum reform and revitalized attitudes toward teaching and learning. The following passage is not one of the more familiar from *The Process of Education*, but it summarizes well the intellectual justification for reform that one was to hear repeatedly in subsequent years:

> ... The curriculum of a subject should be determined by the most fundamental understanding that can be achieved of the underlying principles that give structure to that subject. Teaching specific topics or skills without making clear their context in the broader fundamental structure of a field of knowledge is uneconomical in several deep senses. In the first place, such teaching makes it exceedingly difficult for the student to generalize from what he has learned to what he will encounter later. In the second place, learning that has fallen short of a grasp of general principles has little reward in terms of intellectual excitement. The best way to create interest in a subject is to render it worth knowing, which means to make the knowledge gained usable in one's thinking beyond the situation in which the learning has occurred. Third, knowledge one has acquired without sufficient structure to tie it together is knowledge that is likely to be forgotten. An unconnected set of facts has a pitiably short half-life memory. Organizing facts in terms of principles and ideas from which they may be inferred is the only known way of reducing the quick rate of loss of human memory.
>
> Designing curricula in a way that reflects the basic structure of a field of knowledge requires the most fundamental understanding of that field. It is a task that cannot be carried out without the active participation of the ablest scholars and scientists. The experience of the past several years has shown that such scholars and scientists, working in conjunction with experienced teachers and students of child development, can prepare curricula of the sort we have been considering.[3]

If this sounds more directly applicable to the education of older students than to that of preschool children—and clearly, it does—its relevance to young children was established firmly in what might be called "the Bruner hypothesis" (and this must be one of the most oft quoted educational sentences of the century). "We begin with the hypothesis that any subject can be taught effectively in some intellectually honest form to any child at any stage of development."[4] The importance of this statement lies not in its literal truth, but rather in the fact that school was beginning to be thought of again, after a long hiatus, as primarily a place of instruction where the cognitive powers might be developed; indeed, that learning to think and to know were the most significant occupations of enrollees in school. A belief so powerfully stated, wed to such an overwhelming sense of new excitement by teachers and scholars at all levels, was destined to make its mark on attitudes regarding the earliest years of schooling.

The Bloom Hypothesis

The Bruner hypothesis was a far cry from prevailing ideas of readiness championed especially by Arnold Gesell, but it remained more an intriguing concept than a call to action. Four years later, in 1964, the implications of Bloom's *Stability and Change in Human Characteristics* could not be denied. In what was to become one of the most influential books of the decade, he suggested that up to half the development present by the late teens is attained by the age of four and up to 30 percent more by the age of seven or eight. Even by age four, it may be difficult to change the course of development. The following passages suggest some of the problems of intervention posed by the passage of time in the life of a human being:

> A central thesis of this work is that change in many human characteristics becomes more and more difficult as the characteristics become more fully developed. Although there may be some change in a particular characteristic at almost any point in the individual's history, the amount of change possible is a declining function as the characteristic becomes increasingly stabilized.
>
> Furthermore, to produce a given amount of change (an elusive concept) requires more and more powerful environments and increased amounts of effort and attention as the characteristic becomes stabilized, but change, if it can be produced, must be made at greater cost to the individual. All this is merely to repeat once again a point made throughout this work: it is less difficult for the individual and for the society to bring about a particular type of development early in the history of an individual than it is at a later point in his history. There is an increasing level of determinism in the individual's characteristics with increasing age and this is reflected both in the increased predictability of the char-

acteristic and in the decreased amount of change in measurements of the characteristic from one point in time to another.[5]

Bloom's study involved the careful analysis and evaluation by statistical means of all major longitudinal studies done in the United States up to the early sixties. He investigated many human characteristics, but the mood and concern of the times were such that the central focus was on what he had to say about intellectual development. This made a powerful impact on those already concerned with cognitive development and the education of young children. The crucial material reads as follows:

> ... We may now begin to describe the development of general intelligence. Using either Bayley's correlation data (r^2) or the Thorndike absolute scale (both of which yield essentially the same results), it is possible to say, that in terms of intelligence measured at age 17, at least 20% is developed by age 1, 50% by about age 4, 80% by about age 8 and 92% by age 13. Put in terms of intelligence measured at age 17, from conception to age 4, the individual develops 50% of his mature intelligence, from ages 4 to 8 he develops another 30%, and from 8 to 18 the remaining 20%....
>
> With this in mind, we would question the notion of an absolutely constant I.Q. Intelligence is a developmental concept, just as is height, weight, or strength. There is increased stability in intelligence measurements with time. However, we should be quick to point out that by about age 4, 50% of the variation in intelligence at age 17 is accounted for. This would suggest the very rapid growth of intelligence in the early years and the possible great influence of the early environment on this development.
>
> We would expect the variations in the environments to have relatively little effect on the I.Q. after age 8, but we would expect such variation to have marked effect on the I.Q. before that age, with the greatest effect likely to take place between the ages of about 1 to 5.[6]

This statement provided at once both an explanation for the observed intellectual limitations of children from deprived home settings and a call to action, since, presumably, changed settings in the earliest years would result in changed behavior in school and in adult life. Certainly, programs of early intervention, regardless of their theoretical basis, more closely approximate the timing of stimulation in the good middle-class home, which we know to be a milieu fostering enduring intellectual development from the beginning.

Urban Decay and Socioeconomic Deprivation

When intellectual forces from within and societal forces from without coalesce, educational change frequently results. Such was the case with the highly productive period of the sixties, especially with respect to higher education on the one hand and early childhood education on the other. In fact, the general ferment in education starting about 1957 was so active that the period might well be called "The Education Decade."[7] The impact of ideas such as those expressed by Bruner, Bloom, and others would have been much slighter and developed more slowly had there not been a concurrent rapidly increasing awareness of the implications of urban blight and its accompanying conditions.

Though the latter did not come upon the scene suddenly, full-blown in all their stark reality, we seemed suddenly to be aware of them. The drift to the city had been well under way since Depression days; World War II accelerated it. Affluence for whites in the postwar years provided them the opportunity to move out to the more attractive suburban green. They were replaced in the cities by poor whites and, increasingly, blacks and other relatively impoverished groups unable to pay for the maintenance of public facilities, particularly schools. From 1930 to 1960 the national cost of schooling per pupil rose 331 percent, but the per capita value of taxable property in large cities rose only 97 percent.[8] By contrast, the suburbs were capable of providing better education with comparatively much less strain on the taxpayer. In his *Slums and Suburbs*, James B. Conant, who was then the country's most respected educational spokesman, in 1962 described the inner-city condition as "social dynamite."[9]

It is possible to trace some of the most influential factors converging in the mid-sixties to produce an active commitment to compensatory education for disadvantaged children of preschool age. Research evidence pointed to the importance of early intervention; the Israeli experience with early schooling for immigrant children, the so-called "Oriental Jews," provided a glimpse of the possible;[10] the social climate of the inner city was explosive; black and other minority group leaders were becoming militant and raising strident voices. All this produced a political response in the Economic Opportunity Act of 1964 and the Elementary and Secondary Education Act of 1965, two historic pieces of social legislation.

Started the Kindergarten Headstart

The former created Headstart. The largest project for young children ever backed by the federal government, it combined medical and psychological services with educational services in an effort to prepare children to succeed in school. By the summer of 1965, more than 550,000 children were enrolled in six- or eight-week programs in 2,500 Child Development Centers throughout the country.[11] Since all children eligible for Headstart were from families whose income fell below an established minimum, it was clear that without the program they would not have been in preschool at all. It soon became equally clear, however, that a few weeks or even a full year of compensatory experience before entry into the public schools was not sufficient to bring about enduring developmental gains. Consequently, a second federally financed program, Follow Through, was added to Headstart to give children who particularly needed it a longer-lasting, more coherent series of educational experiences.

For large numbers of disadvantaged children in many areas of the country, no kindergarten classes were available. Since Headstart was designed to take children directly before their first school entry, it naturally replaced all or part of the missing conventional kindergarten year. This meant that a majority of Headstart children already were five. But experience and research alike indicated that for children from severely limited backgrounds this was too late. They could not retain what they had learned in Headstart when they entered "real" school. If the money, time, and energy poured into the Headstart programs were not to be wasted, the federal effort must be extended downward as well. In 1967, Parent and Child Centers were established in some thirty communities as pilot projects.[12] To these centers mothers brought their babies and toddlers and stayed with them to observe the care they received and to be instructed in child-rearing and household skills. Though this program also was largely federally funded, community involvement was stressed, and local attitudes and needs were encouraged to shape each center's procedures in ways appropriate to its locale.

Titles I, III, and IV of the ESEA contributed to early childhood schooling in a variety of ways, but not all their good intentions were fulfilled. A project growing out of Title IV, of particular promise for the improvement of programs through professional research, was born deprived into an environment grown less supportive only two short years after passage of the Act. This was the National Laboratory in Early Childhood Education, created in 1967. The intent was to fund up to ten or twelve university centers, each with a different focus but each committed to include a full span of activity from research to program development to training and dissemination. A coordinated type of collaboration would assure attention to all major aspects of productive intervention and rapid communication of research and programs. Presumably, such a Laboratory would furnish a knowledge base for a national commitment to educating the young.

But funds for realization of these plans were not forthcoming.[13] The debilitating costs of the Vietnam War were taking their toll, drawing resources away from fully implementing the ambitious social legislation of preceding years. The half-dozen or so centers and the headquarters office making up the National Laboratory received only a modest trickle of financial support. Meanwhile, a more ambitious proposal for a nationwide effort in early childhood schooling was championed by James C. Russell of the Educational Policies Commission. The objective was to make available nursery schooling for all four-year-olds, beginning with the disadvantaged and ultimately extending to all children, supported by an annual federal appropriation of approximately four billion dollars. The effort, which proved to be the last of the EPC, failed to get off the ground.

The Education Decade was ushered in, then, with a Russian satellite and ushered out with the United States President who had made its accompanying legislation virtually a personal crusade. One thing that emerges clearly from the period is the shaping impact of federal funding on preschool and particularly prekindergarten education. First-rate scholars were brought into the field and, as we shall see in Chapter Two, from their work there developed considerable theoretical momentum to guide experimentation and practice. On the immediately practical front, a tremendous amount of growth and change in the accessibility of preschool education had occurred, especially during the middle five years of the sixties. In this regard, a 1970 report covering the years 1964–1968 is revealing:

> Throughout this period, a greater percentage of white 5-year-olds were enrolled than non-white 5-year-olds. Yet, during the same period, a greater proportion of both non-white 3-year-olds and non-white 4-year-olds were enrolled than their white counterparts. Although the reasons have not been determined, the disparity for the 3- and 4-year-olds may be partly explained by the greater proportion of working mothers among non-whites and concentration of both Federal and State preprimary programs in the major central cities where higher proportions of non-whites

reside. This same phenomenon is reflected in the more accelerated increase in enrollment for non-whites during the time span. The enrollment of non-white 3- to 5-year-olds rose by 40.5 percent (440,000 to 618,000), while that of whites increased by 20.5 percent (2,747,000 to 3,310,000). As a result, in 1968 the percentage of non-whites enrolled (31.9 percent) nearly equalled the percentage of whites enrolled (33.2 percent). . . . It is noteworthy that the enrollment rates of 3- and 4-year-olds in families whose household head is either unemployed or not in the labor force are higher than those of children of manual/service workers or farm workers. One may conclude that the programs designed to equalize opportunity for children have at least been successful in focusing their efforts on the most disadvantaged. . . .[14]

In brief, two remarkable things had happened in the short sequence of ten years. First, the young had been discovered, educationally speaking. Early childhood schooling no longer was an enclave apart; it had moved into the mainstream of inquiry and practice. Second, the focus of attention came to be placed upon compensatory education for disadvantaged children. In sharp contrast to the mid-fifties, it was now more likely that a precocious child would be denied rather than granted access to one of a limited number of publicly supported preschool places.

SOME RECENT DEVELOPMENTS

There is no doubt that educational activity in general suffered from a reduction in availability of federal monies during the late sixties and early seventies. Supplementary educational centers financed under Title III of ESEA through the states virtually disappeared; the regional laboratories and research and development centers financed under Title IV were reduced in both number and funding. Research funds for early education declined markedly. However, although funds allotted for early schooling were less than they had been, both the interest and growth in preschool enrollments continued.

In the fifties, the focus in preschool education was on providing kindergarten for thousands of children who normally began their school experience with grade one. Nursery schools took in only a privileged few. Today, one of the most rapidly expanding preschool fields is that of the nursery school, enrolling three- and four-year-olds, with the emphasis already shifting to day care for the very young. A dozen years ago, it would have seemed almost bizarre to speak of infants and toddlers in school-like situations, unless traumatic home circumstances made this obligatory. Now, even mothers who have no economic necessity to work, as well as those who must gain a livelihood, are thinking favorably of day care for their very young children.

The U.S. Department of Labor reports that 40 percent of the married women in the United States were members of the labor force during 1970, and of these some 10,200,000 had children under eighteen. About one-fourth of all mothers with children under three years of age held jobs, as did about one-third of those with children between the ages of three and five. This is an enormous number of children whose mothers are not at home, day in and day out. Very often the mother works because she must—there is no father or for some other reason she is the sole breadwinner. But increasingly, middle-class mothers who need not work in order to eat, work to bring in income for the extras, or to meet payments on the house, or because they have professional training they want to use, or simply because it is the thing to do and they want to do it. Someone must look after the young children.

Many children are left with relatives or neighbors on a regular basis for a fee. Some mothers employ baby-sitters; a few, but only a very few, have live-in help. Some children attend private nursery schools (but generally these are available only in urban or suburban areas for well-to-do families). Some hundreds of thousands of children attend Headstart programs, but since these usually are conducted only in the mornings, other arrangements must be made for after-preschool hours. Consequently, thousands of modern Dame Schools have sprung up: friendly, warm-hearted, middle-aged women take little groups of children into their homes and look after them. Since they may charge only a small fee, the temptation clearly is to give minimal food and severely to limit the children's materials. Such well-meaning schoolkeepers typically know nothing about contemporary ideas on education of young children. The ideal is to keep them quiet, neat, well-behaved, and clean—characteristics not necessarily typical of the active, involved, learning child. With rare exceptions, day care in such settings is a custodial operation; a mother is lucky if her child is at least in the hands of a well-intentioned person who is kind and reliable, for many such schoolkeepers are not. Few are equipped to guide those vital early learning years as they ought to be: for growth and discovery, for joy and security.

The need for expanded preschool provision increases as more

and more mothers enter the work force. Some industry-sponsored child care centers offer relatively good care with professionally trained staffs and adequate space and equipment. Sometimes, these services are provided free as a fringe benefit negotiated as part of the labor package; sometimes parents pay a small fee. One such operation is run for children of employees and neighboring residents by KLH, a manufacturer of high-fidelity equipment in Cambridge, Massachusetts. Established in 1968 with a federal grant of $324,000, the program is now operating entirely on funds from KLH, the Massachusetts Institute of Technology, and the Massachusetts Public Welfare Department, with parents paying a portion of the weekly costs. Public funding meets the payments of families on welfare.

Skyland Textile Company of Morgantown, North Carolina, 96 percent of whose workers are women, opened a day care center in July 1969, and credits it with "lowering incidence of employee absenteeism, improving productivity, and attracting and holding a more stable group of workers."[15] Other large companies employing a high percentage of women have initiated or are seriously studying such operations. Numerous universities are beginning to provide them for children of staff, faculty, and graduate students. They are generally subsidized liberally enough so that pennypinching is not a must, unlike the situation of so many of the small proprietary operations, and they can attract competent personnel. Since they often need not break even financially, they can spend the money required for materials, varied equipment, and nourishing food. Their ratio of teachers to children often is set at the federally recommended standard of one adult to four babies or toddlers, one adult to five 3-year-olds, and one adult to eight 4-year-olds.

With inflated prospects of success, commercial day care chains were making their entry into the preschool scene during the late sixties and early seventies. In 1970, *Business Week* reported that, "at least 25 and perhaps as many as 50 companies are now actively in the field," and went on to say: "Not even the Health, Education, and Welfare Department knows who all the entrants are—or who will offer education rather than simply offering parking lots for children."[16]

Market tests discouraged some companies; some were started up and quickly floundered; others are in deep trouble; and some appear to be making a go of it. There are two alternative plans by means of which commercial concerns have gone into the day care market. One is through chains of centers owned and run by a central company, with each center staffed and run by professional and quasi-professional employees. The other is the franchise method, under which individuals purchase each center for a given sum, using the name and format of the parent organization and conforming to its criteria, while assisted in such areas as advertising, accounting, and (supposedly) staff training. Grave questions may be raised about each method of operation, but franchising seems to be the more fraught with possible ills and abuses. Alice Lake described the scene, circa 1970, in *McCall's:*

> Brand-new a year ago, the large-scale day-care business is rapidly gathering steam. A dozen of the biggest companies already operate over 100 child centers in 21 states. But the reality is nothing compared with the promise. Half a dozen companies expect to serve close to 50,000 children by the end of 1971. One outfit alone plans to open 1,000 centers in the next few years, with close to 100,000 preschoolers eventually under a single corporate wing.
>
> A few of the companies intend to run their child-care centers like a chain of look-alike grocery stores, but a majority want to franchise them —to lease their name and know-how to local owner-operators exactly the way Howard Johnson licenses restaurants and Colonel Harland Sanders leases Kentucky-Fried-Chicken stands. The names they have chosen give a hint of what's in store, for although a few are sober (American Child Centers, in Nashville), some are pretentious (Les Petites Académies, in Kansas City), and many are downright cute (Mary Moppet's, in Arizona; Little Shaver's, in Florida and Rhode Island; Kay's Kiddie Kollege, in Florida).[17]

It is clear that operations with such names are geared to catch the eye of the parent who knows little about education or the development and needs of young children by people who are similarly ignorant. Even many businessmen are skeptical of whether commercial day care can function simultaneously as good day care:

> They are not against commercial day care, but they believe franchising is the wrong way to go about it. Conformity to a pat formula is the secret of successful franchising. "You can train anyone to produce a hamburger that tastes the same in California and New York," one business consultant says, "but there isn't any rule book for running a day-care center. It's too complex."[18]

Verifiable statistics regarding total preschool enrollments are hard to come by; available figures vary widely and change rapidly. Often, they confuse more than they help because of failure to clarify whether some or all types of kindergarten enrollments are included or excluded. A 1971 report issued by the National Center for Educational Statistics appears to be making the necessary distinction by defining its population as children enrolled in preprimary programs below the first-grade level, excluding day care centers. It must be assumed, therefore, that 5-year-olds attending kindergarten are included. On this basis, the estimate is that 40 percent of the nation's children between the ages of 3 and 5 were attending preprimary school programs in 1970, in contrast to about 25 percent in 1964.[19]

As one would expect, the highest percentage of enrollment by ages was in the 5-year-old group, the figure of about 70 percent representing only a modest gain from about 60 percent in 1964. Although the percentage for 3-year-olds was only about 13, this represents a substantial increase from approximately 5 percent in 1964. Likewise, the figure for 4-year-olds increased from about 16 percent in 1964 to nearly 30 percent in 1970. As would be expected, the percentage for 5-year-old whites was significantly higher than for blacks in the same age group. Among 3- and 4-year-olds, however, slightly higher percentages of black than of white children were enrolled, reflecting the growing interest in compensatory early schooling for minority group children.

Even if these data are wide of the mark, it is clear that early schooling now encompasses rather large numbers of children, mostly in urban and suburban communities. Interestingly and rather surprisingly, we have very little information regarding the day-to-day operations of schooling in the thousands of installations conducting some kind of educational activity below the level of kindergarten. Descriptions of practices in other countries are becoming available,[20] and in 1970, Weber provided an excellent analysis of both theories and practices in selected experimental centers in the United States, based on first-hand observation.[21] But what goes on in the general run of nursery schools? What kinds of people operate them and what theories do they employ in devising preschool programs? To what extent and in what ways have they been influenced by the ferment in early education?

Answers to these questions are sought in Part Two of this volume. First, however, we look at the legacy of ideas surrounding the educational discovery of young children during the sixties, some of the research behind them, and selected experimentally oriented programs emanating from them. As will be seen, what is described in the following chapter is, in general, a far cry from the broader picture of practice sketched and analyzed in Part Two.

It would be a gross oversight to close the present chapter on the educational discovery of young children without drawing attention to three conclusions emerging with increasing visibility from recent research and practice. First, the school, for any age group, is simply part of the total educational experience, contributing for better or for worse. At best, it can help compensate for home and other environmental deficiencies or enrich an already productive environment outside of school. Second, the very early years are exceedingly formative, setting patterns and directions for much of what will characterize later life. To long-standing interest in early cognitive stimulation have been added concern for a full range of social services contributing to a healthful, sound beginning in life.

These two conclusions lead to an obvious third; that early social and educational services are most effective when joined collaboratively with the home. It is not at all surprising, then, that the political response to early education increasingly leans toward support of comprehensive child care programs of various kinds, beginning with prenatal and even prepregnancy parent education and moving on to child care centers offering health and educational services for family units. "Home Start" enjoys the appeal associated with Headstart just a few short years ago. It would appear that the cradle part, at least, of the old adage, "education from cradle to grave" is about to move from slogan to reality. Other writers have documented how close we are to achieving the second part of the phrase, at least for thousands of senior citizens. Our long-standing concepts of universal education are in process of redefinition.

NOTES

1   James L. Hymes, Jr., "The Kaiser Answer: Child Service Centers," *Kaiser Pamphlets for Teachers,* Portland, Ore., n.d.

2   John I. Goodlad, with Renata von Stoephasius and M. Frances Klein, *The Changing School Curriculum,* The Fund for the Advancement of Education, New York, 1966.

3   Jerome S. Bruner, *The Process of Education,* Harvard University Press, Cambridge, Mass., 1960, pp. 31–32. (Reprinted by permission.)

4   Ibid., p. 33.

5   Benjamin S. Bloom, *Stability and Change in Human Characteristics,* Wiley, New York, 1964, p. 229–230. (Reprinted by permission.)

6 Ibid., p. 68.

7 See John I. Goodlad, "Schooling and Education," *The Great Ideas Today* (edited by Otto Bird), Encyclopaedia Britannica, Chicago, 1969, pp. 101–145.

8 H. Thomas James, James A. Kelly, and Walter I. Garms, *Determinants of Education Expenditures in Large Cities of the United States* (Cooperative Research Project No. 2389), Stanford University, School of Education, Stanford, Calif., 1966.

9 James B. Conant, *Slums and Suburbs*, McGraw-Hill, New York, 1962.

10 See, for example, Moshe and Sarah Smilansky, "Intellectual Advancement of Culturally Disadvantaged Children: An Israeli Approach for Research and Action," *International Review of Education*, vol. 13, no. 4, 1967.

11 Keith Osborn, "Project Head Start—An Assessment," *Educational Leadership*, vol. 23, November 1965, p. 98.

12 Richard E. Orton, "Head Start Moves Down to Prenatal Period," *Washington Monitor*, Sept. 18, 1967, p. 17.

13 The Committee, conducting its work during 1965–1966 under the chairmanship of John I. Goodlad, had been instructed by officials in the Office of the Commissioner, USOE, to plan for support for the Laboratory in the amount of from $5 million to $10 million per year over a period of from five to ten years. In the short period of transition from one commissioner to his successor, the prospect for funds had diminished to zero. The commitment to establish the National Laboratory in Early Childhood Education ultimately was fulfilled, thanks in large measure to the Office of the Commissioner, but at a drastically reduced level of funding.

14 Gordon E. Hurd, *Preprimary Enrollment Trends of Children Under Six: 1964–1968*, USOE, Washington, 1970, pp. 2–4.

15 J. B. Quinn (ed.), *The Business Week Letter*, McGraw-Hill, New York, n.d.

16 *Business Week*, Oct. 31, 1970, p. 50.

17 Alice Lake, "The Day-Care Business: Which Comes First, the Child or the Dollar?" *McCall's Magazine*, vol. 98, no. 2, November 1970, p. 61. (Reprinted by permission.)

18 Ibid., p. 96.

19 National Center for Educational Statistics, *Report on Pre-school Education*, Oct. 20, 1971, p. 8.

20 See, for example, Norma D. Feshbach, John I. Goodlad, and Avima Lombard, *Early Schooling in England and Israel*, McGraw-Hill, New York, 1973.

21 Evelyn Weber, *Early Childhood Education: Perspectives on Change*, Charles A. Jones, Worthington, Ohio, 1970.

CHAPTER 2

THEORY INTO PRACTICE

Let us open our exploration of the nursery school in the United States with a visit to what is perhaps a typical example of the species. The school, in the words of its principal, proudly bills itself as traditional. "Our children are here to play and enjoy themselves, to learn to get along well with others, and to be given the opportunity to develop into warm and happy little individuals," she tells us. "We don't believe in pushing them to learn when they are not ready. There will be plenty of time for reading and writing when they get into first grade."

She invites us to observe a class of four-year-olds. The room is sunny and cheerful, with pictures of animals on the walls and brightly colored tables and chairs. The children are busily involved in various activities. Some are finger painting, some playing with blocks, others with dolls. Two little girls are strutting around in long dresses from the dress-up corner and trying hard not to trip. A group of five is watching the teacher feed the pet rabbit. This done, she comes over to greet us.

Miss Myra informs us that this is free play activity, but that she will now be preparing for juice and story time. Before she can do so, though, Sally, a slight, pretty little girl runs up to complain that Billy is trying to take away her finger paints. The teacher accompanies Sally to the finger painting table where Billy has begun to delve into Sally's equipment. "Now, Billy," she says, "you know that you must not take someone else's things. You have to wait your turn to use the toys if one of the other children is using them. But maybe Sally will be a good girl and share the paints with you if you paint your own picture. You wouldn't mind, would you, Sally, if Billy paints a nice picture like yours?" She hugs Sally, pats Billy on the head, and returns to us. "Billy is at rather a selfish stage right now. I have to remind him constantly not to take things that the other children are using and to share his things with them. I'm sure he'll get over it soon, though."

On her way over to the side of the room to get the juice and cookies ready, she calls on two of the children to help her. Under her direction, they put a cookie at each place and carefully carry the cups to the table. Miss Myra then calls to the children to put their toys away and come and have their juice. Peter, very involved in building a tower with his blocks, does not at first seem to hear. The teacher goes over to bring him to the table.

"Look at my tower," he exclaims. "It's so high it almost reaches to the sky!" "It's very nice," Miss Myra agrees. "But why don't you come and have juice now, and maybe afterward, if you still want to work on it, you can show the other children how you did it. Maybe some of them can help you build it even higher." Peter, rather reluctantly, goes along with her to the juice table.

The children make a pretty tableau sitting grouped around the table drinking their juice as the teacher reads them a story. Twelve are white, three black, and they range in size from little Angela, whose feet barely reach the floor, to Tom, a husky boy almost a head taller. Most seem intent upon the story, though a few wander around the room with their eyes, and we see Peter cast some longing glances at his tower of blocks. But, when the story is finished, the teacher announces that all will now go outside to play for a while and then come back and sing some songs. We leave as the children run out the door to climb on the jungle gym and use the swings. The last thing we see is the teacher settling an argument between two boys who want to use the same swing.

The nursery school class described above is typical of the general practices we found during our study. Certain assumptions are inherent in these practices which can be summarized as follows:

1　Preschool children are not ready or able to learn academic skills such as reading and writing.
2　The important learning for the preschool years is in the emotional and social dimension—learning to get along well with others and adjust to the group and fostering creativity and imagination. Therefore, the teacher concentrates on teaching the children to share, to wait their turn, to cooperate with other members of the group. Finger painting and dress-up encourage self-expression.
3　Development of large muscles and coordination skills are important, and so the children play with blocks, and outdoor equipment for climbing and stretching is made available.
4　The children in the classroom, being the same age, are at the same

stage of development, and therefore a series of activities can be planned for the group which will benefit all. Contained within this, of course, is the desirable goal of preparing the child for group activity.

5   The teacher's role is central. She is warm and supportive and provides social approval. Knowing what children of this age need, she directs their activities into the most profitable channels. She is, in many ways, a mother substitute trying to create in her classroom the atmosphere of the ideal home.

6   Several hours a day spent in such surroundings not only will encourage socialization and emotional well-being but also will provide children with experiences which will contribute to their readiness to learn at a later stage. Thus, one is educating the "whole child." "One should not try to teach specific skills in any organized sequence, but let the child learn from experiences that involve all aspects of his life: his emotions, his relations to other children, his fantasies, his surroundings, his actions. Thus, children are expected to learn color concepts simply by having colored toys around and occasionally hearing the teacher refer to them by color. They are supposed to learn number concepts by playing with blocks. Reading readiness is expected to come from recognizing their first names over their coat hooks."[1]

THEORIES SUPPORTING TRADITIONAL NURSERY SCHOOL PRACTICES

All educational practice, even that which has become ingrained through tradition, has its roots in theory in some form or another, whether implicit or explicit. The physical appearance of a classroom, the activities scheduled, the teacher's attitudes and actions, are all based upon some hypothesis about what a child is, how he develops, and how he learns. The assumptions according to which Miss Myra's classroom operates derive their justification from the maturational theories of Gesell and others.[2]

The child, as seen by the maturational theorists, is a potential adult, containing within him at birth (and determined by his genetic inheritance) the seeds of all he will become, seeds which, given proper sunshine and water, will develop or unfold according to some predetermined pattern of time and sequence. The infant will lift his head when his muscles are physically ready to permit him to do so; and the child will learn to read when his perceptual and motor abilities have matured sufficiently. Attempting to rush any stage of development, whether it be walking or reading, can do no good and probably will be harmful to the child's normal growth.

Part of this general theory contends that very little acquisition of cognitive skills occurs during the preschool years. The child has not yet developed sufficient motor control to make possible activities such as reading and writing and is, at this time, exercising control over his large muscles. The desired learning taking place at this time is of a social and emotional nature. The. child goes through reaching and grasping stages and must also learn to let go, both in the literal sense of learning to share and participate in group activities and in the figurative sense of becoming independent of his mother. The best environment which can be provided for him at this juncture will give him plenty of opportunities to practice these physical and emotional skills and to let them develop according to his own inner schedule.

Gesell's theory of child development, whereby many of the current parent generation were raised, is based upon observation of children and emanates from a long and respected tradition—Darwin providing a model of evolution by orderly stages and G. Stanley Hall applying the stages of evolution to the individual members of a species according to the hypothesis that the development of the individual "recapitulates" the development of the species and thus unfolds in an ordered sequence. Miss Myra's reference, along with many parents, to the "stage" Billy is going through springs directly from this tradition. Billy is simply at one station on his road to maturity; he will depart for the next in due time.

Viewing child development in this manner is, in many ways, very comfortable. The children in the classroom we observed were, for the most part, happy, contented, and busily engaged in the "business" of childhood. "At best, these theories produce a special atmosphere of joy and well-being, from which the children come home all aglow, as after a good party."[3] It is reassuring to know that if we love and nourish the child, protect him from danger, and allow him to grow at his own natural pace, he will become a "learner" when he is ready and will be prepared to become a decent and responsible member of society.

WHEN TRADITION FAILS

However, children were not always learning when the maturationists said they should be ready to do so. In the late fifties, as described in

Chapter 1, an increasing outcry was heard that the schools were failing, that children were not being equipped to function in an increasingly technological society. In addition, there was the conspicuous widespread failure in school of children from inner-city minority backgrounds—the so-called "disadvantaged." Unless one were prepared to write off an entire segment of American society as "naturally" unfit, a new way of looking at early childhood development had to be found, a way which could provide an explanation of the difference between the advantaged and disadvantaged and that would at the same time offer some hope for amelioration of the disadvantaged condition.

Deutsch has pointed out the dilemma of the disadvantaged:

> The children most in need of help are from the economically and socially marginal and quasi-marginal segments of the community. These groups are the ones most caught in the technological and social changes; in many of our metropolitan areas they are becoming the majority of the center city population. It is in these groups that we find the highest proportion of unemployment, welfare support, and broken families. And it is in their children that we see the highest proportion of learning disabilities and school dropouts. While in the past it was possible to absorb most of such youth in unskilled, low-paying jobs, now the current adult generation is increasingly being replaced in such jobs by machines. With the number of unskilled and semiskilled jobs decreasing, in order to find any place in the job market youth must now learn more complex functions, for which a successful educational experience is a prerequisite. This is a central problem for the total community, and a challenge for education.[4]

As evidenced by Headstart, it was to early childhood schooling that the decade of the sixties turned for solutions to this problem. A model for such a program already existed in the preschool classroom that we observed at the beginning of this chapter. Perhaps the answer was simply to open the doors of schools such as these to the children of the slums as well as to the middle class. However, both empirical evidence and emerging educational theory indicated that this "solution" would be incomplete and inadequate.

In the first place, the maturational theory of Gesell was based on careful study of children at the Yale Clinic. This small sample was composed overwhelmingly of the children of university staff—children of middle-class, highly educated parents who most probably provided for their children the "ideal home" mirrored in the nursery school classroom. From this vantage point, Gesell and his followers generalized a description of the development of all children. However, as Deutsch points out, the home environment of a slum child is vastly different from this ideal:

> ... There are crowded and dilapidated tenements ... in a more-or-less segregated community. There are likely to be extremely crowded apartments, high rates of unemployment, chronic economic insecurity, a disproportionate number of broken families, and ... continual exposure to denigration and social ostracism of varying degrees. The educational level of the adults tends to be quite limited. In the homes, there is likely to be a nearly complete absence of books, relatively few toys, and, in many instances, nothing except a few normal home objects which may be adapted as playthings. In addition ... there is a great deal of horizontal mobility. The result is a pattern of life that exposes a child to a minimum of direct contacts with the central channels of our culture. The conditions of social inequality, the absence of an accessible opportunity structure, and the frequent nonavailability of successful adult male models create an atmosphere that is just not facilitating to individual development. Moreover, the everyday problems of living, particularly those of economic insecurity and a multiplicity of children, leave minimal time for the adults who may be present to assist the child in exploring the world, to reward him for successful completion of tasks, or to help him in the development of a differentiated self-concept.[5]

Secondly, new interpretations of child development (and those which were not so new but were just then gaining wide acceptance) questioned the idea that readiness for cognitive learning emerges from the child's natural development without intervention. The environment and family interaction of the typical middle-class home was perhaps itself an important intervention in the development of the child and one which could be duplicated outside the homes where it was lacking. These cognitive theories of development, which will be discussed in more detail below, could find justification in two learning models which viewed the environment as the determinant of what was learned and how it was accomplished, rather than a preexistent inner "seed" which naturally unfolded into bloom. The earlier of the two models was the stimulus-response pattern of learning hypothesized by Skinner and other behaviorists. They looked upon man as passive until acted upon by stimuli from outside his neurological system: physical drives and needs; sensory cues from the environment; and later on, secondary, learned drives. Trial and error was the original paradigm of learning. Having made the correct choice in a given situation by chance and having been rewarded by a favorable outcome, the individual was more apt to decide in the same way again, thus building up associative bonds. The complex attainments of adulthood were the result of long chains of such bonds. In this model, the human brain could be compared to a telephone switchboard with certain stimuli automatically leading directly to certain responses.

The second of these learning models was postulated by Donald O. Hebb, who in 1949 published *Organization of Behavior,* in which he offered a theory of human cortical development which amplified the behaviorists' simple, direct telephone-switchboard concept of the human brain into a vastly more convoluted and complex set of connections, by which a degree of voluntary, rational control by the individual of his own thinking processes became a respectable hypothesis. Instead of man being passively acted upon by external stimuli alone, Hebb proposed that his conscious intellectual life was the product of two streams of energy fusing, each affecting the other. Stimuli from the world outside, transmitted through the senses into the sensory cortex and thence into the entire neurological system, are, of course, an essential part of the whole process; but these meet and harmonize with the individual's "autonomous central processes," the inner energy of psychic life, continuously welling up within him, part of the very core of his life and independently active so long as that life endures. Hebb formulated two distinct phases in human learning. There was the characteristic learning of the infant and very young child, which was basically acquisition of the meaning of his perceptions: how to recognize, interpret, and respond to color, form, sound, distance, texture, and all the rest. This was a foundation task for all future intellectual development, and it began with, if not before, birth. Internally, this sort of learning resulted from the formation of many neurological connections between sensory and motor neurons. Most of these are highly complex, as many cells, lying all over the cortex, are built into a "cell assembly" such that the reaction to a perceptual stimulus becomes something far more intricate than the direct telephone line connection.

Once basic cell assemblies are established, later learning consists of the creation of new connections between those already in existence. These insights into the relationship between phenomena comprise a very rational kind of learning and offer a more personal and self-directed view of man than does the mechanistic interpretation proposed by the behaviorists.

Hebb had thus provided a theory which afforded several essential prerequisites for the arousal of interest in cognition, which was to vitalize American psychology in the next years. He provided a reasonable basis for belief that man was active in his own thinking and learning. He offered a model of early learning based on sensory stimulation repeatedly activating certain groups of cells and causing physiological changes which established neural pathways—learning that arises from repetition gained through appropriate experience. His model of later learning emphasized rationality. Early learning had constructed the neurological analogues of conceptual frameworks, and now mature learning intercombined these freshly in essentially symbolic ways. He saw the infant's and the young child's experience as vital to all that he could become and could come to know in later life, because it established, made possible, but also limited the ground of all learning. Hebb's work contributed to the intellectual climate of the time. Research in neurophysiology, in learning theory, in instructional theory was stimulated and is still lively and strong. This, too, was bound in time to affect profoundly what was considered good school practice for young children.

Thus, the conceptual and theoretical lines of division are drawn. On one side are the Miss Myras, loving the children, making them happy, preserving their normal childhood, making possible their "natural" development, and protecting them from the "vultures of experimental education poaching on this tender territory, forcing advanced curricula. . . ."[6] This position "holds that readiness is a phenomenon determined by the child's own rate of development, that academic pressure adds burdensome pressures upon the child, and that one of the prime aims of the nursery school is to foster self-expression and creativity."[7] The child's socioemotional development is the main concern. On the other side stand those who are anxious to activate the potential of the early childhood years for learning—both in order to negate a disadvantaged environment and to offer to all children the joyous experience of learning, whether it be in school or throughout life. They maintain that "early stimulation results in superior achievement without negative personality or social effects, that we have underestimated the abilities of our children, who can learn faster than we now have them learning, and that children's creative as well as intellectual energies should be channeled more appropriately."[8] Deutsch summarizes the view of these "vultures":

> The overgeneralized influence on some sections of early childhood education of the emphasis in the child guidance movement upon protecting the child from stress, creating a supportive environment, and resolving emotional conflicts has done more to misdirect and retard the

fields of child care, guidance, and development than any other single influence. The effect has especially operated to make these fields ineffective in responding to the problems of integrating and educating the non-white urban child. These orientations have conceived of the child as being always on the verge of some disease process, and have assigned to themselves the role of protecting the child in the same manner that a zoo-keeper arranges for the survival of his charges. Too frequently a philosophy of protectiveness that asks only about possible dangers has prevailed over any question of potential stimulation of development. ... The child is a far healthier and stronger little organism, with more intrinsic motivation for variegated experience and learning, than the overprotectionists have traditionally given him credit for.[9]

THEORIES SUPPORTING NEW PRACTICES

As was stated earlier, educational practice finds its justification in theories of child development and learning. Considerable support for the stress on cognitive learning in early childhood schooling is lent by the work of Jean Piaget.

Like Gesell, Piaget sees the development of a child as taking place in sequential stages. These stages, however, do not consist of the outward expressions of predetermined inner attributes and physical maturation, but rather of different forms of interaction with the environment. Growth is a process of exploring, manipulating, adapting, and assimilating the environment, and the child goes through various stages in the process in the attempt to integrate or organize what is observed (referred to as *assimilation*) and to cope with and adapt to the outer reality (*accommodation*).

Cowles sums up Piaget's theory of development as follows:

> According to Piaget, the child is born with a set of sensorimotor operations (or responses) to perform upon his environment in order to "know" it and himself. As a result of these transactions, and physiological maturation, the original sensorimotor operations are: (a) built into increasingly more complex patterns; (b) internalized so they can be carried on mentally; and (c) tied to language symbols and language systems.
>
> This development takes place on a continuum of three main hierarchical stages: the sensorimotor, in which the physical environment is acted upon directly; the concrete operations stage, in which classes of objects and actions are formed, mentally related to each other, and represented in language; and the stage in which formal operations are performed upon the classes and series of the second stage with the addition

of hypothetical-deductive thinking and problem solving. The main mechanism for this process is cognitive dissonance, or the confrontation of discrepancies between the child's current conceptions of aspects of the world and input that does not fit. If there is an event which he cannot assimilate to his existing mental structures, he must accommodate those structures to it. This mechanism is called by Piaget "equilibration."[10]

Piaget thus describes the early childhood years in terms of the learning which takes place during that time. The child evolves through stages of "knowing," and his experiences and interactions with the environment and with other people are extremely important determinants of his competence in cognitive and intellectual functions. Logical thought is a product of these interactions with the environment, and when they are severely limited in number and variety, development of logical thought processes will be retarded.

This point of view has very different implications for preschool programs from those of Gesell's maturational theory. The focus of the early childhood years can no longer remain solely on fostering social development and emotional well-being. It can no longer be claimed that "learning" must be put off until the elementary school, because Piaget has shown the significance of the preschool years for the acquisition of those skills which are felt to be so necessary for school achievement. Also, Piaget has furnished the justification for intervention programs which seek to manipulate the child's environment in order to provide the kinds of experiences necessary to insure that the child will proceed successfully through the stages of cognition.

Burgess has pointed out five direct implications for early childhood education which can be derived from Piaget's work:

1. The importance of sensorimotor experience is underlined.
2. Language, especially that which relates to labeling, categorizing and expressing, is intimately tied to developing greater facility in thinking.
3. New experiences are more readily assimilated when built on the familiar.
4. Repeated exposure to a thing or an idea in different contexts contributes to the clarity and flexibility of a growing concept of the thing or idea.
5. Accelerated learning of abstract concepts without sufficient related direct experience may result in symbols without meaning.[11]

The third corollary above is perhaps most closely associated with the problem of school failure among disadvantaged children. Although Piaget states that children learn through equilibration—the resolution of dissonance between what they have assimilated before and the new situation that confronts them—he has observed also that too great a discrepancy will lead to frustration caused by the child's inability to cope with such large differences. It is necessary to fit the experiences presented to the child to what the child has already experienced. This has been referred to as the problem of the "match." Miss Myra's classroom, patterned as it is after the ideal middle-class home, may match very closely the previous and present experiences of the middle-class students in her class. Whether such a classroom environment would also be useful in dealing with a disadvantaged child is highly questionable. Therefore, the early childhood educator must re-examine the environment and procedures of the traditional nursery school because, as Hunt points out, "the coded information stored in culturally deprived children from lower-class backgrounds differs from that stored in children with middle-class backgrounds. This difference makes it dangerous for middle-class teachers to prescribe intuitively on the basis of their own experiences or of their experiences in teaching middle-class youngsters."[12] In this connection, it should again be noted that the theory upon which Miss Myra has based her procedures was derived from the study of middle-class, advantaged children.

Piaget's work provides a theoretical foundation for emphasizing cognitive development in the preschool years. Evidence from other sources has reinforced this conclusion. Bloom's study, discussed in Chapter 1, pointed to the preschool years as the time of most rapid growth in intelligence and to the importance of the early environment in encouraging this development. He also suggested that intervention to alter a characteristic would have the most marked effect if it were brought to bear during the period of most rapid growth. Thus, early childhood schooling should be prepared to intercede so as to change or enrich the environment when necessary in order to foster cognitive development in the preschool years.

Further support for the stress on the child's cognitive growth during early childhood is proffered by the work of Hunt. Perhaps his most important contribution to the field is hope. If one subscribes to the maturational theory and holds that a child's development and intellectual ability are genetically determined at birth, it would seem rather futile to pour a great deal of money into compensatory education, which at best could do nothing to affect the child's growth and at worst could do irreparable harm by pushing the child beyond his natural pace. This concept implies that intelligence, or IQ, is fixed at the moment of birth and is not to be modified by environment or education. Hunt, however, "integrated classical and new data from the study of intellectual development and its measurement in ways that permit a reinterpretation of the concept of intelligence."[13] Rather than being viewed as a fixed quantity, intelligence could be defined as "a network of central neural processes and information processing strategies, the quality of which is affected significantly by the kinds of encounters a child has with his environment."[14] Accepting the idea that the limits of an individual's intelligence are fixed by his genes, Hunt nevertheless maintained that it is environmental factors which determine whether these limits will be reached. Again, his work pointed to the importance of the preschool years as a time to intervene to promote children's intellectual development, especially when their disadvantaged milieu is likely to cause retardation. Hunt has said that "so long as it was assumed that intelligence is fixed and development predetermined, the intellectual inferiority of children from families of low educational and socioeconomic status had to be considered an unalterable consequence of their genes. With the changes in our conception of man's intellectual development, . . . there emerges a hope of combating such inferiority by altering, for part of their waking hours, the conditions under which such children develop. The question is 'how'?"[15]

"But," goes the counter-argument, "children are not ready to learn before the age of six. They don't have the eye-muscle coordination to enable them to learn to read, nor do they have a long enough attention span to learn the required concepts. Also, these years should be a time of happiness and play, not of arduous work." However, since the turn of the century, the children taught by Maria Montessori and her followers offer support to the interventionists.

YOUNG CHILDREN CAN LEARN: THE MONTESSORI METHOD

The Montessori method begins with careful study of the nature of the child. The principles which Dr. Montessori discovered during her years of working with children directly are to control all aspects of the child's world when he is in a Montessori classroom—the atmosphere, physical set-up, materials provided, and the teacher's activities.

The method is based on the fundamental idea that children are different from adults: "The child is in a state of continuous and intense transformation, of both body and mind, whereas the adult has reached the norm of the species."[16] His concentration, his interests, the things that motivate him are all different from those of an adult. Further, the child is essentially inner-directed, and his activities have little reference to external goals or standards. This is what makes it so difficult for a teacher to prescribe what a child should be doing at any given time and thus leads to a second principle: The child should be given liberty to select his own activities—"education by self-activity . . . in a prepared environment."[17]

The key words here are "prepared environment." "For Montessori, a spontaneous natural process of education is primarily a function of learners acting upon their environment—it is not something a teacher does to a child."[18] It was Montessori's belief that the child, allowed the opportunity, will select an activity which is right for him at that time and will stay with it as long as is necessary to master the principles involved. In addition, children *enjoy* repetition and actually maintain a much longer attention span than do adults if they are engaged in something which interests them. Therefore, she designed a series of materials of the type that children enjoy—blocks, beads, tracing and drawing paper and pencils, rods, bells, and so on. Each item was designed so that the child, when using it correctly, would learn directly from the activity. Each deals with only one principle at a time; for example, a set of blocks intended to teach color differentiation is identical in every aspect—size, shape, and texture—except for color. However, some activities are meant to serve more than one purpose. For example, cylinders of different widths, which sharpen visual perception of sizes, are fitted into their proper holes by means of grasping a knob at the top of each. The knob must be held with the thumb and first two fingers the way a pencil will later be positioned for writing.

Major emphasis is on sharpening the senses, since Montessori believed that all learning has a sensorimotor base, and "acquisition of knowledge rests upon the development and refinement of motor and perceptual skills."[19] Bells teach gradations in sounds, differences in texture are learned by stroking sandpaper tablets, and the eye is trained to take in differences in all dimensions—size, shape, width, height, color. There are even activities which heighten the sense of smell. In addition, manipulating the materials provides practice in muscular coordination and motor skills. The exercise in sensory discrimination and muscular control leads directly to accomplishment in the skills of reading and writing.

The teacher's role in a Montessori classroom is to prepare the environment so that a child can teach himself. This means making sure that all requisite materials are available and in their place for the children's use. When a child has indicated interest in an activity, the teacher demonstrates the proper way to use the material and then offers further assistance only when the child requests help. Instruction, for the most part, is carried on by other members of the class. A single nursery classroom in a Montessori school will include children from three to six years of age, permitting the older children to instruct and help the younger and giving the younger children examples to follow.

Evans calls the Montessori method the "first truly systematic attempt to educate children under six years of age."[20] Some children taught according to its principles are reading and writing at the age of four and a few even earlier. Traditional early childhood educators have invoked the sweatshop image for schools emphasizing academic skills at this tender age. However, as Hunt points out, Montessori "based her teaching methods on children's spontaneous interest in learning."[21] Nancy Rambusch, a moving force behind the Montessori revival in the United States in the 1960s, "criticized nursery and kindergarten teachers who, when they see a child eager to begin reading at three or four, reroute him into bead-stringing and block play because they believe he is not ready to learn." She wrote, "What does it merit a five-year-old to *read*, one is told, if he doesn't *jump* satisfactorily? These teachers find repugnant the notion that children actually derive pleasure from the exertion involved in what is to them 'work.' "[22]

Even within Miss Myra's classroom, some confirmation for this view of the child's nature can be found. Peter has become so preoccupied with his work with the building blocks that he does not want to leave them even to have juice and cookies. Although the teacher implies that because of his short attention span he will forget about his tower ("... afterward, if you still want to work on it..."), Peter keeps looking at it throughout the story period and would surely rather be back with his blocks than where he is. Nursery school teachers have always spoken of the child's inability to concentrate for long periods of time. Montessori would point out that it is perhaps the fault of the activities that have been selected for the children rather than an attribute of the children themselves.

NURSERY SCHOOL PROGRAMS WITH A COGNITIVE EMPHASIS

Even among educators who agree that the early childhood years should be a time to intervene to promote cognitive learning and ability—especially among the disadvantaged whose early home environment fails to provide experiences which encourage such learning —there is little agreement as to the form such intervention should take. Experimental and research-oriented programs with cognitive emphasis presently range from those employing direct instruction in specific skills to those which are only slight modifications of the traditional nursery school program.

Direct Instruction: Bereiter and Engelmann

The work of Bereiter and Engelmann at the University of Illinois at Urbana is an example of the direct instruction approach. In aiming their study toward the disadvantaged child, the two educators began with a pair of major premises:

1. Mere enrichment of experience is not sufficient to enable the culturally deprived child to overcome his backwardness in skills necessary for later academic success. . . . For this reason we were led to reject the approach of the typical nursery school, which appears to be based upon mimicry of those aspects of the culturally privileged home environment which are deemed significant for intellectual and personality growth. A more fruitful approach appeared to be that of selecting specific and significant educational objectives and teaching them in the most direct manner possible, as is done in the intermediate and secondary school grades.

2. The outstanding deficiencies of culturally deprived children are in the area of language. Language covers such an enormous territory, however, that setting up language development as an objective for preschool education narrows the field hardly at all. The field can be narrowed considerably by separating out those aspects of language which mainly serve purposes of social communication from those aspects which are more directly involved in logical thinking. The former include lexical terms—nouns, verbs, and modifiers—and idiomatic expressions. The out-

standing feature of the latter aspect of language is the manipulation of statement patterns according to grammatical and syntactical rules.[23]

Children attend the Bereiter-Engelmann preschool program for two hours each day. Three twenty-minute periods daily are devoted to small-group instruction. Groups of five children with a teacher intensively drilling according to a carefully formulated set of instructions work successively on language, reading, and arithmetic. The language teaching emphasizes linguistic structure: categorization ("Trains, automobiles, bicycles are all vehicles"), the use of the negative ("This is *not* a spoon"), the truth-testability of statements, and so on. Definite goals are set up in each area which the children are expected to reach, for only through such goals, meticulously thought-out and achieved sequentially, can the preschool accomplish the task of bringing the disadvantaged children up to a level necessary for later success. Direct instruction is the mode used to give the children mastery of each step. The teaching is quick-paced, high-pressured; children are encouraged to shout out their answers as a means of discharging some of the tensions created by the program's demands.

> The school as a whole is run in a highly task-oriented, no-nonsense manner. Full participation of all children in the learning tasks is treated as a requirement to which the children must conform (much like the hand-washing requirement in a conventional nursery school) rather than as a developmental goal toward which the children are allowed to progress at their own rate. Emphasis is placed upon effort, attention, and mastery, but not upon competition, as is so damagingly done in many of our more achievement-oriented elementary schools. It may be mentioned in passing that the morale and self-confidence of the children appear to be very high and that there are relatively few signs of psychological stress.[24]

Bereiter and Engelmann conceive of their program as a means for enhancing learning in certain very specific key areas in order to provide children who would otherwise fail in school with the means for success. The proper evaluation of this project concerns itself with whether these objectives have in fact been reached, and test results have demonstrated that, at least on a short-term basis, they have been. Results of a follow-up study have indicated, however, that despite the initial skills the children possessed as they entered first grade, they had not been able to maintain the advances they had made, and within the public school setting had slid back until they were then (three years later) largely doing poor or failing work.[25] This problem of not maintaining early gains in specific learning areas has plagued educators throughout the world.

The Bereiter-Engelmann "structural pedagogy"[26] method has been called the "pressure-cooker approach."[27] Instruction carried out in a series of rapid-fire shouts on the part of both teachers and students has led to comparison of the classroom atmosphere to a marine corps drill.[28] The material to be learned is treated as a foreign language (whether it be language structure, reading, or arithmetic), no prior knowledge on the part of the student is assumed, and no provision is made for individual differences in ability, learning style, or earlier experiences. The pace, the material to be presented, and the manner of its presentation are decided in advance by the teacher and the curriculum. These facets of the program have led many cognitively oriented critics to question the approach in the light of Piaget's work.

The Environment as Teacher

The Montessori method of instruction fits more easily into Piaget's formulation. The child in choosing his own activity presumably will select one which will provide the appropriate degree of dissonance at that particular time. The activities, however, are intended to be undertaken in a predetermined sequence, since each builds upon or expands a skill learned in the preceding one. The child's liberty comes in deciding when he wishes to undertake an activity, how long he will spend with it at any one time, and when he will go on to the next. In schools true to Montessori, the teacher will never interfere to urge a child to move on to the next step or to abandon an activity he is involved in, but if the student attempts to work with material for which he theoretically is not yet ready, she will gently lead him into choosing something more suitable for his abilities at the time.

The Montessori method is, in many ways, highly structured, with its programmed sequence of activities and insistence that there is only one correct way to use each of the materials. Many critics have asked if the method really allows for individual differences since the prescribed order of activities might not be optimal for every child. Others have accused the system of being a way to "individualize conformity."[29]

Other criticisms of Montessori have focused on the lack of emphasis on verbalization and language development. When a child indicates a readiness to undertake a new activity, the teacher demonstrates the proper use of the material. She does not "teach" in the accepted sense of the word, since she does not explain any of the *principles* involved. The child will learn by inferring principles through repeated manipulation of the material. In her demonstration, the teacher uses as few words as possible, limiting herself to naming the equipment and stating what she is about to do. Since, as Bereiter and Engelmann have pointed out, verbal skills are very undeveloped in the disadvantaged child, this might be a serious shortcoming in an intervention program based strictly on Montessori precepts.

An attempt to remove the structuring so objectionable to many in the Bereiter-Engelmann program and present even in Montessorian "liberty" is a teaching method such as O. K. Moore's Talking Typewriter. Pines describes it as follows:

> This method consists of letting the child teach himself skills in his own way, without adult interference. In principle, at least, the child always takes the initiative. The environment—both man and machine—simply responds in certain ways, depending on what the child has done. This means that no two programs are alike—each child faces puzzles that are programmed just for him, and that keep changing as he goes along. He never needs to please an adult, or to achieve anything. But if he keeps at it, he gradually makes a series of interlocking discoveries about sounds, words, and sentences, much in the way that young children learn to talk.[30]

The New Nursery School: A Synthesis of Practices

Perhaps the most successful projects stressing cognitive achievement are those combining aspects of various methods. An example is the New Nursery School at Greely, Colorado. The program has a definite cognitive emphasis and was designed to meet the needs of Spanish-speaking children whose older brothers and sisters had encountered difficulty and failure in school. Nimnicht, the director, was very anxious, however, not to interfere with the child's natural pace, since many new problems could be created by pushing a child beyond his ability. Butler describes the school as follows:

> The New Nursery School is organized as an autotelic responsive environment. An autotelic activity is done for its own sake rather than for obtaining rewards or avoiding punishment that have no connection with the activity itself. A responsive environment satisfies the following conditions: (1) It permits the learner to explore freely. (2) It informs the learner immediately about the consequences of his actions. (3) It is self-

pacing, i.e., events happen in the environment at a rate determined by the learner. (4) It permits the learner to make full use of his capacity for discovering relationships of various kinds. (5) Its structure is such that the learner is likely to make a series of interconnected discoveries about the physical, cultural or social world.

The teachers are a part of the responsive environment and therefore respond to the child. The teachers do not "teach"; they facilitate the child's learning. A child is not asked to give up an activity to do something else, nor does he have to be part of any group activity.[31]

It is clear that the guiding principles of the New Nursery School are based closely upon Montessori. There is no predetermined sequence of activities, however, and each child, in effect, designs his own program. A variation of the Talking Typewriter is one means that is used, and many Montessori-style materials also are available.

Despite the stated emphasis on the individual child selecting his own activities, the program also utilizes group sessions intended to teach certain basic concepts in much the same way as the Bereiter-Engelmann curriculum was devised (although the teaching styles are not at all similar). Weber observed "very didactic group times where the learning of concepts of color and size, or same and not same, or sound perception form the objectives."[32]

One of the rules stringently observed within the New Nursery School classrooms is that a conversation with the teacher can be initiated only by the child, in order to insure that verbalization will always be on a subject of interest to the child. This seems to imply that the teachers will be rather withdrawn and verbal communication would remain at a minimum (and, indeed, Weber observed such an atmosphere at times), but the Nimnicht system differs from the Montessori in that certain times of the day are set aside for purposes of stressing verbalization and language. When the children are playing outside or carrying out several indoor activities such as sponge-painting or dropping colors into water, they are "subjected to a kindly, but constant verbal bombardment. The nearby teacher puts into words the motor activities of the children.... During outdoor play the teachers continuously verbalize a child's activities."[33]

INFLUENCING AND CHANGING THE BEHAVIOR OF THE YOUNG CHILD

We believe that the preschool years should be a time of learning and that to consider them a time of mere socioemotional growth serves only to condemn some children to failure in school and to rob others of their most productive and receptive years, to waste the time when they most want to learn. There is no one "right" program for these years. Each of the methods which has been briefly described here has it strengths and weaknesses. The problem now is to match the program to the child, to find the optimal combination of direct teaching, liberty, individual and group work. Young children can and should learn; as Hunt said, the question is "How?"

Other implications are contained in the idea that the child is malleable, that intervention is possible during the early years to influence his development positively. Miss Myra, secure in the knowledge that Billy is only going through a stage, can be content to remind him of his selfishness and ask him to improve. However, if Billy's actions are a result of his environment and prior experiences, will simply speaking to him about the way he should be acting have any effect? If a child will not cooperate and will not learn, his actions can no longer be accepted as an unalterable consequence of his individual pattern of behavior—not in the primary school years and especially not in the preschool years, which Bloom has shown are the time when the child is most open to influence and change.

The new view of the child provides hope in this realm also. Since he is not developing according to a unique pattern but is instead reflecting the influence of his environment and experience, then it should be possible to ascertain the factors in the environment which are producing negative effects and intercede to either change or counteract them. In addition, useful techniques could be identified which would provide the means to modify all children's behavior and guide them along paths which society feels are desirable.

Conditioning or Behavioral Modification

The behaviorists offer one model for influencing the child. As was mentioned earlier, the behaviorists postulate that learning takes place through the action of the environment upon the learner. The environment provides a *stimulus* (S) which calls forth a specific *response* (R). Whether it will be repeated or not, in other words, learned, depends upon the result, the *reinforcement* the learner receives. If the result is pleasure, social approval, or a tangible reward, the reinforcement is said to be positive and the response is likely to be repeated when the stimulus is received again. If the reinforcement is negative—pain, dis-

approval, withdrawal—the response to the stimulus will be altered.
According to behaviorists:

> ... The child is born with very little patterning of personality or mind.
> Accordingly, it is possible to teach a child almost any behavior pattern,
> provided one teaches in terms of the laws of association learning and
> provided one starts at an early age before competing response patterns
> have been learned.[34]

Several experimental preschool programs make extensive use of
behaviorist theory (now called "operant conditioning"[35] or "behavior
modification"[36]) as a means of instruction in both the cognitive and
socioemotional realms. Kohlberg notes:

> In general, such a program implies a play for shaping the child's be-
> havior by successive approximation from responses. At every step, im-
> mediate feedback or reward is desirable and immediate repetition and
> elaboration of the correct response is used. A careful detailed program-
> ming of learning is required to make sure that (a) each response builds
> on the preceding, (b) incorrect responses are not made since once made
> they persist and interfere with correct responses, and (c) feedback and
> reward are immediate.[37]

The Liverpool Laboratory School at the Research and Development Center in Early Childhood Education at Syracuse University is a
program based directly on reinforcement theory. Its students are not
the disadvantaged but come instead from an essentially middle-class
suburban area. The school is attempting to determine whether children
can learn cognitive skills during the preschool years and to identify
techniques which will be successful in bringing about such learning.

The program is built around a highly detailed schedule of reinforcement. Skills to be taught are broken down into specific components, each of which is immediately reinforced when it appears
correctly. Teachers reinforce in four steps; in the first, raisins or candies are awarded for each correct response; in the second, the candies
are replaced by tokens which can be traded for a small prize; the third
involves distributing tokens which can be exchanged for more valuable
tokens. Two or more of the latter may be traded for a prize. In the
fourth step, four valuable tokens are required to receive a prize.[38]

Bereiter and Engelmann also use operant conditioning in their
program. Their reinforcement program contains both verbal and tangible rewards. Weber describes a rapid-fire sequence in language train-

ing in which the teacher verbally reinforces each response of the students:

Teacher: What is the same as beautiful?
Children: Pretty.
Teacher: Good. You are so good. If someone is beautiful they are pretty. What is the opposite of pretty?
Children: Ugly.
Teacher: I'll have to shake everyone's hand. . . .[39]

She also speaks of an arithmetic lesson in which the children were given a cracker for each correct response.[40]

Teaching and managing behavior by means of operant conditioning does not appeal to all and raises several moral issues. In the first place, it postulates an image of the learner as passive and receptive and leaves little room for individuality and creative thinking. According to Martin:

A science of behavior emphasizes the importance of environmental manipulation and scheduling and thus the mechanization and routinization of experience. Similarly, it stresses performance in the individual. Doing something, doing it efficiently, doing it automatically—these are the goals. It is the mechanization of man as well as the mechanization of the environment. The result is the triumph of technology: a push-button world with well-trained button-pushers.[41]

There is no question that human behavior is powerfully shaped by the response it evokes from others. Thus, many problem behaviors of children were induced initially by unwise responses which "taught" the child that crying, whining, hitting, temper tantrums, and so on were effective means of being noticed or getting what one wanted. Such behavior can be changed relatively easily when it no longer brings about the expected reaction. But what of behavior that springs more deeply and genuinely from the child himself? What of behavior that is temperamentally determined or that expresses inner need or anxiety? To manipulate a child in such a way as to eradicate a symptom will not help him if the underlying cause of his behavior remains untouched. It is this question which one is impelled to raise about even the most humane and positive use of reinforcement techniques in the education of young children. If the inner disturbance is left untouched, yet the child has been so handled as to eradicate his untutored expression of that disturbance, has he not been separated from the roots of his own being? Will it not in time be more and not less difficult for him to come to know himself and thus to guide his own behavior in more positive ways? Evelyn Weber sums it up well:

> Can operant conditioning be coupled with some concern for the affective side of growth? It doesn't seem that it can. By its very nature—doing something to what is considered a passive organism—it turns its back upon these significant realms. Indeed, the addition of extrinsic reinforcements seems to entail a psychological coercion which few children can withstand regardless of their inner feelings.[42]

When we stop to think how deeply young children are affected by their immediate perceptions, and how powerless they are to defend themselves against the impact of their senses, we realize that seemingly innocuous and petty devices such as raisins and candies do in fact wield considerable power—power located not within the individual psyche, but exercised upon it from outside. However benign the use of reinforcement techniques in a given situation may be, they raise some inevitable ethical questions. In the last analysis, their use is a way of playing Pied Piper, no matter how valid the rationale and how beneficial the intended outcome.

The Problem of the Match

According to the behaviorist formulation, a human being is not a self-directing organism but rather acts as a result of either external stimuli or internal instinctual drives such as hunger, pain, sex, and so on. However, as Hunt notes:

> The assertion that all behavior is so motivated implies that organisms become quiescent in the absence of painful stimulation, homeostatic need, and sexual stimulation. Observation stubbornly indicates that they do not. ... Humans work for nothing more substantial than the opportunity to perceive, manipulate, or explore novel circumstances. This evidence implies that there must be some additional basis for motivation.[43]

A second model for interacting with the child postulates therefore that whatever motivation is necessary for learning already exists innately within the child, that learning is fun, and that the child willingly seeks out the challenge inherent in mastering a new situation. Why, then, do children not learn? Why do they withdraw from or disrupt a learning situation?

Hunt suggests that the answer lies in what he calls the problem of "the match." As the individual interacts with the environment, he encounters situations incongruous with information (in Piaget's termi-nology, *schemata*) that he has already assimilated.

> There is evidence that incongruity with such standards will instigate action and produce excitement. There is also evidence that an optimum of such incongruity exists. Too little produces boredom. . . . Too much produces fearful emotional stress.[44]

The problem is to provide for each individual an activity which will match his need at that moment, one which will cause him to continue exploring and learning and not withdraw in either boredom or distress. Hunt suggests that "only the individual himself can choose a source of input which provides him with an optimum of incongruity."[45] There-fore, in providing a child with a flexible situation in which he can choose his activities by himself, the child will be able to find the perfect match.

This thesis, of course, sounds very much like the essence of the Montessori method and programs such as the New Nursery School which have already been discussed. Indeed, meshing as well as they do with Piaget's ideas of child development, Hunt's ideas are widely accepted in many experimental preschool programs with cognitive emphasis. The guiding principle here is that the child wants to learn and is his own best teacher since only he can make an accurate judg-ment as to what is right for him at any particular time. If a child is not learning, it is because what is being presented to him does not match his own unique set of prior perceptions. If a child will not participate or is disruptive, it is because what he is being asked to do has no meaning for him.

The Power of the Environment and Significant Models

A third formulation for dealing with the problem of motivation, the *how* of preschool education, points to the amount of time the child spends *outside* the direct influence of the preschool classroom. Since the home environment plays such a fundamental role in shaping the child's behavior, perhaps an important realm of activity for early edu-cation, compensatory or not, should be the home itself, with the parents as the most significant teachers.

A large part of a child's behavior and attitudes can be traced to the models he chooses to emulate. He tends to mirror the patterns of behavior of the people around him, most significantly, at first, those of his family and then his neighbors and older children he admires. This is true both in obvious areas such as language, where he will learn to speak according to the speech modes he hears around him, and in the affective realm where the child will develop attitudes toward society, school, and himself which reflect those of the people he is closest to, especially his mother. If she is hostile and feels unable to cope, these attitudes will be felt by the child.

In addition, the cognitive style developed by the child is strongly influenced by his mother. Hess and Shipman postulated "that the mother can be viewed as a teacher, as a programmer of input, during the pre-school years and that mothers from different social-class levels will program or socialize the cognitive behavior of their children in different ways."[46] They divided a sample of 152 mothers and their children into four groups based on measures of social class, interviewed and tested them, and observed sessions during which each mother was asked to teach her child three simple tasks. Their conclusion was as follows:

> The cognitive environment of the culturally disadvantaged child is one in which behavior is controlled by imperatives rather than by attention to the individual characteristics of a specific situation, and one in which behavior is neither mediated by verbal cues which offer opportunities for using language as a tool for labeling, ordering, and manipulating stimuli in the environment, nor mediated by teaching that relates events to one another and the present to the future. The meaning of deprivation would thus seem to be a deprivation of meaning in the early cognitive relationships between mother and child. This environment produces a child who relates to authority rather than to rationale, who may often be compliant but is not reflective in his behavior, and for whom the consequences of an act are largely considered in terms of immediate punishment or reward rather than future effects and long-range goals.[47]

The cognitive style encouraged in the culturally deprived home can be accepted as a given by the preschool and the program designed to balance the home environment by teaching or encouraging cognitive styles thought to be more conducive to success in school learning. Another approach is to alter the home environment by teaching the mother rather than the child and to encourage the former in behaviors believed to exercise a positive influence on the child's cognitive development.

A program utilizing this latter method was directed by Ira J. Gordon at the Institute for Development of Human Resources, University of Florida, Gainesville. It is based on six assumptions:

> 1) Attitudes toward learning are learned primarily at home, and the home is thus a central learning place; 2) the parent's self-esteem, attitudes toward school, expectations for success, and provisions of experience influence a child's performance, attitudes, and self-esteem; 3) children learn best when home and school share in the educational experience; 4) children learn best when their own subculture is respected and finds potency both in the classroom and in the general operation of the school; 5) parents themselves gain in self-esteem and feelings of competence when they see themselves able to teach their own children, to teach others, both adults and children, and to function as decision makers in all aspects of the program; 6) when parents are actively involved in the education of their children, they will continue to enhance the child's growth and their own activity after the formal program ends.[48]

An important element in the program is the training of "paraprofessional parent-educators" who visit the home of each enrolled child about once a week, bringing a learning task which has been developed cooperatively by the teachers and the parent-educators. The parents are encouraged to become actively involved in the school and to visit and participate in the classroom work as often as possible. The aim is not only to modify the behavior of the mothers toward their children, but to make the school more responsive to the former's needs by making them an integral part of planning and implementation.

Another project, the Ypsilanti Home Teaching Project, under the direction of David P. Weikart, completely replaced the traditional nursery school with an attempt to reach directly into the home. This "was an effort to explore the feasibility of sending teachers into the homes of disadvantaged families to provide a training program for the mother and a tutoring program for the preschool child without an accompanying classroom program."[49] A certified teacher visited the home once a week for a ninety-minute period and worked directly with the child in a cognitively oriented program adapted to his specific needs. The mother was required to be present and to take part, and the teacher attempted to explain to her what was being done and the principles of child development upon which it was based. The mother was encouraged to continue the activities with the child during the week and to modify her own behavior in interactions with the child according to the procedures she had observed. The project's findings were that the mothers were highly receptive, anxious that their children do well, and willing to try new techniques of interaction.

Many cognitively oriented preschool programs make some use of parent involvement, either as part of a classroom program, directly in the home, or through a combination of both. A stated aim of the Bank Street Early Childhood Center in New York City, for example, is "To evolve programs with and for parents which will help them cope with the life problems adversely affecting their children's growth and educability."[50] Research has shown that when all else is equal, parent involvement increases a program's success.[51] As Weikart and Lambie have pointed out:

> ... It would seem, then, that preschool programs that are directed at the disadvantaged child and do not involve the mother are accepting a challenge beyond the capacity of any educational curriculum. The problem is not to provide enrichment opportunities for the child or even child welfare information to the mother, but to restructure the mother-child interaction pattern. It is to this end that preschool education must turn.[52]

FURTHER DIFFERENCES BETWEEN COGNITIVELY ORIENTED AND TRADITIONAL NURSERY SCHOOLS

It might be well at this point to summarize some of the points of difference which have been discussed between the traditional nursery school and the more cognitively oriented experimental programs just described. Perhaps the most obvious was the principal's statement that the school does not stress learning. Within the classroom, situations which could be made a part of a learning sequence are ignored or used for other purposes. When Peter is so engrossed in building with his blocks, Miss Myra praises him for making it so high—an emphasis on his muscular coordination. She could have taken this as an opportunity to teach numbers, counting, or concepts such as "more and less," "higher," and so on. Miss Myra makes no attempt to match the activities to the children. Her classroom is teacher-directed in that the teacher decides when activities will begin and end and the sequence in which they will be undertaken. Self-discovery methods, whereby the child learns principles through undertaking his own activity, are rarely followed except in periods of free play, and even then the materials which the children use provide little scope for learning specific concepts. Many activities are conducted by the teacher with the children acting as spectators, as when Miss Myra feeds the rabbit while the children watch. The very size of the class, fifteen children to one adult, prohibits very much individualization. No parents are involved here, and neither is use made of teacher aides, as is the case with many new programs.

The Age Factor

The age of the children in the class is another factor upon which a comparison can be made. The four-year-old children in Miss Myra's class are perhaps in their second year of nursery school. Certainly, very few traditional schools would take them before the age of three. But as it becomes more and more clear that intervention at the age of four may be too late to counteract the alienating influence of a disadvantaged environment, cognitively oriented programs are reaching earlier into infancy for their students. A project such as the Nurseries in Cross-Cultural Education (NICE) in San Francisco begins with two-year-old children who remain in the program for three years. And now, with the emerging emphasis on day care, we find cognitively oriented programs serving children as young as six months.

The Children's Center in Syracuse, New York, established under the direction of Julius Richmond and Bettye Caldwell, is an attempt to intervene in the development of infants from disadvantaged backgrounds to prevent the cognitive retardation thought to be a result of a deprived early environment. Children in the program are as young as six months and none is older than three years. Socioemotional development and cognitive growth are treated with equal emphasis, and the curriculum is planned so as to deliberately stimulate concept learning in the Piagetian sense. Situations and activities are arranged for the children in order to foster abilities such as classification and discrimination along various dimensions. As Pines observed the program:

> Even the babies under one year of age do finger painting on plastic trays and take part in special learning games. They may listen to various sounds —bells, whispering, and stones in a box—or smell many odors, including vinegar. A one-year-old may learn object permanence: The teacher puts a toy behind a barrier to see whether the baby can find it. . . . A slightly older child may work on the toy-string problem: He learns to pull a string to reach a toy, a lesson in cause and effect.[53]

Although group care for infants has usually been condemned out of hand, the Syracuse program has demonstrated that at least it is not harmful and has not produced negative effects on the children's emotional development. In fact, since the participants in the program are, on the whole, children of working mothers who would normally be left with an older sibling, overworked neighbor, or even alone, they receive more individual attention in the group context than they could expect at home. An adult is assigned to be primarily responsible for each child and to provide that child with a one-to-one relationship for at least an hour every day. With the growing demand for day care and the rapid proliferation of services, the Syracuse Children's Center could well provide a viable model.

Another factor which may be considered in comparing traditional nursery schools with cognitively oriented programs is the narrow age range of children within the class. Miss Myra's group was made up entirely of four-year-olds, but even so we observed a wide diversity in their physical development as indicated by height and weight. The majority of preschool programs, experimental or traditional, continue to classify by age, and perhaps this is simply a convenience. Piaget's formulation of how children learn and the new stress on self-discovery methods and the child's search for his own match indicate, however, that arrangement by age makes no more sense than any other formula. Indeed, the potency of models in the young child's development makes grouping across ages desirable in order to provide younger children with older examples. Montessori has also shown that having children teach each other is of benefit to both the learner and the teacher and that in a mixed-age group much of the teaching is accomplished by the children themselves.

The Role of Play

One of the arenas of great debate in early childhood education, not only between the traditionalists and those who advocate change but also among the cognitively oriented themselves, is that of the role of play in a preschool program. The majority of time spent in the traditional nursery school is devoted to the children's spontaneous play. During "play period," they are left alone and encouraged to use the materials and equipment however they like. The teacher will intervene only to settle social problems. In Freudian theory and especially in the work of Erik Erikson, spontaneous, uninterrupted play is deemed vital to the child's total growth and development. Erikson feels that in play a child deals with life experiences in an attempt

> ... to repeat, to master, or to negate in order to organize his inner world in relation to his outer. Further, play involves self-teaching and self-heal-ing ... play activity becomes the child's means of reasoning, and permits the child to free himself from the ego boundaries of time, space, and reality, and yet to maintain a reality orientation, because he and others know that it is "just play."[54]

Within the group of educators agreeing that the preschool years should be a time for learning, there is considerable disagreement as to the role that should be assigned to play in a cognitively oriented pro-gram. Some, acknowledging its importance in the child's emotional development, give it much the same emphasis and significance as is found in the traditional nursery school. Others, pointing to the very brief time that the school has the child compared with the home, say that the school must emphasize different areas. Still others create an entirely new function for play.

The Bereiter-Engelmann direct instruction approach is one which discounts the importance of play as part of the preschool program. Spontaneous play can be useful as a means of releasing energy and tension which may have built up during the concentrated drill sessions, but, as Bereiter has pointed out:

> We have virtually no free play—just the first ten minutes, and the sing-ing, which is pretty structured. Free play is too time-consuming, and it is superfluous. "Group experience," "playing with their peers," are the *least* of these kid's needs. In some ways they're much less infantile than middle-class children. It's a rare middle-class child of four who can show genuine compassion; but with these kids, if you suddenly notice one of them is crying and you don't know why, ask the other children—they're *aware* they know what's wrong. Many of these kids have served as baby sitters. They do a great deal of comforting each other.[55]

Other programs, even though labeled cognitively oriented, appear to the casual observer to be devoted almost exclusively to play time. Such programs as Montessori classrooms and the New Nursery School encourage the child to select his own activities and provide materials for him to play with which are designed so that he will learn through manipulating them. These methods stress that learning itself is fun and that the child's enjoyment comes from a sense of control and exploration. They maintain that the most significant and rewarding events to the child are his moments of insight, what Montessori terms "explosions," when he suddenly arrives at some conclusion or connection between events in his environment. In these classrooms, the child is playing continually; his playthings have merely been arranged so as to provide an opportunity for him to experience these explosions. As Evans points out, "the way in which a learning environment is arranged for the occurrence of play activities is perhaps more critical than some might believe."[56]

The play in a Montessori classroom still could not be termed spontaneous, and the true Montessori method makes no provision for dramatic play as dressing-up and acting out roles or for group or social play. In fact, Montessori discouraged fantasy as making it more difficult for the child to cope with reality. Therefore, the problem still remains for those who feel, with Erikson, that fantasy and dramatic play are vitally important in the development of the child's personality. Some may concur with Bereiter and Engelmann that since the disadvantaged child needs so much and so little time is available to work with him, it is necessary to select those activities which are most important and beneficial. Therefore, play must take a back seat to more directed pursuits. Ironically, while it is in the typical "middle-class" type nursery school that spontaneous play is stressed, it is perhaps the disadvantaged child who needs it most within the school situation. The middle-class child normally has at home a variety of toys for all types of play situations along with an adult available and willing to pretend with him. The disadvantaged home, in spite of abundant love, may provide little opportunity and scope for play both in regard to toys and encouragement from adults. This consideration must be borne in mind in designing the ideal preschool program.

DESIGNING A PRESCHOOL PROGRAM

The number and variety of programs and methods devised to teach the preschool child are staggering. Even once having made the decision to abandon or modify the Miss Myra–style classroom, the educator is faced with a bewildering array of contradictory ideas aimed toward the same end—to promote the cognitive skills and abilities of the child. How, then, to choose?

The first assumption, perhaps, should be that there is no one right way. As in many other fields, too strict an adherence to a method or "creed" can be just as limiting and harmful as following no path at all. Weber points out:

> In order to provide truly enriching experiences the total growth of each child as a person must be considered. The complexity of behavior makes it difficult to deal with many aspects of development at once. For this reason we find projects investigating specific aspects and tending to ignore others. Some programs purporting to enhance the intellectual realm neglect the affective side of learning.[57]

Later, she adds:

> Currently, cognitive growth is on the high end of the educational pendulum swing; it is frequently the focus which rides roughshod over other concerns. Cognition tends to be divorced from the totality of human growth in a spurious, injurious manner. By looking at the child only as a knower and failing to utilize what we have learned about him as a reactor and a purposer, many of the newcomers to the field of early childhood education are working ahistorically.[58]

What appears to be needed ideally is a synthesis of various ideas and methods. Several projects now operating provide such a synthesis in that they are based systematically on theories of child development which view the preschool years as important for cognition and have developed their curricula as a result of research and observation of ongoing practices, both traditional and experimental. These have tried to deal with the whole child. Most are intended primarily to serve the disadvantaged child, but there is no reason why their practices could not be incorporated into the preschool experience of all children.

Several examples already have been mentioned, such as the New Nursery School which is avowedly eclectic. The nursery school sponsored by the Institute for Developmental Studies in New York City under the direction of Martin Deutsch is another instance of a synthesis of different streams of thought into a coherent program. Begun in 1962 as a 3-year demonstration and research school, it was founded on five assumptions: that (1) the development of cognitive skills and the ability to use intellectual skills depend mainly on environment; (2) the environment acts selectively on different aspects of development depending on the child's stage of evolution at that time and, therefore, there are optimal times for the stimulation of specific functions and stimuli which encourage one area of development may have no influence on another; (3) some types of environment are more stimulating than others in the realm of cognitive development; (4) cognitive development proceeds by stages which probably follow a consistent order; and (5) there are a few basic skills on which all others are built and acquisition of some skills is a prerequisite for the mastery of others.[59]

The traditional nursery school program provided the basis for the Institute's curriculum, but modifications were introduced as the result of a careful study of disadvantaged children and the skills they were lacking when compared with children who were expected to do well in school. Five areas of deficiency were identified: "language, visual perception, concepts, auditory perception, and lack of a positive self-image."[60] An attempt was made to break down these categories into a sequence of short steps leading to mastery of basic skills, and these were then programmed into activities for both individual and group use.

The four-year-olds' classroom is structured very much like Miss Myra's, with the teacher directing the children into activities and with a scheduled play time, juice time, story time, and so on. The difference is that, in the large proportion of free play time, the child has available a wide variety of materials designed, much like the Montessori materials, to lead him into individual discovery of certain fundamental principles and concepts. Further, group time is devoted to acquisition of cognitive rather than social skills. There are listening booths in which the child works with a tape recorder, listening to stories while following directions for exercises in identifying letters or numbers. There is also much greater stress on verbalization as the children in the housekeeping area and occupied with other activities are constantly encouraged by the teacher to talk. The equipment is always named as it is used; the children are required to ask rather than point when they want something; and they are involved in group stories, songs, and games.[61]

Development of a positive self-image is viewed as an extremely vital part of the method. The children's and the teacher's names are always used, pictures of the children are taken and prominently displayed, along with mirrors, at child-eye level throughout the room. Black and white dolls as well as pictures of children of all races are used to help promote self-identity.

The physical set-up of the room, as in a Montessori classroom's "planned environment," also is very important. Teachers are encouraged to see things from the child's perspective in arranging the classroom and to keep things neat, without distracting clutter. The stress on order, simplicity, and routine are drawn from the Montessori model.[62] The layout of the room and the materials provided are all devised to work toward the curriculum goals. Deutsch has itemized what is considered necessary for an "intervention environment":

> The environment would demand development and stimulate it along certain parameters. The environment would include sensorimotor stimulation, opportunities for making perceptual discriminations, interacting with a verbally adequate adult, receiving some individual attention, linking words and objects and meaningfully relating them in stories or to varying experimental contexts, being assisted in experiencing positive self-identifications, being encouraged toward task perserverance, and being helped to receive both tangible and verbal rewards for relatively competent performance. Such an environment includes stimulation which would be demanding of responses consistent with achieved developmental capabilities, and which would have sufficient and continual feedback from adults.[63]

Elements of many of the theories and practices which have been discussed previously in this chapter can be seen at work here: behavior modification and reinforcement theory, learning through assimilation and accommodation, and learning through observation and imitation of models. The program, in addition, makes an effort to involve parents, although not to the extent found in those programs utilizing home teaching. In reviewing the testing program administered to the children who have gone through the program and control groups, Butler has said, "Tentative results suggest that continuous and carefully planned intervention procedures can have a substantially positive influence on the performance of disadvantaged children and can avoid the cumulative failure all too frequently found."[64] Since traditional nursery school practices form the basis for this system, there is no reason why the modifications which work so well in increasing the cognitive skills of disadvantaged children should not be used to enrich the preschool years of all children.

QUESTIONS FOR THE FUTURE

Despite the persisting resistance to cognitively oriented programs among some of the preschool education establishment, and despite the fact that innovative practices have not, on the whole, filtered into the mainstream of early childhood schooling in this country—as we shall see in the next chapter—we feel that the differences between the Miss Myras and those proposing use of the preschool years for cognitive learning have been decided mostly in favor of the latter—particularly in the realm of intervention on behalf of the development of the disadvantaged child. Like all educational change, implementation will take time.

We should, however, mention a few of the controversies which are only now being joined. One concerns the role of language training in compensatory education. Nearly all the programs which we have discussed have placed primary emphasis on verbalization, although varying techniques for promoting language development have been employed. Most of the fire has been drawn by the Bereiter-Engelmann program, since it subordinates all else to highly structured direct language teaching, but the questions directed to their method should be considered in the context of all compensatory programs.

Bereiter and Engelmann can be described as defining cultural deprivation as "language deprivation."[65] Others, like Deutsch, have alluded to the lack of verbal abilities as a significant difference between the disadvantaged child and his more fortunate peers. Strengthening the facility to use language has been made a primary goal in many of these programs, since "Whorf, Vygotsky and some contemporary theorists have made language the essential ingredient in concept formation, problem solving, and in relating to an interpretation of the environment."[66] It has appeared, therefore, that the most fruitful approach to dealing with a deprived background is to stress language training.

Other educators have suggested that there may be a missing link between acquisition of language and achievement in the spheres of concept formation and problem solving. Some research has indicated that there is no direct connection between language skills and higher mental processes; for example, studies of deaf children have demonstrated that on tests of classification their performance closely matched that of normal children of the same age.[67] Piaget, in defining the stages of cognitive growth, shows language appearing long before the stage of intellectual operations.[68] It may not be sufficient, then, only to stress language as a route to cognitive achievement. Additional research is clearly needed here.

Another area of conflict in early childhood education theory is between those who would educate for the future and those who look essentially to the needs of the present. Future-oriented educators look ahead to the skills that the child will need to succeed in school and in society when he becomes an adult. They see the preschool years as the time to lay a solid foundation for the acquisition of these abilities. Their adversaries, such as many persons identified with the Association for Childhood Education International, warn of the "danger that programs designed with a future orientation may too easily neglect children as *children*."[69] They postulate that a full and rich existence as a child is the best guarantee of a successful life as an adult. The argument here is in many ways a recapitulation of the conflict between the interventionists and those who maintain a hands-off attitude toward childhood. But even in the light of what is known about cognitive development during the early years, a wholly satisfactory solution is yet to be found.

As additional preschool programs are developed and found to be effective in counteracting retardation in the culturally deprived and promoting enrichment and acceleration for all children, another problem will become more acute. Little correspondence often is found between the experiences provided and the skills gained in the successful preschool and the situation which the children encounter when they enter the traditional elementary school classroom. In commenting on the tendency of the advantages gained in compensatory preschools to wear off during the elementary years, Weikart and Lambie have claimed:

> It may be that preschool follow-up data are discouraging because elementary education is not willing to alter curricula so that children given a start in preschool can continue to progress with the assistance of programs designed especially for them. For example, ... [there is] evidence that where poor elementary teaching is current, effects of preschool wear off more quickly than where better teaching is available. Educators evaluating Head Start have reported the same trends.... Because of poor teaching or uninspired curriculum the thirst of Head Start children for further knowledge went largely unquenched and the advantages of preschooling rapidly dissipated.[70]

The implication here is double-edged. If preschool gains are being eradicated by inappropriate education in the elementary school, then the elementary school, too, must change. However, adjustments will have to be made also by those compensatory programs which base their curricula on an analysis of the skills necessary to succeed in the traditional primary school. They may be using entirely the wrong standard.

A fourth battleground is perhaps the most crucial. A major thrust of preschool education today is directed at the disadvantaged child, with the aim of making him more like the middle-class child and thus enabling him to succeed in society. The question is not only whether the middle-class model is most appropriate for all, but also whether it is the optimal form which society can take. The entire concept of intervention in the development of the "disadvantaged" child downgrades and even ignores the existence of his own culture—a concept against which many minority groups are rightly rebelling. The aim of American education has never been to make everyone the same, and care must be taken at this point that, in our zeal to provide what is "missing" in the life of the disadvantaged minority child, we do not destroy things of value already there.

THE TEACHER

A fundamental element in any educational process has largely been ignored in the foregoing discussion: Namely, that no matter what the aims of a program, the materials provided, or the theoretical justification, the responsibility for the success or failure of any method lies primarily with its interpreter—the teacher. Butler has stated that in measuring the impact of educational practices, study of the method itself may be far less informative than observation of teacher style.[71] Regardless of the curriculum, regardless of how detailed its theoretical formulation, it is what the teacher actually does that has an effect on the child.

Miss Myra was a mother substitute. She kept the children busy and happy, settled their quarrels, wiped their noses, hugged them, loved them. Evans points out that the traditional nursery school "stresses the creation of an emotional bond between teacher and child; a strong teacher-pupil relationship is frequently viewed as the key to the child's successful learning."[72] Possibly, though, the ferment in early childhood education during the last decade has obscured this role. If the preschool is to be a place of learning and enrichment, the teacher undoubtedly will play a key role.

Piaget summarized his view of the role of the teacher as follows:

> The best way to facilitate a child's transition from one state of intellectual development to the next is to let the student re-invent by himself whatever we want him to attain. . . . But this makes the teacher's role much more difficult. He must then (1) set problems—the child also does this by himself, but the teacher can prepare the materials, or create appropriate situations; and (2) offer conflicting evidence when the child is too quickly satisfied with his solutions, so as to introduce a temporary lack

of equilibrium that will force him to modify previously assimilated patterns of thought."[73]

The preschool of the future depends heavily upon its teachers. Theory, materials, and equipment by themselves are no substitutes. Whether the teacher is the Montessori directress, who is expected to be a resource person only, a "catalyst for progress,"[74] or the Bereiter-Engelmann drill master, or the model for mother and child, or the key to the perfect "match," the method will be successful only if the teacher is. Children learn when and what they are carefully taught. And this, as later chapters will amplify, is our message.

NOTES

1 Maya Pines, *Revolution in Learning: The Years from Birth to Six,* Harper & Row, New York, 1967, pp. 2–3. (Reprinted by permission.)

2 See, for example, Arnold Gesell, *Studies in Child Development,* Harper & Brothers, New York, 1948.

3 Pines, *Revolution in Learning,* p. 3.

4 Martin Deutsch, "Facilitating Development in the Preschool Child: Social and Psychological Perspectives," in *The Disadvantaged Child: Studies of the Social Environment and the Learning Process by Martin Deutsch and Associates,* Basic Books, New York, 1967, pp. 61–62 (excerpted from Chapter 4 © 1967 by Martin Deutsch).

5 Ibid., pp. 63–64.

6 Pines, *Revolution in Learning,* p. 3.

7 Annie L. Butler, *Current Research in Early Childhood Education: A Compilation and Analysis for Program Planners,* American Association of Elementary-Kindergarten-Nursery Educators [NEA], Washington, 1970, p. 10. (Reprinted by permission.)

8 Ibid., p. 10.

9 Deutsch, "Facilitating Development," pp. 73–74.

10 Milly Cowles, "Four Views of Learning and Development," *Educational Leadership,* vol. 28, no. 8, May 1971, p. 793. (Reprinted by permission.)

11 Evangeline Burgess, *Values in Early Childhood Education,* Department of Elementary-Kindergarten-Nursery Education [NEA], Washington, 1965, p. 35.

12 J. McVicker Hunt, "How Children Develop Intellectually," *Children,* vol. 11, no. 3, pp. 83–91, 1964, p. 90. (Reprinted by permission of the author.)

13 Ellis D. Evans, *Contemporary Influences in Early Childhood Education,* Holt, Rinehart and Winston, New York, 1971, p. 3.

14 Ibid., p. 3.

15 Hunt, "How Children Develop Intellectually," p. 88.

16 E. M. Standing, *The Montessori Revolution in Education,* Schocken Books, New York, 1962, p. 8.

17   Ibid., p. 7.

18   Evans, *Contemporary Influences*, p. 58.

19   Ibid., p. 33.

20   Ibid., p. 30.

21   Hunt, "How Children Develop Intellectually," p. 90.

22   Quoted in Pines, *Revolution in Learning*, p. 114.

23   Carl Bereiter, Siegfried Engelmann, Jean Osborn, and Philip A. Reidford, "An Academically Oriented Preschool for Culturally Deprived Children," in Fred M. Hechinger (ed.), *Preschool Education Today: New Approaches to Teaching Three-, Four-, and Five-Year-Olds*, Doubleday and Company, Garden City, N.Y., 1966, pp. 105–6.

24   Ibid., p. 109.

25   Carl Bereiter and Siegfried Engelmann, *Teaching Disadvantaged Children in Preschool*, Prentice-Hall, Englewood Cliffs, N.J., 1966, p. 54.

26   Evans, *Contemporary Influences*, p. 107.

27   Pines, *Revolution in Learning*, p. 50.

28   Ibid., p. 50.

29   Evans, *Contemporary Influences*, p. 49.

30   Pines, *Revolution in Learning*, pp. 73–74.

31   Butler, *Current Research*, p. 45.

32   Evelyn Weber, *Early Childhood Education: Perspective on Change*, Charles A. Jones, Worthington, Ohio, 1970, p. 108. (Reprinted by permission.)

33   Ibid., p. 108.

34   Lawrence Kohlberg, "Early Education: A Cognitive Developmental View," *Child Development*, vol. 39, pp. 1013–1062, 1968, p. 1020. (Reprinted by permission of the Society for Research in Child Development.)

35   Morris L. Bigge and Maurice P. Hunt, *Psychological Foundations of Education*, 2d edition, Harper & Row, New York, 1968, p. 350.

36   Weber, *Early Childhood Education*, p. 31.

37   Kohlberg, "Early Education," p. 1020.

38   Weber, *Early Childhood Education*, p. 104.

39   Ibid., p. 100.

40   Ibid., p. 26.

41   William E. Martin, "Rediscovering the Mind of the Child," *Merrill-Palmer Quarterly*, vol. 6, no. 2, Jan., 1960, p. 70.

42   Weber, *Early Childhood Education*, p. 105.

43   Hunt, "How Children Develop Intellectually," pp. 85–86.

44   Ibid., p. 86.

45   Ibid., p. 86.

46   Robert D. Hess and Virginia C. Shipman, "Maternal Influence upon Early Learning: The Cognitive Environment of Urban Pre-School Children," in Robert D. Hess and Roberta Meyer Bear (eds.), *Early Education*, Aldine Publishing, Chicago, 1968, p. 92. (Reprinted by permission.)

47   Ibid., p. 103.

48 Ira J. Gordon, "Parent Involvement in Early Childhood Education," *The National Elementary Principal,* vol. 51, no. 1, Sept., 1971, p. 28. (© 1971, National Association of Elementary School Principals. All rights reserved.)

49 David P. Weikart and Dolores Z. Lambie, "Preschool Intervention Through a Home Teaching Program," in Jerome Hellmuth (ed.), *Disadvantaged Child,* vol. 2, Brunner and Mazel Publishers, New York, 1968, p. 442.

50 Weber, *Early Childhood Education,* p. 77.

51 Evans, *Contemporary Influences,* p. 79.

52 Weikart and Lambie, "Preschool Intervention," p. 441.

53 Pines, *Revolution in Learning,* pp. 162–163.

54 Henry W. Maier, *Three Theories of Child Development: The Contributions of Erik H. Erikson, Jean Piaget, and Robert R. Sears, and Their Applications,* Harper & Row, New York, 1965, pp. 24–25.

55 Pines, *Revolution in Learning,* pp. 54–55.

56 Evans, *Contemporary Influences,* p. 19.

57 Weber, *Early Childhood Education,* p. 23.

58 Ibid., p. 170.

59 Cynthia P. Deutsch and Martin Deutsch, "Brief Reflections on the Theory of Early Childhood Enrichment Programs," in Deutsch and Associates, *The Disadvantaged Child,* pp. 379–381 (excerpted from Chapter 20 © 1967 by Martin Deutsch).

60 Weber, *Early Childhood Education,* p. 97.

61 Shirley Feldmann, "A Pre-School Enrichment Program for Disadvantaged Children," in Hechinger (ed.), *Preschool Education Today,* p. 100.

62 Ibid., p. 99.

63 Deutsch and Deutsch, "Brief Reflections," pp. 384–385.

64 Butler, *Current Research,* p. 44.

65 Evans, *Contemporary Influences,* p. 105.

66 Martin Deutsch, "The Disadvantaged Child and the Learning Process," in Deutsch and Associates, *The Disadvantaged Child,* p. 53 (excerpted from Chapter 3 © 1967 by Martin Deutsch).

67 Katrina de Hirsch, "Preschool Intervention," in Eloise O. Calkins (ed.), *Reading Forum: A Collection of Reference Papers Concerned with Reading Disability,* monograph no. 11, National Institute of Neurological Diseases and Stroke, Bethesda, Md., PHS, NIH, U.S. Department of Health, Education, and Welfare, n.d., p. 87.

68 Ibid., p. 87.

69 Evans, *Contemporary Influences,* p. 10.

70 Weikart and Lambie, "Preschool Intervention," p. 440.

71 Butler, *Current Research,* p. 39.

72 Evans, *Contemporary Influences,* p. 41.

73 Pines, *Revolution in Learning,* p. 42.

74 Evans, *Contemporary Influences,* p. 40.

TWO

A TALE OF NINE CITIES

CHAPTER 3

201 NURSERY SCHOOLS

As stated in Chapter 2, a major purpose of this study was to ascertain what is happening "out there" in the mainstream of preschool education in the United States. In that chapter, by examining theories of child development and learning and innovative programs, we investigated the headwaters, some of the sources of information and ideas for the practitioners in the mainstream. We now look to see if these headwaters are flowing smoothly into the stream and refreshing and replenishing it.

THE SURVEY

Nursery schools in nine cities were surveyed in an attempt to observe, describe, summarize, and analyze what is actually going on in a sample of early schooling in the United States. The cities included—Atlanta, Chicago, Houston, Kansas City, Los Angeles, Nashville, Philadelphia, Rochester, and Seattle—were selected in order to provide a reasonably representative geographical distribution throughout the nation.

For each city, a specialist in early childhood education was chosen who then became the coordinator for data collection in that city.*

Both for financial and practical reasons, it was decided to use local coordinators to survey each city rather than a central staff person. Our budget would not permit the considerable travel expenditure required to send observers all over the country. Funds were sufficient,

---

* The coordinators and their institutional affiliations at the time the study was conducted were: Atlanta, Lois Sauer (Emory University); Chicago, Alice Burnett (Indiana University); Houston, Robert Williams and R. Bernice McLaren (University of Houston); Kansas City, Edna Mitchell (William Jewell College); Los Angeles, Judith Ramirez (University of California, Los Angeles); Nashville, Else W. Hjertholm (George Peabody College); Philadelphia, Joanna Williams (University of Pennsylvania); Rochester, David Elkind (University of Rochester); and Seattle, Frances Prindle (Seattle Community College).

however, to bring the local coordinators together for one initial series of meetings to decide upon strategy. The practical consideration grew out of our assumption that nursery schools in any cities we selected would be difficult for an outsider to locate, and therefore someone should conduct the survey who was familiar with not only the early childhood education field but the specific metropolitan area as well.

The Instruments

One problem to anticipate was a possible lack of consistency among data gathered in this manner. In order to avoid this as far as possible, two forms were drawn up to be used as the basis for interviews and observations. The first, called the Director Interview Form, was intended to elicit general information about the school itself—its goals, curricula, facilities, personnel, and philosophy. This information was to be obtained through an interview with the head of the school. The second form was to supply the basis for comprehensively observing what actually went on in the given school. Called the Classroom Observation Form, it instructed the observer to record the activities, materials, interactions, attitudes, and organization of individual classrooms within the school. Both forms, which may be found in Appendix B, were based on instruments which the Research Division of |I|D|E|A| had developed for surveys of preschool education undertaken in England, Israel, and selected countries of Asia.

After drafts of the two forms had been made, the coordinators were invited to attend a two-day conference to make final plans for conducting the survey. The forms were the main topic of discussion, and they were carefully analyzed and modified according to suggestions made by the coordinators. Each coordinator then used them in interviews and visits to selected preschools in the Los Angeles area. Working in pairs, they collected the same information that would be gathered from the schools in their particular cities. On the basis of these visits, the forms were discussed and analyzed again, and further changes were made so that they more nearly complied with conditions actually observed. Definitions and terminology were discussed and agreed upon and impressions compared so that judgments to be made later would be consistent in terms of these common definitions and assumptions.

Another decision made by the coordinators at this conference was the working definition of *preschool* or *early schooling* to be used for the purposes of the survey: namely, "organized educational care outside the home for children before the age of entry into the formal public or private school structure." Information was to be collected on nursery schooling for children in the age range of two to five. Five-year-olds were to be included only where kindergartens were considered an integral part of the nursery school.

Identifying the Population

As we predicted, locating the nursery schools in each city proved to be a problem. After the coordinators returned home, their first task was to identify all the schools within their city in order to select a representative sample. In most cases this proved to be impossible. None of the cities had a central licensing bureau or directory in which all schools were listed. Not only did licensing procedures and agencies vary from city to city, but even within given cities records varied according to the source of funding or whether food was served or safety standards met. We found that backyard playgroups and other types of informally organized installations could not be included at all in our sample. No one officially knew of their existence, and there was no means of locating them in any systematic way.

Kansas City presents the situation in microcosm. Beyond the problems faced in other cities, additional confusion was created by the fact that the state line runs through the urban area, dividing the city into a Kansas sector and a Missouri sector. In the Kansas precinct, at the time the study was conducted, the state Child Welfare Office maintained a file by county for each person who applied for a child-care license. Hard data on installations were difficult to obtain, however, because of bureaucratic red tape resulting in part from competition among governmental agencies. Several were struggling jealously to maintain possession of the responsibility for licensing, which led in many cases to a situation of double licensing. When the survey was begun, the Kansas Department of Health (Division of Child Health) and the Department of Social Welfare both were licensing and inspecting all centers which provided education or care of preschool children. Later, the situation was remedied somewhat when the responsibility of licensing was assigned to the Department of Health with the approval of the Department of Social Welfare, but some overlap of inspection teams still continued.

In Missouri, licensing was mandatory only for day care centers and was handled through the state office in Jefferson City. The local Office of Child Welfare employed teams of supervisors to inspect the day care centers, but no supervision or licensing regulations had been established for preschools or for private homes in which small groups of children are assembled. If the number of children was more than six, an approval study was made and a license might subsequently be granted. At the same time, the state delegated to each city and town the right to formulate its own regulations governing preschools and child care.

The Public Health Department of Kansas City, Missouri, also took responsibility for approving applicants for child care. A city permit, costing $1, was required for a group of children up to six in number. More than six required a state permit. A city ordinance dictated minimum safety inspection for fire protection, space and ventilation, kitchen standards, and health certification of employees working with the children.

Preschools which offer an educational program rather than merely supplying day care do not fit comfortably into any of these categories and were apparently a source of some confusion among different agencies. The Health Department, for example, appeared to assume that health examinations for preschool teachers fell under the jurisdiction of the board of education. It is not known if anyone at all visited these schools for health inspections.

The fact became clear that there were no specific regulations for a half-day preschool. Fire inspection was obligatory for a public building, but no public agency seemed willing to assume the responsibility of licensing the preschool. One school director informed us that someone came out from the Public Health Department and looked over their equipment, but that the inspector had no authority to aprove or disapprove of their facilities. This means that in Kansas City, Missouri, at the time when our study was in progress, anyone could start a preschool with no specific standards or educational requirements to be met and with no one in the state prescribing basic guidelines.

Selecting the Sample

The sampling procedures followed in Houston, Texas offer an example of the methods used in most cities. As a first step, to identify the number and type of preschool facilities available, we contacted preschool associations and interviewed their officers. Unfortunately, it readily became apparent that these officials were by no means well-acquainted with the members of the association and their activities. Their offices were able to provide lists of names and the approximate number of members, but the lists did not prove to be of great help since subsequent investigation revealed that many persons operating preschool facilities were not members of any organization.

The next step, then, was to contact religious and church groups to request lists of their educational facilities. In many cases, it was not possible to tell from the information obtained whether a preschool facility was included in a specific school, and it was necessary to reach the schools directly to find out. Subsequently, state welfare offices were consulted, since Texas has a licensing law. At the time, however, the law applied only to those centers which care for children more than four hours a day, regardless of program; consequently, half-day programs did not come under the law and thus were omitted from the lists procured from the welfare office.

Ironically, the most useful tool for locating preschool facilities turned out to be the telephone directory, since most nursery schools were recorded in the Yellow Pages. The list provided here was incomplete, however, because many church-related programs were not categorized separately as a preschool facility but were included under the church's listing. The last resort proved to be personal contact with persons in the field and keeping a sharp lookout when driving through the city for signs advertising centers.

More than six hundred preschool facilities were thus eventually identified in Houston and the surrounding area. From these, representative centers were selected for the Houston sample by controlling for such variables as geographic location, public or private control, socioeconomic status of clientele, type of program, etc. The final sample comprised eight semiprivate programs, five Headstart programs, five which were strongly church-related, two university laboratory schools, two bilingual programs, one Montessori program, one wholly commercial venture, and one upper-class private institution. A total of twenty-two schools was visited in Houston, with three schools fitting into two of the classifications listed above.

Similar procedures for locating the schools to be sampled were followed in most of the cities surveyed. The guidelines established for selection of the sample within each city were as follows: (1) the number of schools in each category was to be generally proportional to the number of children enrolled in preschools in that category; (2) some schools in each of the categories identified in that city were to be included; (3) the schools were to be as "typical" as possible of the type of program as far as the knowledge of the coordinator allowed, though it was suggested that if an outstanding school in a category were known, that school also should be included in the sample; (4) most, or all, of the college laboratory schools in the area were to be visited because it was thought that these schools would be the pacesetters for preschool education; and (5) typical Headstart schools would be limited in the sample since they have been extensively studied elsewhere and we believed that our efforts could be more productive and informative if focused on other types of institutions. Certain selected Headstart schools with unusual programs, however, were to be included in the sample. It can be seen, therefore, that although our intention was to make the sample as typical and as randomly selected as possible, it might tend to be skewed slightly toward schools likely to be the most innovative. However, the sample as a whole probably was made up of largely "average" nursery schools in each of our nine cities.

Observation Procedures and Data Collection

After the sample was selected in each city, we contacted the schools in question to obtain permission for observers to visit. Although several coordinators reported instances where they were met with suspicion and resistance, in most cases no problems were encountered and the large majority of the schools cooperated willingly and even eagerly. The manner in which visits to the schools were conducted and data gathered was left to the discretion of the individual coordinator. Some observers held on to the forms and filled in the information as discussions and observation proceeded. Others gave the Director Interview Form to the head of the school and asked her to fill in certain sections. It was then completed by the observer during later interviews. At the coordinators' meeting, however, the need for uniform interpretation of questions and the requirement that an attempt be made to answer each and every question had been stressed. No matter how the data were collected, these two specifications were to be honored.

The time devoted to observation in individual classrooms ranged from one-half hour to nine hours, with the median time spent in any one observation being two hours. The greatest number of observations took place in the morning. Very few surveyors visited exclusively in the afternoons, and several reported visiting the schools in both the morning and afternoon.

Two other requests regarding the compilation of data had been made at the coordinators' general conference. One was that the observations be initiated as soon as possible after the conference so that the guidelines and procedures would be easily remembered. This also would assure that the observations would not be delayed until toward the end of the school term when programs might not be as typical. The other was that the data be forwarded to us as collected instead of being held until all observations and interviews were completed. It was thought that this method would facilitate the summary and analysis of data in two ways. First, if consistent misinterpretations or omissions of questions on the forms were made, time would still be available for their correction. Second, any desirable modifications of sampling could be made when the data suggested hunches or trends.

A total of 201 schools was visited, as indicated in Table 3.1.

TABLE 3.1. SCHOOL VISITATIONS

City	Number of Schools Visited
Atlanta, Georgia	17
Chicago, Illinois	25
Houston, Texas	22
Kansas City, Missouri	38
Los Angeles, California	22
Nashville, Tennessee	14
Philadelphia, Pennsylvania	22
Rochester, New York	20
Seattle, Washington	21
Total	201

Analysis of the Data

The data gathered by the observers were recorded on Director Interview Forms and Classroom Observation Forms, one for each school and classroom visited. The completed questionnaires were then sent to us for processing.

The first step in analysis of the data was to compile the responses to each item on the forms. For multiple-choice items, a simple tally was made of the number of responses to each alternative, and then percentages of the total number of responses were computed for each category. The total number of responses to each item always was used as the basis for finding the percent of the total for each alternative offered for that item. For example, if there were only 150 responses to a certain item, a classification containing 15 responses would be scored as 10 percent of the 150 actual responses—*not* 7.5 percent of the 201 potential responses.

Items calling for open-ended responses demanded an extra step. First, a tally was made simply by recording summary phrases for each response given. No attempt was made at this point to interpret the data, but only to record them. The tally of responses was then examined in order to determine categories of similar responses or those which said the same thing in different words. The number of responses in each group could then be established and percentages computed. Again, the total number of responses to each item was the basis for tabulation of percentages for that item.

For each item, a count was also kept of the number of blanks, called "no tallies." Then, when we knew that there was a large number of no tallies for any item, we had less confidence in generalizations based on data therefrom. Further, in some cases, a large number of no tallies could in itself be taken as indication of a trend; that is, as an absence of conditions or activities we had predicated at the outset.

In addition to computing the percentages for the responses of the total sample, we also extracted from the total three groups of programs which were clearly identifiable as discrete types. These were schools which the observers classified as college laboratories, Montessori schools, or parent cooperatives. We anticipated that these programs might be unique or at least palpably different from the other nursery schools in the total sample. College labs, for example, might be expected to be innovative, and thus we felt it would be interesting to look for trends among them. They are, supposedly, a testing ground for experimental educational practices, and the schools in this category that we looked at were, indeed, engaged in psychological and educational research, teacher training, and product development.

Montessori schools were examined separately because it was assumed that they would follow the well-defined Montessori program described in Chapter 2 and would thus provide a contrast to practices in other schools in the sample. It was our perception, however, that many schools calling themselves Montessori do not always adhere strictly to the program's basic concepts and principles. This may be accounted for partly because Montessori has now become fashionable and many schools have jumped on the bandwagon with inadequate orientation. Also, many practitioners have constructed their programs on the Montessori model but have modified them to meet common criticisms such as those summarized in Chapter 2. Nonetheless, we believe that our sample reflects a cross-section of schools which call themselves Montessori.

Parent coops were chosen for additional analysis because, for one thing, they constitute a rather clear-cut classification. In addition, we thought that the parent involvement in these schools might have some special impact on philosophy and practices that should be noted and analyzed.

Parent cooperatives throughout the country tend to be quite similar in their basic organization. Most are wholly run and financed by the parents of the children enrolled. In most instances, parents are required to participate in the classroom as assistant teachers and also to serve on various committees such as membership, purchasing, finance, and health. The educational program is usually the responsibility of a professional staff of teachers, but the underlying educational philosophy is controlled by the parents, who hire the director and staff. The schools thus run the gamut of preschool theories and practices. One common factor, at least, found in all these schools is the regular presence of mothers (and fathers) in the classroom.

It should be noted that the number of each of these three types of schools in the total sample is small, and therefore, any generalizations which are drawn about their programs are suggestive rather than definitive. Percentages of responses for each of the three were computed only for those items which we felt might prove to be important on the basis of tentative hypotheses beginning to emerge from the general data. Once percentages had been ascertained, the data were compiled into tables so that they could be studied in clustered, summary form likely to suggest trends. In cases where the data seemed to warrant it, a more critical analysis of statistical significance (a chi-square analysis) was carried out in order to test several hypotheses. As a rule, these analyses are not reported here, although they were used as the basis for many generalizations. Tables containing the most significant data and the results of these analyses may be found in Appendix A.

Some of the terminology and phraseology used in this chapter may be repetitious, but this is deliberate. For example, it is important that the data be viewed in most cases as a percent of *responses,* not as the number of schools or classrooms reporting. This is so because in some instances schools or classrooms may not have responded to the item. Elsewhere, a single school or classroom may have provided multiple responses to the item. This accounts for the different number used as the basis in reporting the responses to each item in the forms. At any point where the percentages reported do not add up to 100, the difference is made up by those cases where no observation was made or where, for one reason or another, a tally could not be made of the response given. All these problems begin to suggest the enormous complexity involved in getting a picture of school practice as it actually exists at any one specified time.

Problems and Limitations in Conducting the Study

Certain problems and limitations are inherent in conducting a survey of nursery schools in the United States. In the first place, the reason we decided to undertake the study at all was that so little was known about day-to-day practice in American preschools. One difficulty which became apparent immediately was the paucity of instruments which could be used for data collection. This led us to develop our own, and the evident need for such instruments has been demonstrated by the number of subsequent requests which we have received for ours.

Another obstacle is that extant data about the schools are skimpy. There are no widely accepted achievement tests which can be administered to five-year-olds on a national scale. No quantitative method is available for recording the philosophy of the school directors or the activities of the teachers. Any effort to describe what is going on in the classroom calls for subjective impressions on the part of the observer: Are the children happy? Is the teacher enthusiastic? We can prescribe guidelines to use when making these judgments, but judgments seem always to call for going beyond hard data.

Several other limitations already have been mentioned. Lack of funds made it impossible to send a single team of observers to every school. Though we tried to prevent it, this may have led to inconsistencies in the data. Finding an adequate sample was extremely complicated, so that, in spite of our intentions, the sample may not be as representative as we would wish. The number of schools and classes observed and used for drawing generalizations is fairly low, although probably the largest ever observed intensively in a single study. However, the consistency found among the data gathered in cities widely separated both geographically and sociologically supports the validity of the procedures used.

In summary, this survey was conducted because it was necessary. At the time it was begun, a great deal of money was being poured into early childhood schooling with very little information about what was actually happening in the field. We should know where we are before we try to move forward, and therefore, instead of conducting one more experimental manipulation of various factors which might affect the learning of young children, we decided to undertake a field study designed to provide a description of the day-to-day practices in typical nursery schools in major cities throughout the country.

GENERAL CHARACTERISTICS OF NURSERY SCHOOLS

Schools of our sample were categorized in two ways: (1) according to who was in control, and (2) according to the program emphasis. Following our classification, the sample included:

17 college laboratory schools
21 Headstart centers
72 independent schools
20 parent cooperatives
39 church-controlled schools
29 under federal, state, or city control (other than Headstarts)
15 miscellaneously controlled schools (largely under the aegis of public or private philanthropic organizations)
1 unclassified school.*

The directors of the schools were asked to specify the general emphasis of their programs. The following classifications resulted:

72 custodial or day care
55 emphasizing parent education
39 emphasizing the preparation of professionals (teachers and other workers)
38 compensatory education
36 emphasizing the use and training of paraprofessionals
29 emphasizing research and program development
26 stressing Montessori methodology.

* A few schools spread across two classifications of control. This accounts for the larger total of 214 rather than the previously reported total of 201 schools.

There was also a rather sizable number grouped under "other" and "miscellaneous program emphases" which were not listed separately on the data collection instrument. A further breakdown of the schools stressing research and program development and those utilizing Montessori methodology revealed:

16 schools concerned with child development
13 developing exemplar educational programs
9 concerned most with readiness for later schooling
9 emphasizing the training of exceptional children
5 with traditional preschool programs
4 emphasizing socialization of children
3 providing a community service
4 with unidentified program emphases.

Many schools were classified as having more than one program emphasis. For example, the same school might have been categorized as providing an educational program for children, dealing with parent education, and being involved in research and program development. It must be remembered that these groupings resulted from information provided by the directors and not from direct observation.

The primary source of funds for more than half the schools was fees or tuition. The amount of such fees varied widely according to the type of program offered and the number of hours children were in attendance, ranging from 0 (for children on scholarships or the school being entirely dependent on funds other than tuition) to $1,650 per year. Other financial sources, each accounting for less than 10 percent of the responses, were churches; federal government; charities, foundations and community agencies; gifts, grants, and contributions; state governments; colleges or universities; fund drives; a combination of federal and state governments; and finally, support by city governments alone.

The school buildings characterized by the observers ranged from old frame houses which were hardly suitable for young children and, in some cases, bordering on unsafe, to structures which had been built specifically to suit the program of the school. Less than half the schools had facilities of their own; almost a third shared space with a church group. Such sharing usually meant that space was simply rented from the congregation, but in several instances, materials and equipment were shared with Sunday school groups.

Classroom observers generally found rooms to be safe and spacious or at least adequate. Ventilation was nearly always rated as comfortable. As a rule, the classrooms were considered cheerful and sunny, although at least one-quarter were deemed not especially cheerful places for children. When each of the three special types of program (college labs, Montessori, and parent coops) were analyzed separately on this dimension, we were surprised to find that a substantial number of classrooms for all three were rated as neither cheerful and sunny nor dingy and depressing. Many of these classrooms apparently left a rather bland impression on the observers.

The Staff

Most schools visited were administered by a director or head teacher. They were usually in attendance at the school full-time each day and possessed either a bachelor's or graduate degree. Customarily, their backgrounds included considerable experience in nursery school education, the range running from six months to forty years. The largest number of responses clustered in the three- to eight-year province. The number of years of other types of teaching experience for directors went from one to thirty years, with the largest number of responses clustering in the two- to eight-year grouping.

Among the teaching staff, a college degree or at least some college training was common. The best trained teachers, in terms of academic preparation, were found in the college lab schools, while teachers in parent coop schools had had the least amount of preparation. Many teachers in all types of schools had had formal training and experience in early childhood education, though one school reported that it was mandatory that the teachers they hired have *no* formal training in education. Assistant teachers, present in some schools, were high school graduates or may have had some college work but usually had little or no teaching experience.

A little less than half the teachers in the sample were rated as being very enthusiastic, cheerful, and eager. Almost all the others were judged to be at least moderately happy and enthusiastic. Parent coop teachers showed a slight tendency to be rated more often as very enthusiastic, while Montessori teachers tended to be more often observed as somewhat less enthusiastic and more subdued in their work than were those of other schools.

Less than half the classrooms had aides available as resources. Aides were classified as either persons related to the children (parents) or as those who were not related. As might be expected, teachers in parent coops were more likely to be assisted by parent aides than were those in other types of schools. It also appeared that in college lab schools the teachers more often than in other programs had more than one aide. These aides were usually not related to the children.

The role of the aide varied considerably among classrooms. Some assisted in teaching and worked with groups of children or with individuals. Some performed nonprofessional tasks such as mixing paints, serving snacks, or straightening up the room. Few had had any formal preparation for work with young children, but generally they supported the teacher in the overall program. In a few instances, however, the aides appeared to conflict with the personality of the teacher or with the classroom procedure.

A number of schools had additional staff resources, most frequently social workers, music teachers, psychologists, speech therapists, nurses, and medical doctors. Further, those with an all-day program provided lunch and often employed a cook, housekeeper, or custodian. A few schools availed themselves of a secretary or a bus driver. Few instances of involving persons from the broader community as a resource for the school in any role were reported. Thus, little use was made of outside persons with special expertise who might enrich the school's program.

The directors were requested to estimate the average ratio of adults to children in the school. Unfortunately, it is not known to what extent only professional people and/or aides were used as a basis for the estimate or to what extent all adults in the school, including cooks, custodians, and secretaries, were included. At any rate, the adult-pupil ratio reported was generally in the range of 1:5 to 1:10.

The Pupils

We were interested in the criteria which the various schools used to select their students, and therefore the directors were asked about entrance requirements. The largest category of responses involved the child's physical health, though fewer than one-third of the directors mentioned any such standards as obligatory. In those schools where good health was a prerequisite for entrance, it appeared in most cases that the school's decision to accept the student was based on the results of a rather routine medical check-up. The only other category which accounted for over 10 percent of the responses was criteria pertaining to specific needs of the child or his family. For example, some schools require that the parents be in a low-income bracket or that both parents be working, and others that the child have physical or emotional problems. Other prerequisites, such as toilet-training, age-maturity, and ability to function in a group, met with small numbers of responses.

In almost half the schools we visited, a child would have to wait at least some time after making application before being accepted. The waiting period ranged from a few days to a few years, but from the clustering of the responses, it seemed that if it was necessary at all, the wait tended to be long rather than short. However, about one-fourth of the directors indicated that there was no waiting period at their schools and that students would be admitted immediately upon application (assuming fulfillment of entrance requirements).

Half the schools in the sample served children who were mostly from middle or upper socioeconomic class families. One-third of the schools enrolled primarily children from a low socioeconomic class. College labs, Montessori schools, and parent coops appeared to serve children from the middle rather than either high or low socioeconomic groups.

Observers were asked to note when they were in the classroom the ethnic composition of the groups. Half the classrooms were reported to be racially or ethnically mixed. One-fourth were all-white and one-sixth were all-black. The remaining fractions were accounted for by classrooms made up of other ethnic groups, such as all Jewish or Mexican-American or Chinese.

As could be expected, the amount of time that the individual child spent at the school depended upon the type of program offered. Day care programs usually ran all day; parent coops were likely to have staggered-days attendance; and other institutions had some children attending all day, some half-days. The latter programs were scheduled primarily in the morning. Some schools had classes every weekday; others Monday, Wednesday, and Friday, or Tuesday and Thursday.

Within a single school, attendance patterns often varied, with some children present every day of the week and some only three days, some a half-day and others all day. A clear pattern seemed to emerge for Montessori schools, with twenty of the twenty-four sampled reporting that all or some of their pupils were at school for a half-day every day. Fourteen of these advised that *all* pupils were in attendance every day for a half-day. It is also interesting to note that none of the parent coops mentioned children who attend their schools all day every day of the week.

The youngest child enrolled in any of the sample schools was six months; the oldest was six years. Although these ages fall outside the age range we established in our definition of "preschool," schools serving these children were included in the sample because they were typical of schools in the area. In any case, the classrooms observed in these schools were only those containing children whose ages fit into our definition.

Most of the schools accepted children from two-and-a-half to six years, with about half the schools reporting that their students ranged from three to five years in age. College labs appeared to have a more limited age range than the general sample, with their students being primarily four- and five-year-olds.

In general, the children seemed to be enjoying their nursery schools, regardless of the type of program. However, children of this age tend to be happy, anyway, and so it is not possible to determine from our study whether happiness in the life of a preschool child is due to the nursery school or just to being a child.

The Classrooms

As noted above, the majority of the classrooms visited were rated as cheerful and sunny. In about half, the arrangement of the room (distribution of furniture and materials and division of the room into areas) sufficed to allow the children freedom of movement with little disruption of or by fellow students. However, in over one-quarter of the sample, the physical organization of the classroom seemed inadequate to permit proper utilization of space and nondisruptive movement of the pupils and, indeed, served to restrict or impede movement.

Our observers rated about half the classrooms they visited as placing some emphasis on routines and rules, but commented that attitudes toward them were fairly casual. A fourth were classified as having a high emphasis on the children following routines and rules. College labs were judged to put slightly less emphasis on routines and rules than the general sample. Montessori classes, on the other hand, tended to have more emphasis on rules and regulations than was generally observed. The noise level of most classrooms was said to be reasonable and appropriate, with less than 10 percent regarded as unnaturally quiet for a preschool and an equal number as chaotic and noisy to the point of discomfort.

The Program

In most of the classrooms studied, it appeared that whatever program was offered was integrated, organized, and well-planned. Forty-five percent of the classes were deemed coherent and directed with smooth transitions and implementation of the program, while another 42 percent were judged to be moderate in organization and planning. College lab programs were more likely to be considered coherent and well-planned than was the general sample.

The children, on the whole, seemed to be active participants in the program. Over half were rated as busily engaged and involved in their tasks and an additional one-third as generally busy though not greatly involved. Only 5 percent were reported as being lethargic and showing very little activity.

Half the teachers were viewed as highly engaged and busy with the program and the children, with an additional one-fourth as moderately engaged. Thirteen percent were reported as busy with routines but showing little involvement with the children. Nearly 8 percent were seen to be unobtrusive with the children but engaged in observation of the children and the program.

Less than half the classroom aides were rated as highly engaged and busy with the children and program, and slightly more than a fourth were considered to be moderately engaged. However, about one-fourth of the aides were found to have little or minimal involvement with the children.

Teacher reinforcement of children's behavior was generally positive and constructive. Reasoning or talking to the child was the technique most often witnessed. In addition, physical rewards (smiles and pats on the head), diverting the child to a new activity, scolding, warning or threatening, and ignoring the situation were noticeable to some extent. Punitive isolation, loss of privileges, group pressure, tangible rewards (candy or toy), planned time-out or temporary withdrawal, and physical punishment were rare.

The foregoing provides a general description of the 201 nursery schools making up our sample. Let us turn now to matters of philosophy, function, daily program, materials, and the like providing the basic ingredients of the children's preschool education.

CHAPTER 4

HOW NURSERY SCHOOLS SEE THEMSELVES

Our first concern, after describing the general characteristics and atmosphere of the schools we visited, was to identify at least the rhetoric conveying the philosophical and theoretical conceptions of the school programs. Therefore, the director was asked a set of questions designed to provide information about the school's basic philosophy and the theories of child development and learning to which she and, presumably, the school program, adhered. The responses drew upon concepts and methods of the kinds discussed in preceding chapters. Clearly, the ideas of Gesell, Piaget, Bruner, Hunt, and others were not foreign to these administrators even if they did not refer to them by name. It should be noted, however, that the answers elicited rarely constituted any consistent theoretical position.

The Importance of Developmental Areas in the School Program

The respondents were requested to rank eleven development areas according to their importance in the school's program. In addition, an open-ended question at the end permitted them to add any additional areas they felt to be crucial. To be rated were:

1 Academic skills (reading, writing, drawing, arithmetic)
2 Arts and creative expression
3 Cognitive-intellectual development
4 Concept acquisition (concepts of time, color, size)
5 Emotional development (self-confidence, self-esteem, etc.)
6 Language skills
    a oral development
    b reading and vocabulary development
7 Motor skills (large muscle)

8   Sensory awareness
9   Sensorimotor skills (visual and auditory training)
10   Social-interpersonal skills (cooperation, rules, etc.)
11   Verbalizing feelings

The data regarding replies to our queries in this area are summarized in Table 4.1.

The general tendency here was for the directors to rate all the developmental categories as being of high importance in their programs. Two exceptions appeared: Ratings of academic skills were rather evenly distributed in the sample as being of low, medium, or high importance to the program, and evaluations of the importance of reading and vocabulary language skill development also were rather evenly divided along the same lines.

As can be seen from Table 4.1, several interesting trends emerged. For example, by far the greatest agreement among nursery school administrators seems to be about the importance of the traditional goals of the developmental psychologists (Gesell and others) in the nursery school program. Over 75 percent of the respondents in the total sample characterized emotional development, social-interpersonal skills, and arts and creative expression as being of high importance in their programs. However, it is encouraging to note that over two-thirds of the directors also ranked as highly important four areas included in most of the cognitively oriented innovative programs we examined previously: sensory awareness, oral language skills, verbalizing feelings, and concept acquisition. In addition, over half of them added sensorimotor skills and motor skills. The only areas which were not esteemed as highly important by over half of the directors were reading and vocabulary development and academic skills.

The directors of the parent cooperatives, more than any other identifiable group, most closely mirrored the responses of the total sample. Over 75 percent also ranked emotional development, social-interpersonal skills, and arts and creative expression as of high importance. The remaining areas, however, tended to be placed lower in importance than for the general sample. The only additional developmental area reported as being of high importance by more than two-thirds of the parent coop administrators was verbalizing feelings, while less than half ranked cognitive-intellectual skills as high. Only 10 percent judged reading and vocabulary skills as highly important, and 5 percent reported the same for academic skills.

TABLE 4.1 AREAS OF EMPHASIS IN PROGRAM

Areas of Emphasis	Total Sample Percent of Responses				College Labs Percent of Responses				Montessori Percent of Responses				Parent Coops Percent of Responses			
	High	Medium	Low	No Tally and Other	High	Medium	Low	No Tally and Other	High	Medium	Low	No Tally and Other	High	Medium	Low	No Tally and Other
Academic Skills	31.53	33.97	36.96	3.8	29.41	35.29	23.52	11.76	62.50	16.66	8.33	12.50	5.00	30.00	60.00	5.00
Arts and Creative Expression	75.00	20.50	3.00	1.50	82.35	11.76		5.88	58.33	37.50		4.16	75.00	15.00	5.00	5.00
Cognitive-Intellectual Development	61.18	30.33	3.97	2.97	70.58	17.64		11.76	87.50	8.33		4.16	50.00	35.00	10.00	5.00
Concept Acquisition	67.00	26.00	5.50	1.50	88.23	11.76			87.50	4.16	4.16	4.16	50.00	40.00	5.00	5.00
Emotional Development	85.50	10.50	3.00	1.00	88.23	5.88	5.88		87.50	8.33	4.16		90.00	5.00		5.00
Language Skills: Oral Development	70.00	23.50	4.50	2.00	100.00				70.83	12.50	4.16	12.50	50.00	35.00	10.00	5.00
Language Skills: Reading and Vocabulary Development	32.32	32.35	18.87	8.34	41.17	5.88	5.88	47.05	62.50	29.16		8.33	10.00	35.00	40.00	15.00
Motor Skills	62.93	20.29	8.11	.50	94.11	5.88			75.00	12.50	12.50		50.00	35.00	10.00	5.00
Sensory Awareness	71.84	19.09	4.52	4.52	100.00				91.66	4.16		4.16	55.00	25.00	5.00	15.00
Sensory-Motor Skills	65.30	27.13	4.51	2.51	100.00				79.16	16.66		4.16	55.00	25.00	10.00	10.00
Social-Interpersonal Skills	76.10	20.38	.98	2.98	82.35	5.88	5.88	5.88	75.00	16.66	4.16	4.16	80.00	15.00		5.00
Verbalizing Feelings	67.68	21.20	6.55	1.51	88.23	5.88	5.88		70.83	20.83	8.33		70.00	20.00	5.00	5.00

College labs tended to consider all developmental areas as highly important in their programs. *All* their directors maintained that oral language skills, sensory awareness, and sensorimotor skills were highly important, and over three-quarters added motor skills, concept acquisition, emotional development, verbalizing feelings, arts and creative expression, and social-interpersonal skills. Two-thirds of them also included cognitive-intellectual skills. As in the general sample, less than half ranked reading and vocabulary skills and academic skills as highly important.

At least half the Montessori directors viewed all the developmental areas as being of high importance in their programs. Sensory awareness, cognitive-intellectual development, concept acquisition, emotional development, sensorimotor skills, and social-interpersonal skills were all ranked high by more than three-fourths. More than two-thirds similarly characterized oral language and verbalizing feelings. Of all the developmental areas, arts and creative expression received the smallest number of high rankings from Montessori directors.

If we turn to a consideration of the developmental areas rated by directors as being of *low* importance in their programs, it is interesting to note that over one-third of the total sample placed academic skills in this category. Over half the parent coop directors ranked academic skills as low, while less than 10 percent of the Montessori schools did so. In the general sample, the only other area which was called low in importance by more than 10 percent of the directors was reading and vocabulary skills. At the same time, again indicating the importance of traditional values, less than 1 percent of the sample considered social-interpersonal skills as unimportant.

It should also be pointed out that although Montessori schools appeared to ascribe less importance to arts and creative expression as indicated by the number of responses rating it as of high importance (and, indeed, as was mentioned earlier, Montessori herself did not encourage fantasizing, which would appear to be related), none of the Montessori directors specified arts and creative expression as being of low importance.

There was a total of sixty-four responses in the space provided for the directors to name any other area in the curriculum and to rate its importance in relation to the general program. Nearly all of these were described as being high in importance. Only three responses were named by three or more directors. Independence was listed by six, development of self-concept and self-image by five, and decision-making by three. Examples of other listings in this category were Jewish cultural content, scripture learning, self-discipline, sketching, black image, day care, and adult encounter techniques adapted for children.

FUNCTIONS OF THE SCHOOLS

Another way of ascertaining the director's values and philosophy of nursery school was to ask her to record what she considered the primary functions of her school. The question was open-ended, but the following aspects were expressly listed in order to suggest the kinds of things we had in mind: child care, readiness for school, child development program. The director could give as many answers as she chose, but most tended to limit themselves to the categories which we suggested.

To tabulate the data obtained from this question, the individual responses were categorized. For example, the largest group comprised those functions which pertained to general child development, in other words, assisting the child to grow in various facets of development. Over one-fourth of the directors listed this as one of the primary functions of their schools. An almost equal number reported education and readiness for elementary school as fundamental, including both a general focus on education as well as the development of very specific skills which were thought to contribute to success in a child's continuing education.

Ranking third in number among the responses was child care. Most dealt with the physical care and well-being of the child such that he was safe and relatively happy at a place away from home. About one-seventh of the directors gave responses in this category. All other classifications accounted for less than 10 percent of the total and included a great variety of answers. Mentioned were development of self-awareness, self-motivation, self-image, and self-confidence; socialization; parent education; preparation of personnel; research and program development; transmission of religious values; and fostering individual creativity.

Although it is hard to generalize from such varied responses, it is provocative to observe that, along with general child development, the largest group of responses involved academic preparation of the child for later schooling, thus apparently recognizing the potential of the preschool years for learning. One would have to question, of course, what the directors meant by this response, bearing in mind the distinction between *academic* learning which anticipates the traditional elementary school and the development of *cognitive* skills which help the child to think and enable him to find his own solutions to problems—help him to learn how to learn. In this regard, there appears to be some inconsistency between the directors' ratings of developmental areas and their responses to this more open-ended category of school function.

Responses to this question by directors of college labs, Montessori schools, and parent coops were studied separately to see if any trends could be discovered. The types of responses from these three programs were similar to those in the general sample, but the order in which they were mentioned and the frequency with which they appeared differed somewhat. The primary function of college labs, according to the administrators, encompassed the education of personnel, research, and program development to a greater extent than was true for the other samples. Parent education was named by college lab directors as a primary function more often than any other program except the parent coops. But the two largest categories of responses here, as in the general sample, were child development and education and readiness for school.

Montessori directors also reported categories similar to those in the total sample, but none listed child care as a function of her school. As in the general sample, parent coop directors enumerated general child development and readiness for school as the two major categories, but the third largest category for these schools centered on parent education.

OBJECTIVES OF THE SCHOOLS

The directors were also asked to identify the specific objectives of their programs, the attainment of which would contribute directly to fulfilling the schools' primary functions. The question again was open-ended, and it is of interest that considerable overlap was found between the responses given this question and those given the preceding item concerning the functions of the school. One could thus inquire whether the respondents could adequately separate general functions from specific objectives in their thinking. Again, the responses were categorized, and they proved to be mainly of three kinds: (1) those dealing with development of self, personality traits, and attitudes; (2)

those suggesting preparation for school and the development of specific skills thought to contribute to success in schooling; and (3) those generally involving child development. These categories accounted for almost half the responses. All other classifications each received less than 10 percent of the total responses and included such objectives as child socialization; child care; parent education and participation; education of personnel; creation of a learning atmosphere throughout the school; teaching religious tenets; concept development; research and program development; preparation for living; compensatory education; development of creativity; broadening of child's experiences; providing bilingual or cultural programs; and rendering service to the community or church.

Sixty percent of the responses made by directors of college lab schools fell into three categories, each comprising an equal number of responses: training of personnel, child development, and readiness for school. The only other categories named were development of aspects of the self, socialization, parent education and participation, and research and program development.

The range of objectives listed by Montessori directors was more restricted than in the case of any of the other schools. Only four categories of responses were given. One-third mentioned child development and one-fourth specified readiness for school. About 12 percent mentioned development of self, personality traits and attitudes, and an equal number reported research and program development.

The responses from parent coops fell into rather equal categories. Socialization appeared to be a greater concern than for other schools in the sample, however, as about one-fifth of the directors listed it as a specific objective. Other categories mentioned in these schools were, in descending order of frequency: child development; readiness for school and specific skills thought to contribute to success in school; development of self, personality traits, and attitudes; parent education and participation; development of creativity; research and program development; and service to the community or church. The last two categories received only one response each.

PROBLEMS OF THE SCHOOLS

The directors were also asked what they considered to be the major problems of their schools, since we felt that responses to this question would indicate the concerns of the director and the aspects of nursery schooling which she considered significant. The question once more was open-ended and worded in such a way as to call for several responses rather than one overriding concern. Therefore, the responses tended to range widely over many subjects, and no one category was mentioned by more than one-fifth of the respondents.

Although the largest number of responses (17.77 percent) fell into the classification of program or curricular problems, we found it disappointing that relatively few directors seemed to find this area a difficulty even in a time of so much ferment and experimentation regarding what is appropriate early schooling. It is difficult, of course, to know if the program was not considered a trouble spot because the directors were satisfied with their efforts to plan a suitable program and revise it periodically or merely because of complacency in accepting a curriculum always followed and considered "right" for preschool children.

In any case, among those administrators who did mention the program as a problem, several groupings of responses were evident. Development of new aspects of the program and program changes were the most often referred to, but even here, only nine directors noted this concern. Other difficulties listed by more than five directors were those which arose in trying to extend the present program and in attempting to meet the needs of the child and his family.

An almost equal number of directors (17.42 percent) indicated that they had problems in the category of physical facilities or equipment. These included the lack of facilities and equipment and hindrances caused by sharing thereof. The third largest category of responses incorporated personnel problems (16.72 percent of the responses), primarily the lack of staff and volunteers. Other related dilemmas included low pay, lack of custodial help, and teacher work demands.

Surprisingly, the problem of funding the nursery school was mentioned by only 11.84 percent of the respondents. The general lack of funds for running the school was most frequently named, but three directors also mentioned the need for funds to provide scholarships for less privileged children.

Ten percent of the directors indicated that they had trouble with parents, as regards such matters as parental pressure to influence the program, parents being too busy to have time for their children, getting parents to understand the value of a preschool rather than seeing it as a baby-sitting service, communication barriers, and parents' mobility. The next largest category of responses also had to do with parents, but these were related to the education of the parents themselves and their participation in the school, such as difficulties in getting parents involved in, oriented to, and receptive to the program, and in developing programs of parent education.

Other categories reported each made up less than 5 percent of the total responses. Some directors listed neighborhood problems (concern about burglary, vandalism, and trespassers), and others indicated the need for transportation of the children or improvement in their present system of transportation. Other problems which each accounted for little better than 1 percent of the responses were those pertaining to the racial-ethnic composition of the group (all but one director responding in this category indicated that a balance was desired); to interpersonal relations within the school or with other groups; to maintaining discipline; and to sporadic attendance.

A larger percentage of college lab directors indicated problems with their program than was true of the general sample. Nearly 30 percent noted concern in this area. Personnel matters were listed by about 25 percent, while more than 10 percent complained about physical facilities or equipment and lack of funds or the need for high financial status in order to be able to attend the school. Less than 5 percent listed difficulties with security, interpersonal relations, neighborhood problems, or parent education and participation.

Only 5.88 percent of the Montessori directors claimed that problems with the program and curriculum was one of their main concerns. Again, there is little evidence upon which to base a valid interpretation, but in this case it may be that since a well-defined Montessori program does exist, directors do not worry themselves with further program development. For the Montessori directors, personnel problems were uppermost and were alluded to by almost one-fourth of those responding. One-fifth indicated that parent education and participation were stumbling blocks, and other responses dealt with such subjects as transportation, parental concern and unrest, funding, physical facilities and equipment, sporadic attendance, and neighborhood problems.

An even smaller percentage of the parent cooperative directors (3.70 percent) indicated that dissatisfaction with the program and curriculum was a major concern. The largest number of responses here came under the category of parent education and participation, with more than 20 percent listing problems in this area. Another 15 percent named difficulties with parental personal problems and parent concern and unrest. This is perhaps logical considering the nature of the parent cooperative schools themselves. Other areas enumerated were funding, interpersonal relationships, physical facilities and equipment, transportation of children, and personnel.

SUCCESSES OF THE SCHOOLS

It was our impression that the program of the school, rather than being a subject of concern for the directors, was instead essentially a source of satisfaction. When the respondents were asked to tell us what they considered unique or particularly successful about their school, by far the largest category of replies concerned the general program impetus or a particular curricular emphasis. As the question was open-ended, a large scattering of responses could be expected, but in this case over 30 percent of the directors maintained that their program or some aspect of it made their school unique or successful. Some unique program considerations which were reported were development of imagination, increased bilingual skills, and development of independence and self-reliance. Curricular offerings which the directors mentioned as being extraordinary included music, field trips, academic skills, and teaching of such subjects as French and tap dancing.

Only two other categories of responses to this item were listed by over 10 percent of the administrators. The first included those responses which revolved around the school staff, such as educational preparation and experience of the teachers, mutual support among them, similar philosophical stance, willingness for staff involvement in the total program, and the staff turnover requiring children to adapt to many adults. The other feature was the parent education program which the school provided and the degree of parent participation in the school's general program.

Smaller numbers of directors offered responses to this question about the uniqueness or success of the school which came under several other categories. Some listed the general atmosphere of the school and noted that the children were happy or that they loved each other, that the children seem to be secure or that their school was a comfortable place for children to live and learn. Also named were exceptional facilities and equipment, such as the presence of sufficient materials for the number of students, the modern construction of the school, accessibility of Montessori equipment, and the amount of land on which the school was located. Other classifications, which accounted for very limited numbers of responses, were concerned with the interpersonal relationships within the school or with other groups; the freedom of the school; community involvement, relations, and support; staff and paraprofessional educational programs; the socioeconomic, ethnic, or racial integration of the student body; staff relationships with parents; other miscellaneous offerings of the school, such as bus service; the organization of the school itself (responses here usually indicated that the school was nongraded); and the school's sources of funding.

Forty percent of the responses from college laboratory school directors suggested that the program emphasis or curricular aims were the school's most successful or unique aspect. The only other category receiving more than 10 percent of the replies from this group of directors pertained to staff qualifications and attributes. Nearly 40 percent of the Montessori directors also reported that the most unique or successful characteristic of their school was the program or curriculum. Three other categories each garnered over 10 percent of the responses from these directors: the general atmosphere of the school itself, its facilities and equipment, and staff qualifications and attributes.

No single program characteristic was reported consistently by parent coop directors as unique. Four classifications received about the same number of responses, each receiving over 10 percent of the total. Not surprisingly, parent education and involvement were mentioned as unique and successful most often, followed by interpersonal relationships within the school or with other groups, program emphasis or curricular aims, and qualifications and attributes of the staff.

CHAPTER 5

BEHIND SCHOOL AND CLASSROOM DOORS

From the data presented in the preceding chapter, one would certainly have to conclude that the source waters of theory and innovation are to some degree flowing into the mainstream of preschooling practice in the United States. Directors of average nursery schools appear to be aware of the developmental areas stressed in many of the controversial and innovative early schooling programs, since most indicate that these areas have an important place in their own programs. Only a very small percentage of the administrators saw the function of their schools as being solely that of child care. In other words, it appears that few nursery schools see themselves as providing merely baby-sitting services, but instead accept their responsibility and role in the child's overall development and preparation for later schooling. Since most directors also express satisfaction with their programs, the logical assumption would be that the program and curriculum of the average nursery school are designed and implemented for these ends. Unfortunately, our data indicate that this assumption is false. The flow from the headwaters to the mainstream is making at most a surface ripple. The current is flowing along virtually undisturbed.

The Curriculum

Many of the items in our questionnaire and instructions for the observers were devised to provide information about the workings of the nursery school program so that we could examine and determine what was actually being done rather than what the director said her school was doing. For example, more than half the directors in the general sample had rated ten of the twelve developmental areas that we listed as being of high importance in their program. Seven of the twelve were so rated by more than two-thirds of the respondents. In order to ascertain whether these were actually incorporated into the curriculum, we asked the directors to indicate the frequency with which basic curricular areas and activities appeared in their programs.

We listed twenty-eight curricular areas and activities and instructed the director to specify whether they appeared daily, frequently, occasionally, or rarely or never in the school program. Further, an open-ended section gave the administrator the opportunity to list any areas which we had not included. Our list was compiled at the coordinators' meeting described earlier, and it should be pointed out that, in addition to being the product of our research staff, it represented the thinking of a group of early childhood education specialists from throughout the country.

The list of curricular areas and activities and a summary of the data collected in response to this item are presented in Table 5.1.

Several conclusions may be drawn from these data. Only six of the twenty-eight listed areas were rated as appearing daily in the program of at least two-thirds of the schools in the total sample. These were art, informal language, informal music, blocks, outdoor play, and story time. Only two additional areas appear daily when ratings made by over half the schools are considered: informal reading readiness and informal science.

Some activities may constitute an integral part of the school program even though they are not included on a daily basis. In order to identify these, responses in the "frequently" and "occasionally" columns were combined. Even this analysis, however, yielded only one activity—cooking (here play could not be separated from actual cooking)—which could be added to our previous list of activities occurring daily in over two-thirds of the schools. When looking at responses made by over half the directors, four additional categories could be considered frequent: dramatization and role-playing, nature walks, rhythms, and trips.

We found these figures extremely discouraging. Out of the universe of activities available to occupy, encourage, stimulate, and instruct preschool children, we could pinpoint only seven which constituted an integral part of the program (even given our loose definition of "integral") in at least two-thirds of the schools we surveyed. Thirteen can be named when we compile a list of activities found in the programs of at least half the schools. This does not comprise even half of the twenty-eight areas which we chose to list as most likely to appear in a preschool program. It does not begin to cover all the possible activities.

An additional breakdown into the three program groups provided little basis for encouragement. Parent cooperatives are, again, most like the total sample. In these schools, however, only four activities— art, blocks, outdoor play, and story time—were included in the daily program of more than two-thirds of the schools. Using 50 percent of the schools as the cut-off point adds only informal language and informal music. Other activities mentioned as turning up in the program frequently or occasionally by two-thirds or more of the directors of parent coop schools were carpentry, cooking, nature walks, and trips. Informal arithmetic, dramatization and role-playing, organized group games, and rhythms were rated "frequently" or "occasionally" by over half these directors. Thus, a total of fourteen activities could be considered an integral component of the parent cooperative school programs.

College laboratory directors reported a larger number of activities taking place on a daily basis in two-thirds of the classrooms. Nine activities—informal arithmetic, art, informal language, informal music, informal reading readiness, informal science, blocks, outdoor play, and story time—were so rated. Over half the directors listed four additional activities as part of the daily program: informal social studies, dramatization and role-playing, informal rest, and rhythms. A combination of the activities rated as undertaken either frequently or occasionally yielded three which were included in more than two-thirds of the schools: cooking, nature walks, and trips. A total of sixteen activities can thus be seen as a fundamental part of the program of college laboratory schools.

The list of activities which appear in the daily program of at least two-thirds of the schools is the same for the Montessori schools as for the college lab schools. Of the Montessori directors, 50 percent also add four others to the daily program: informal social studies, organized group games, reading, and formal reading readiness, which may bespeak the more academic emphasis of the Montessori programs. By looking at the "frequently" and "occasionally" columns, it can be seen that Montessori schools tend to include the more formal instructional areas which the other types of schools and the general sample do not. Formal science and formal social studies were specified by half the Montessori sample as appearing frequently or occasionally. Half the schools also named dramatization and role-playing and rhythms, and two-thirds noted that nature walks and trips were frequently or occasionally part of the program. Thus, a total of nineteen activities appear as an integral part of Montessori school programs.

TABLE 5.1　FREQUENCY OF CURRICULAR AREAS AND ACTIVITIES

Curricular Area or Activity	Daily				Frequently			
	Total Sample	Col. Lab	Mont.	Par. Coop	Total Sample	Col. Lab	Mont.	Par. Coop
Informal Arithmetic	50.22*	76.47	76.16	30.00	27.57	11.76	16.67	40.00
Formal Arithmetic	17.26	23.52	45.83	0.00	10.09	11.76	12.50	0.00
Art	82.50	88.23	83.33	85.00	11.50	0.00	12.50	10.00
Foreign Languages	8.95	0.00	16.66	0.00	4.96	11.76	29.16	0.00
Informal Language	68.02	88.23	75.00	55.00	10.65	5.88	8.33	25.00
Formal Language	20.60	35.29	45.83	0.00	10.55	11.76	20.83	10.00
Informal Music	77.22	94.11	62.50	60.00	15.84	5.88	25.00	30.00
Formal Music	19.58	23.52	29.16	15.00	18.07	5.88	25.00	10.00
Music Instrument Instruction	5.58	11.76	12.50	5.00	12.69	5.88	16.66	15.00
Informal Reading Readiness	62.18	82.35	91.66	45.00	15.91	5.88	0.00	15.00
Formal Reading Readiness	21.71	35.29	50.00	5.00	11.11	11.76	16.67	10.00
Reading	15.81	17.64	54.16	5.00	3.57	17.64	8.33	0.00
Informal Science	50.99	76.47	62.50	45.00	26.25	23.52	20.83	25.00
Formal Science	10.04	17.64	20.83	0.00	13.04	17.64	25.00	0Ɫ.00
Informal Social Studies	36.86	58.82	50.00	30.00	27.25	29.41	29.16	25.00
Formal Social Studies	6.08	11.76	8.33	0.00	13.16	11.76	33.33	5.00
Blocks	81.30	88.23	62.50	70.00	9.08	5.88	0.00	20.00
Carpentry	20.00	47.05	25.00	25.00	21.00	35.29	8.33	45.00
Cooking	7.06	17.64	25.00	5.00	23.21	64.70	4.17	25.00
Dramatization and Role Playing	32.82	64.70	16.67	30.00	35.81	23.52	29.16	30.00
Organized Group Games	35.64	11.76	50.00	25.00	29.20	41.17	12.50	30.00
Informal Rest	45.95	64.70	25.00	30.00	4.02	5.88	4.17	5.00
Naps	43.00	23.52	25.00	5.00	.50	0.00	0.00	0.00
Nature Walks	4.51	5.88	8.34	5.00	44.71	70.58	33.33	15.00
Outdoor Play	82.82	88.23	87.50	70.00	11.10	5.88	8.33	20.00
Rhythms	38.69	52.94	45.83	30.00	47.23	35.29	45.83	45.00
Story Time	85.34	82.35	79.16	85.00	10.10	11.76	8.33	10.00
Trips	0.00	0.00	0.00	0.00	33.32	41.17	16.16	25.00

* Percent of directors who indicated that informal arithmetic occurred daily in their program.

IN PROGRAM

Occasionally				Rarely or Never				No Tally			
Total Sample	Col. Lab	Mont.	Par. Coop	Total Sample	Col. Lab	Mont.	Par. Coop	Total Sample	Col. Lab	Mont.	Par. Coop
12.30	5.88	0.00	15.00	7.87	0.00	4.17	10.00	2.45	5.88	0.00	5.00
7.06	17.64	8.33	5.00	38.88	35.29	16.67	50.00	27.27	11.76	16.67	45.00
2.00	0.00	4.17	0.00	1.00	0.00	0.00	0.00	2.50	11.76	0.00	5.00
9.93	17.64	12.50	5.00	58.69	52.94	37.50	75.00	15.40	17.64	4.17	20.00
4.06	0.00	4.17	0.00	4.56	0.00	0.00	5.00	12.69	5.88	12.50	15.00
5.02	0.00	0.00	15.00	34.67	35.29	20.83	35.00	29.14	17.64	12.50	40.00
2.97	0.00	4.17	5.00	.99	0.00	4.17	0.00	2.97	0.00	4.17	5.00
7.52	23.52	12.50	15.00	30.63	35.29	12.50	30.00	24.11	11.76	28.83	30.00
21.31	17.64	25.00	30.00	44.16	52.94	33.33	40.00	13.19	11.76	12.50	10.00
5.47	0.00	0.00	15.00	6.96	0.00	0.00	15.00	8.44	11.76	8.33	10.00
7.06	11.76	4.17	5.00	37.36	35.29	16.67	45.00	22.71	5.88	12.50	35.00
7.65	5.88	16.67	15.00	53.56	29.41	16.67	70.00	17.34	29.41	4.17	10.00
14.13	0.00	12.50	20.00	4.54	0.00	0.00	0.00	4.03	0.00	4.17	10.00
15.05	11.76	25.00	15.00	37.16	35.29	16.67	35.00	24.60	17.64	12.50	7.00
16.15	11.76	8.33	15.00	12.61	0.00	4.17	15.00	6.56	0.00	8.33	15.00
10.13	11.76	20.83	15.00	42.63	47.05	25.00	40.00	28.41	17.64	12.50	40.00
2.52	0.00	8.33	5.00	3.53	0.00	25.00	0.00	3.02	5.88	4.17	5.00
21.50	5.88	16.67	20.00	31.00	11.76	45.83	5.00	5.00	0.00	4.17	5.00
43.93	11.76	41.66	55.00	21.20	5.88	29.16	10.00	4.04	0.00	0.00	5.00
18.69	5.88	29.16	20.00	7.94	5.88	25.00	10.00	2.97	0.00	0.00	10.00
19.30	11.76	25.00	20.00	12.87	35.29	12.50	20.00	2.47	0.00	0.00	5.00
11.10	5.88	8.33	10.00	29.28	17.64	50.00	45.00	7.57	5.88	12.50	10.00
2.00	5.88	0.00	0.00	47.00	70.58	54.16	85.00	6.00	0.00	20.83	10.00
39.18	11.76	41.66	70.00	8.00	5.88	8.33	5.00	2.51	5.88	8.33	5.00
2.52	0.00	0.00	0.00	2.02	5.88	0.00	5.00	1.51	0.00	4.17	5.00
11.05	11.76	8.33	15.00	1.00	0.00	0.00	5.00	1.50	0.00	0.00	5.00
2.01	5.88	4.17	0.00	1.01	0.00	8.33	0.00	1.01	0.00	0.00	5.00
49.98	41.17	50.00	65.00	14.64	17.64	29.16	0.00	2.02	0.00	4.17	10.00

Although the three types of programs analyzed separately do show some increase over the general sample in the number of activities included in their programs, one is still led to the conclusion that programs in the different types of preschools existing in this country lack the variety and richness implied by recent ferment in the field. What is even sadder is that the indications are that the typical nursery school provides limited opportunities for expression of individual differences and offers a narrow range of activities to encourage a child's development.

Program Evaluation

Another item on the Director Interview Form was intended to discover whether the schools were attempting to incorporate new ideas into their programs in any systematic way. No matter how much a director or a teacher might talk about and express agreement with new theories, we felt that innovative ideas could not make their way into the classroom program in any useful form unless there was evidence that the school was looking at itself and its program in order to know what it was actually doing and whether it was successful. Thus, it would have to be engaged in some kind of self-analysis and evaluation not only of its students but also of its curriculum and classroom practices.

Directors were asked two questions about evaluation. One requested information about whether the program was evaluated and how it was done, and the other concerned methods of assessing and evaluating student growth. Responses to both queries would seem to indicate that when evaluation is made, it is generally a loose, informal, and rather sporadic process. Examination of the data on evaluation of the school's program offered little evidence of any systematic attempt to look at the program either to examine the efficacy of current practices or to provide information for instituting change.

Of the directors sampled, 10 percent indicated that there was *no* evaluation, in any form, of their school's program. Over one-fourth related that their programs were evaluated by the school staff. There were few intimations, however, that such evaluations were carried out in any systematic fashion. The next largest category of responses (about 15 percent) included evaluations by state, county, or city officials, but these were most often concerned only with licensing standards, fire regulations, building inspection, and so on. Approximately the same number of respondents asserted that their schools were evaluated by the sponsoring or funding agency, usually by means of visits by ministers of the sponsoring church (for parochial schools) or by representatives of foundations and charities.

Just over 5 percent of the administrators reported evaluation of the program through parent involvement in the school and its educational program, and less than 5 percent described evaluation by independent associations or by owners or directors of the school only. Other scattered responses named appraisal by university or professional persons, use of standardized tests, evaluation by visitors to the program and by students and trainees, formal or informal follow-up studies, and formal research. Some replies were called evaluation procedures by the directors but seem to be of questionable value in the actual assessment of the school's program. These included such methods as auditing of the budget or a yearly report to a central office.

Nearly 40 percent of the college lab directors reported that evaluations of their program were conducted by members of the school staff. Evaluations by university or professional persons accounted for just over 20 percent of the responses, and those by students or trainees were listed in 17 percent of the cases. Five other categories each received less than 5 percent of the responses to this item: evaluation by sponsoring or funding agency, by the state, by visitors, and by parent involvement. Less than 5 percent of the college lab directors reported that there was no evaluation of their programs.

One-third of the Montessori directors claimed that they were evaluated by independent associations, usually either the American Montessori Society or the International Montessori Society. Over 20 percent of these directors did not respond to this question at all, however, and more than 10 percent indicated that no evaluation of the program was carried out. Equal numbers (just more than 10 percent in each case) mentioned evaluation by the owner, by the state, or by the staff.

Twenty percent of the parent cooperative directors stated that there was no evaluation of their programs. Equal numbers (20.83 percent in each case) cited evaluation by the staff, by university or professional persons, or through parent involvement. Three other categories each received less than 5 percent of the responses: evaluation by the sponsoring or funding agency, state evaluations, and a reply suggesting that evaluation of the program did occur but with no process designated.

Collecting Information About the Children

The individual child is the starting point in almost all the innovative programs we investigated in Chapter 2 and in all theories of how children develop and learn. We were therefore interested in seeing the extent to which the school conceived of each child as an individual, collected data about his needs, and attempted to adapt the program to meet them.

Directors were asked whether they gathered any information about the child or his family at the time of registration. Only about 1 percent of the replies indicated that no attempt was made to do this. Well over half the responses showed that some type of a written form requesting information about the child from his parents was included as part of the registration procedure. Where it was available, our observers usually procured a copy of the form and sent it to us. These forms most often contained only general questions eliciting names of adults to call in an emergency, addresses, and medical information. Only rarely was inquiry made about the developmental history of the child or his family background.

The only other mode of acquiring information about the child prior to his enrollment in the school receiving any significant number of responses was an interview or conference between the parent and the director of the school, a teacher, or a social worker. About one-fourth of the respondents stated that such consultations were common at their schools. Home visits were mentioned by about 5 percent of the directors. It would seem that these two procedures would be more likely than others to provide accurate information for the school about the needs of the child and his developmental and family history, but of course, there is no way for us to know from the data exactly what the school sought to find out through such conferences or visits.

Evaluation of Students

About two-thirds of the administrators indicated that their schools evaluated student growth through observations by individual teachers or the director and through maintaining written records. It is our impression that almost all these evaluations were of a perfunctory and unstructured nature. We could find little evidence of guidelines or checklists provided by the school which the teachers were to use. If these observations are as loose and casual as they appear, the information yielded by them must be fairly superficial and of little use in diagnosing individual needs. This inference, of course, is subjective and is based on what our observers were *not* given by school directors and information which they did *not* include in their reports.

About 17 percent of the directors asserted that student evaluation in their schools was made through a testing program. Less than 5 percent responded that no evaluation was made of the students, and even fewer that evaluations were based on collective staff observations, the compilation of sociometric data, parent comment, specialist assessments (by speech therapists, dentists, and medical doctors), appraisals by students or trainees, or by testing prior to enrollment.

Over 50 percent of the college labs noted that pupil evaluation was undertaken by observation and records, presumably by the teacher. About 25 percent reported the use of tests. Less than 10 percent of the evaluations derived from student teacher or trainee observations.

Evaluation of students in Montessori schools appeared to be achieved primarily by means of teacher observations, records, and reports, as these methods accounted for over three-fourths of the Montessori responses. About 10 percent of the directors maintained that they used tests. An equal number responded that there was *no* evaluation of pupil growth. This was a much larger percentage than was found for either of the other two types of schools or for the sample as a whole and is rather surprising in view of the more academic emphasis of these schools implied by the data reported previously.

As might be expected from the nature of the parent cooperative program, parent observation as a means of evaluating pupil development was used more heavily than in the general sample. About one-quarter of the responses fell into this category. However, for these schools, too, the most common means of appraisal was through teacher observations, with more than half the directors responding in this way. Only about 6 percent of parent coop administrators said they used tests to assess their students' growth.

Individualization of Instruction

We looked for evidence in the classroom that the teacher was, indeed, as many directors said, observing and evaluating her students by asking our observers to rate teachers on their attempts to individualize instruction for the children in their classes. Individualization was judged to be occurring in the class if there was indication that individual children were being diagnosed in terms of their special needs and that educational decisions attuned to these needs were then made and implemented. On this basis, only a third of the classrooms sampled were rated as making an attempt to individualize their programs; slightly less than a third showed a little evidence; and about one-third offered almost no evidence of any such effort. Further, when observers were asked to note particularly successful or unique aspects of the classroom program, in only 5.88 percent of the cases did they specify that any individualization was conspicuous in the class. This is hardly an encouraging situation.

Reports to Parents

The schools we surveyed did not, on the whole, appear to have any formal system for reporting to parents on their children's progress. When directors were asked what procedures they utilized to report to parents, they usually listed several methods. Over half the responses in the total sample fell into two categories: conferences by teachers and social workers, and informal contacts with parents—largely as children were delivered to school or picked up. There was no suggestion that such conferences, whether formal or informal, were initiated on any regular basis or that they provided any in-depth information about the child for either parent or the teacher. The next largest category of methods was telephone calls, which came to just under 15 percent of the responses. Only about 10 percent of the respondents indicated that they made written reports on the students. These were used in some cases where parents were absent or separated.

Other means of notifying parents each accounted for less than 10 percent of the replies. These included parent group meetings and programs, home visits, newsletters and impersonal notes, parent observations, and casework consultation. Fewer than 1 percent of the directors said that they made no reports in any form to the parents.

College labs and Montessori schools were more likely than the general sample to use conferences as a means of informing the parents. Thirty percent of college lab directors and 50 percent of the Montessori stated that they used this method. The college labs tended to follow the total sample in the other categories of responses. Montessori schools differed, though, in maintaining that written reports to parents were used by 25 percent, with three additional categories each accounting for less than 10 percent of the responses: informal contacts, parent observations, and phone calls.

Parent coops were more likely to utilize informal talks (over 30 percent of responses) and conferences (25 percent) as ways of communicating with parents. Over 15 percent claimed that parent group meetings were set up to discuss pupil progress, and about 10 percent mentioned the use of phone calls and written reports. Just over 2 percent responded that no reporting procedures were employed.

To summarize briefly: We have discussed here our attempts to unearth direct evidence from what the directors reported and our observers saw as to whether school personnel visualize each child as an individual and adjust the program to his needs. What we found was not auspicious. There is little indication that the schools gather developmental information about the child when he enters in order to establish a base line for his progress. Most attempts at evaluating his growth within the program apparently are so informal that it is doubtful that useful information could be amassed. In fact, within the individual classrooms, we found little evidence that the observation and evaluation that directors claimed to be taking place was, in fact, going on. Finally, since methods of reporting to parents again seemed to be very informal, it is doubtful if systematic reviews of student progress and discussion of corrective measures constitute a regular part of the schools' procedures.

Classroom Equipment and Learning Materials

Our next step was to search out indirect evidence which might imply that individualization was indeed happening and that the school recognized its obligation to provide for all their children and to analyze and adjust in correspondence with their individual needs.

One indication that the schools were aware of the "problem of the match," previously discussed, and attempt to provide for it might be in the amount and variety of equipment and learning materials accessible in the classroom and play yard. At our meeting of coordinators, we drew up a long list of such items which, in the opinion of these experts in early childhood education, might reasonably be expected to be found in a nursery school classroom or outdoor play area. The list was not meant to be exhaustive, and considerable space was provided on the Classroom Observation Form for the observer to note the presence of any other apparatus not named on the form. The material was defined as being present if it was clearly visible to the observer and not hidden away under things or in cupboards or cabinets. If it was clearly observable to us, then we could assume that it was easily available to the children in the classroom. A summary of these data is found in Table 5.2.

We named 65 different types of materials and equipment on the checklist. Of these, only fourteen were found in at least three-fourths of the classrooms visited: child-size straight chairs, phonographs, running water, tables for working, toilets, real animals, unit table blocks, library picture books, crayons, dolls and accessories, housekeeping toys, music listening materials, wood inlay puzzles, and table toys. It is disturbing to note that this grouping does not contain any items commonly associated with boys but does include dolls and housekeeping toys traditionally regarded as being for girls.

Four additional kinds of equipment were in evidence when observations for two-thirds of the classrooms were compiled: chalkboards, cubbies or lockers, easels and paints, and science materials. Eleven more were found in at least one-half of the classes: bulletin boards; adult chairs; piano or organ; floor crate blocks; clay; collage materials; dress-up clothes; math materials; rhythm instruments; highly defined trucks, cars, and trains; and creative play trucks, cars, and trains. Thus, out of the innumerable kinds of equipment and materials which can be ordered commercially, collected from many homes, or constructed from easily obtainable everyday items, only twenty-nine could be said to be present in at least half the classrooms in our sample, and of these, many were basic necessities such as tables, chairs, and toilets.

There was quite an array of other materials and equipment omitted from our list but which the observers noted. These ranged from commercially produced materials to highly creative products designed for the needs of a particular group of children. In no case, however, did any of these items approach 50 percent of the responses —in fact, none was mentioned in even 10 percent.

A total of thirty-four kinds of equipment and materials was noted in at least half the classrooms of college laboratory schools. In addition to equipment found in classes of the total sample were child-size rocking chairs, mechanical toys, programmed materials, stuffed animals, and water play areas. When three-fourths of the classrooms were considered, college lab schools had more kinds of equipment available than the general sample or either of the other types of special programs. Nineteen items were discerned in 75 percent of the rooms. Cubbies or lockers, pianos or organs, easels and paints, rhythm instruments, and science materials were added to materials visible in three-fourths of the classrooms of the total sample.

According to our observations, Montessori schools had fewer kinds of equipment and materials available than did either of the other two separately identified programs or, for that matter, the sample as a whole. Only eight items were found in more than three-fourths of the Montessori classrooms: child-size rockers, cubbies or lockers, tables for working, real animals, library picture books, crayons, math materials, and wood inlay puzzles. Fourteen more were on hand in more than one-half of these rooms: science materials, bulletin boards, adult chairs, phonographs, running water, toilets, unit table blocks, collage materials, easels and paints, housekeeping toys, mats for working, programmed materials, rhythm instruments, and water play area. In Montessori schools, a lack of conventional toys such as dolls and trucks might be expected, but we found the general paucity of overall material difficult to account for. Several tentative explanations may be advanced. First, Montessori techniques call for all material to be in its place when not in use by the children. It is possible that our observers did not see a great deal of material because it was stored away. Second, they may have included in the category of math materials specialized Montessori equipment such as counting rods, golden beads, and others which teach number concepts, thereby lumping together the wide variety of mathematical materials which Montessori designed. The third explanation might be that many of these schools call themselves Montessori but simply are not in regard to their programs. They may have a few of the best-known Montessori materials and nothing much beyond that.

Parent cooperative schools had thirty kinds of equipment and materials which were found in 50 percent or more of their classrooms. Beyond the list for 75 percent of the classrooms in the general sample, 75 percent of the parent coop classes had bulletin boards, dress-up clothes, easels and paints, science materials, and creative play cars. Over half these rooms had three kinds of materials missing from the total sample and the other types of programs: textbooks, carriages and buggies, and woodworking materials. It is hard to reconcile here the presence of textbooks with the very low rating awarded academic

TABLE 5.2 MATERIALS AND EQUIPMENT, PERCENT BY TYPE OF PRESCHOOL CLASSROOM AND BY ALL CLASSROOMS

Equipment	Indoors				Outdoors			
	All N=216	P N=20	CL N=20	Mont. N=26	All N=216	P N=20	CL N=20	Mont. N=26
Bulletin Boards	56.94	75.00	70.00	61.53	1.38	*	10.00	
Adult Chairs	61.11	35.00	70.00	50.00	3.70	5.00		
Comfortable Chairs	10.18	15.00	10.00	15.38	0.46			
Child-size Straight Chairs	94.90	90.00	95.00	15.38	4.16		20.00	
Child-size Rockers	33.79	25.00	50.00	84.61	0.46			
Chalk Board	70.37	50.00	55.00	11.53				
Cots	37.96	5.00	25.00	11.53				
Cubbies or Lockers	69.90	50.00	90.00	76.93	0.46			
Desks for Working	14.35	5.00	15.00	26.92				
Mats for Resting	25.00	25.00	20.00	34.61				
Phonograph	83.33	90.00	75.00	50.00				
Piano (organ)	57.87	50.00	80.00	46.15				
Running Water	77.77	90.00	95.00	65.38	11.11	20.00	35.00	
Tables for Working	96.29	90.00	90.00	84.61	5.55	5.00	30.00	
Television	30.55	10.00	15.00	15.38				
Toilets	93.05	90.00	100.00	57.69	2.31			
Animals (real)	76.85	35.00	75.00	100.00	14.35			19.23
Balls	37.96	40.00	20.00	26.92	24.53	20.00	35.00	15.38
Blocks (unit/table)	84.25	85.00	90.00	61.53	3.70	5.00	10.00	
Blocks, Crates (floor)	55.55	65.00	55.00	15.38	11.11		35.00	
Books: Texts—Primers Pre-primers	24.53	50.00	25.00	38.46				
Books: Library (picture)	93.51	100.00	90.00	88.46	0.46			
Carriages, Buggies	37.03	55.00	40.00	7.69	4.62		5.00	
Clay	57.40	55.00	55.00	30.76	0.92		5.00	
Climbing Apparatus	21.75	45.00	25.00	3.84	63.88	60.00	80.00	50.00
Collage Materials	62.96	70.00	65.00	53.84				
Cooking Materials (toy & real)	37.96	45.00	40.00	46.15				
Crayons	87.96	85.00	90.00	84.61				
Dolls & Accessories	82.87	95.00	95.00	19.23	0.92		5.00	
Dress-up Clothes	63.42	80.00	70.00	15.38	1.85		5.00	
Easels/paints	74.53	80.00	75.00	57.69	7.40	10.00	20.00	7.69
Filmstrips & Projector	12.96	5.00	10.00	3.84				
Finger Paints	43.98	65.00	35.00	23.07	0.46		5.00	

* Empty cells indicate no cases.

TABLE 5.2   MATERIALS AND EQUIPMENT, PERCENT BY TYPE OF
PRESCHOOL CLASSROOM AND BY ALL CLASSROOMS (Continued)

Equipment	Indoors				Outdoors			
	All N=216	P N=20	CL N=20	Mont. N=26	All N=216	P N=20	CL N=20	Mont. N=26
Housekeeping Toys	88.88	95.00	85.00	69.23	0.92	5.00	10.00	
Jump Ropes	19.44	20.00	10.00	7.69	10.64		35.00	11.53
Math Materials	63.88	60.00	70.00	92.30				
Mats for Working	22.22	15.00	30.00	69.23	0.46			
Mechanical Toys	47.68	30.00	60.00	30.76				
Movies	9.72		20.00	7.69				
Music Listening	76.85	85.00	75.00	34.61				
Programmed Materials	39.81	35.00	50.00	50.00				
Puppets	32.40	45.00	40.00	11.53				
Puzzles (wood inlay)	81.94	80.00	85.00	76.92				
Puzzles (cardboard)	37.50	40.00	45.00	26.92				
Riding Equipment: Bicycles	4.62				10.18	10.00	35.00	7.69
Riding Equipment: Tricycles	13.88	15.00	20.00	3.84	31.48	50.00	65.00	7.69
Riding Equipment: Scooters	4.16	5.00			7.87	5.00	35.00	3.84
Riding Equipment: Wagons	16.20	25.00	15.00	3.84	27.77	45.00	65.00	7.69
Riding Equipment: Cars	14.81	5.00	5.00	3.84	11.11	10.00	40.00	7.69
Rhythm Instruments	62.96	50.00	85.00	53.84				
Sand & Accessories (and Substitutes)	16.66	15.00	25.00	7.69	46.29	50.00	65.00	23.07
Science Materials & Corner	70.37	85.00	80.00	69.23	4.16	5.00	20.00	
Slides	9.25	10.00	15.00	3.84	30.09	20.00	60.00	26.93
Store Equipment	27.77	40.00	45.00	11.53	3.24		10.00	
Stuffed Animals	48.14	35.00	50.00	19.53	0.92			
Swings	5.09	5.00			47.68	40.00	60.00	34.61
Table Toys	80.09	80.00	85.00	42.30	1.85		5.00	3.84
Tools	5.55	5.00		7.69	18.98	20.00	50.00	15.38
Trucks/Cars/Trains (Highly Defined)	59.25	55.00	55.00	30.76	8.79	15.00	20.00	7.69
Trucks/Cars/Trains (Creative Play)	56.48	75.00	65.00	23.07	8.33		20.00	11.53
Water Play Area	33.33	40.00	50.00	50.00	12.96	30.00	30.00	7.69
Water Toys	27.77	35.00	35.00	46.15	8.33	30.00	20.00	3.84
Woodworking Materials	31.48	55.00	40.00	19.23	8.33	45.00	35.00	
Workbooks (Non-Programmed)	10.18		5.00	23.07	0.46		5.00	

skills and reading by parent coop directors. The only items not found in half the parent coop classrooms which were observed in the rest of the sample were adult chairs and real animals.

For the total sample, only one item was found in the outdoor play area of 50 percent or more of the schools: a climbing apparatus. In half the college lab schools, in addition to the climbing apparatus, tricycles, wagons, sand and accessories, slides, swings, and tools were present. Parent coops had the climbing apparatus, tricycles, sand and accessories, while at least half the Montessori schools had only the climbing apparatus. No single item was located in at least three-fourths of the schools of either the total sample or the special programs. This offers a rather bleak picture of playgrounds which do little more than allow children to stretch and run. We could find little evidence that the outdoor area, if the school had one at all, was viewed as a place in which the school's program could be continued and extended. The large number of no tallies in response to this item should be noted, however.

In addition to noting the kinds of equipment and materials available in the classrooms they visited, the observers were instructed to give a subjective rating of the variety and quantity of these materials. Most classrooms were judged as having an adequate variety. Just over 17 percent were characterized as being very well equipped with a rich array of materials providing variety. Slightly less than 35 percent were called ample, with a wide breadth of materials available. About 26 percent were deemed to have a moderate variety, and 11 percent to be somewhat below average, with some equipment and material available. Eight percent of the classrooms were considered to be sparsely equipped, with a minimum of materials available.

Over half the classrooms (51.38 percent) were rated by the observers as having an ample quantity of equipment and material for the number of children in the class. About 36 percent were called adequate, meaning that the children had to take turns in using the material but not so much so as to cause frustration. About 10 percent were rated as limited and insufficient.

Teaching Methods

One focus of our observation was to ascertain whether the activities of the teachers within the classroom and in their interactions with the children tend to follow the kinds of behaviors which are thought to promote cognitive development according to the theories of Piaget, Hunt, and others and are reflected in certain experimental or innovative programs. We could also seek out evidence of self-directed creative activities found in many innovative programs.

The same curricular areas which were evaluated by the directors as to the frequency with which they appeared in their programs were listed in the Classroom Observation Form. Here, the observers were requested to rank the activities occurring in each area as to the degree of structure imposed upon the activity by the teacher. The intent was to determine the degree to which the teacher directed and controlled the children while they were engaged in that activity or the degree to which teacher expectations dominated the activity or use of materials. In a classroom influenced by the child development theories of Piaget, one would expect most activities to be unstructured, with the teacher allowing the child to proceed at his own pace and to manipulate the material in his own way. This was not what we found. A summary of the data for this item may be seen in Table 5.3.

Of the thirteen areas claimed to be an integral part of the program of their school by at least half the directors in the general sample (see page 94), only three were rated by our observers as unstructured in more than half the cases in which they were observed: blocks, outdoor play, and dramatization and role-playing. Each of these, in fact, was considered unstructured in more than two-thirds of the observations.

None of the thirteen activities was judged to be highly regulated by the teacher in more than half the observations; however, seven were judged as having some structure imposed on them by the teacher. Those characterized as having some teacher structuring in over two-thirds of the cases were nature walks and trips. Informal music, story time, informal reading readiness, cooking, and rhythms were so described in over half the classrooms.

For three of the activities, the evaluations were too scattered to enable us to say that over half the cases observed were highly regulated, had some structure, or were unstructured. However, for informal language, art, and informal science, by adding together the ratings for "highly structured" and "having some structure," it was possible to see again that in over half the classrooms these activities tended to be more structured than unstructured. Art was either highly structured

TABLE 5.3 DEGREE OF STRUCTURE OBSERVED IN CURRICULAR AREAS AND ACTIVITIES

Curricular Area or Activity	Highly Regulated				Some Structure				Unstructured			
	Total Sample	College Lab	Mont.	Parent Coop	Total Sample	College Lab	Mont.	Parent Coop	Total Sample	College Lab	Mont.	Parent Coop
Informal Arithmetic	13.11	18.18	21.73	16.66	51.63	27.27	56.52	41.67	35.24	54.54	21.73	41.67
Formal Arithmetic	59.45	75.00	50.00	100.00	37.83	25.00	50.00	0.00	2.70	0.00	0.00	0.00
Art	13.57	5.26	12.50	5.55	47.91	36.84	45.83	55.56	35.93	57.89	41.66	38.89
Foreign Languages	30.00	100.00	37.50	*	65.00	0.00	62.50		5.00	0.00	0.00	
Informal Language	9.93	17.64	17.64	15.38	46.58	17.64	47.05	46.15	43.47	64.70	35.29	38.46
Formal Language	58.33	5.00	21.42	75.00	37.50		64.28	25.00	4.16		14.28	0.00
Informal Music	13.42	6.25		13.33	61.74	50.00		53.33	24.83	43.75		33.33
Formal Music	46.51	5.00	60.00	33.33	53.48		15.00	66.66	0.00			0.00
Musical Instrument Instruction	16.66	100.00	20.00		54.16	0.00	80.00	100.00	29.16	0.00	0.00	0.00
Informal Reading Readiness	10.65	13.33	12.50	8.33	53.27	26.66	75.00	50.00	36.06	60.00	12.50	41.66
Formal Reading Readiness	52.17	62.50	45.45	100.00	41.30	37.50	54.54	0.00	6.52	0.00	0.00	0.00
Reading	22.85	0.00	33.33	25.00	45.71	75.00	44.44	75.00	31.42	25.00	22.22	0.00
Informal Science	6.14	0.00	20.00	7.69	46.49	30.00	40.00	23.07	47.36	70.00	40.00	69.23
Formal Science	26.08	0.00	40.00	0.00	60.86	100.00	40.00	66.66	13.04	0.00	20.00	33.33
Informal Social Studies	11.76	11.11	36.36	16.66	42.35	22.22	36.36	83.33	45.88	66.66	27.27	0.00
Formal Social Studies	47.61	100.00	50.00	100.00	47.61	0.00	50.00	0.00	4.76	0.00	0.00	0.00
Blocks	12.82	16.66	25.00	0.00	24.16	21.42	33.33	17.64	69.79	71.42	41.66	82.35
Carpentry	6.04	7.14	25.00	0.00	20.51	16.66	25.00	22.22	66.66	66.66	50.00	77.77
Cooking	23.40	0.00	44.44	0.00	65.95	75.00	55.55	80.00	10.63	25.00	0.00	20.00
Dramatization and Role-Playing	3.36	0.00	0.00	0.00	26.89	14.28	33.33	20.00	69.74	85.71	66.66	80.00
Organized Group Games	28.40	33.33	45.45	0.00	57.95	33.33	54.54	50.00	13.63	33.33	0.00	50.00
Informal Rest	25.00	20.00	20.20	33.33	43.75	0.00	60.00	0.00	31.25	80.00	20.00	66.66
Naps	55.10	100.00	50.00		44.89	0.00	50.00		0.00	0.00	0.00	
Nature Walks	12.82	33.33	0.00	0.00	69.23	66.66	75.00	66.66	17.94	0.00	25.00	33.33
Outdoor Play	2.68	0.00	0.00	7.14	30.87	20.00	38.46	28.57	66.44	80.00	61.53	64.28
Rhythms	26.04	22.22	27.27	22.22	63.54	11.11	72.72	66.66	10.41	66.66	0.00	11.11
Story Time	27.51	25.00	44.44	31.25	61.74	41.66	44.44	56.25	10.73	33.33	11.11	12.50
Trips	20.51	0.00	0.00	0.00	66.82	80.00	100.00	66.66	12.82	20.00	0.00	33.33

* Empty cells indicate no cases.

or had some structure in 61.48 percent of the cases, informal language in 56.51 percent, and informal science in 52.63 percent.

Other curricular areas which were not noted by the directors as appearing daily or frequently in their programs were also seen and categorized by our observers, though in fewer numbers than the other activities. Of these, only one—carpentry—was considered unstructured in at least half the classrooms. Four activities were listed as being highly regulated by the teacher in over half the cases: formal arithmetic, formal language, formal reading readiness, and naps. Six were seen to have some teacher structuring imposed upon them: informal arithmetic, foreign language, formal music, music instrument instruction, organized group games, and formal science.

For four other areas, no single category received over 50 percent of the ratings. However, by adding the "highly structured" and "some structure" columns, it could be seen that with these activities, too, the tendency was toward structuring of the activity. Reading was called highly structured or some structure in 68.56 percent of the cases, informal social studies in 54.11 percent, formal social studies in 95.22 percent, and informal rest in 68.75 percent of the cases where they were observed.

It can thus be seen that of the twenty-eight pertinent curricular areas, only playing and constructing with blocks, outdoor play, dramatization and role-playing, and carpentry could be viewed as unstructured by the teacher such that the children direct their own activity. It certainly does not appear that self-discovery methods have been incorporated by the average nursery school teacher.

Of the three separate programs, college laboratory schools had more of their activities deemed unstructured than did the other types of program or the sample as a whole. Eight areas were listed as unstructured in over two-thirds of the college lab classrooms: informal science, informal social studies, blocks, carpentry, dramatization and role-playing, informal rest, outdoor play, and rhythms. Four other activities were described as unstructured in over half the classes: informal arithmetic, art, informal language, and informal reading readiness. Parent coops also had more activities designated as unstructured than did the total sample. Eight such activities were found, six in more than two-thirds of the classes—informal rest, dramatization and role-playing, carpentry, blocks, informal social studies, and informal science— and two others in over half the classes—organized group games and outdoor play. Montessori classes had the fewest unstructured activities.

Dramatization and role-playing was the only area listed as unstructured in over two-thirds of the classes observed. Carpentry and outdoor play were added in over half the classes.

It is intriguing to note that in addition to having more unstructured activities than did the other programs or the general sample, college lab schools also had more activities which the observers construed as being highly regulated by the teacher. There were seven such activities, six of them in more than two-thirds of the classes: formal arithmetic, foreign language, formal music, music instrument instruction, formal social studies, and naps. Formal reading readiness was deemed highly structured in more than half these classes.

The Montessorian ideal of "liberty" might lead one to anticipate that more of the activities in Montessori classrooms would have had little or no teacher structuring than was reported above. However, the Montessori insistence that there is only one right way to use each piece of equipment would entail the probability that most activities carried on by the children, while having little formal teacher supervision or direction, would have at least some degree of teacher structure or expectation imposed upon them. This was, indeed, what we found. Although no activity was reported to be highly regulated by the teacher in more than two-thirds of the Montessori classrooms, in over half the classes four activities were so rated: formal arithmetic, formal music, formal social studies, and naps. The majority of the activities observed in Montessori classes were described as having some degree of structure exercised over them by the teacher. Fifteen were classified in this way in over half the classes, and five in over two-thirds. Though it is impossible to determine the kind of structure in question from the form in which the data were collected, the activities may have been judged in this way because it was observed that the teacher structured how the child was to use the material and then left him to work with it at his own rate and in his own time. This is only conjecture, however.

The Teacher's Role

Several other multiple-choice questions on the Classroom Observation Form requested the observer to make a judgment about the teacher's style, methods, and behavior. The data collected here also seem to indicate that traditional teaching methods are still the rule in most nursery school classrooms. For example, when asked about the locus of control and decision-making within the class, the observers rated 31.94 percent of the classes as teacher-controlled. In 38.79 percent, it was noted that children had opportunities to make decisions, but that the class was teacher-directed most of the time. Therefore, two-thirds of the classes in the sample were seen as primarily teacher-directed. In fewer than a third of the cases were the children considered to have many opportunities to make decisions.

Observers were asked to classify the role of the teacher within the classroom as either the authority in charge and highly directive; directive but unobstrusively so; as a resource for children to use; or as providing little direction or interaction with the children unless necessary. The greatest number of teachers were categorized as directive but not obtrusive—44.90 percent. More than one-fourth (26.28 percent) were viewed as authoritative and highly directive; less than a quarter (22.39 percent) appeared to consider themselves as a resource for the children to use; and 6.02 percent were described as giving little direction to the children or having little interaction with children except where necessary.

Classroom Interactions

A series of items was concerned with the interactions occurring within the classroom. It would appear from these data that most interactions between teacher and child are initiated by the teacher, and that when the child does initiate an interaction, it is usually for the purpose of obtaining permission for something or for routine requests. For example, when the observers were instructed to rate the degree of teacher-child interaction, 45.35 percent of the classes were determined as having some degree of physical or verbal interaction stemming primarily from teacher initiation. These usually took the form of pats on the head or body, or some individual verbal recognition of children. A high degree of either physical or verbal interaction was found in 37.49 percent of the classes. Only 8.77 percent were rated as having little interaction initiated by the teacher but with the teacher being readily available and active when needed (probably the role which would be considered most appropriate in many of the innovative programs described in Chapter 2). Another 6.93 percent were judged as having little interaction though physical proximity might be high, as when the teacher distributes food to the children but does not interact with them.

The overwhelming majority of teacher-to-child interactions were ascertained by our observers to be warm and supportive, with 46.31 percent rated as very warm, supportive, and accepting, and an additional 48.14 percent as moderately so. Only 3.20 percent were rated as cold, critical, disinterested, and punitive.

When child-to-teacher interaction was ranked, in the majority of classrooms (52.04 percent) the number of such interactions was deemed moderate. Only a third of the classes (33.61 percent) were considered to have a high degree of child-to-teacher interaction, with many children initiating contact with the teacher. However, in only 12.89 percent was the amount of interaction considered low and were the children rarely or never seen to initiate contact with the teacher.

When the quality of interactions between the child and the teacher is scrutinized, it can be clearly seen that children perceive the teacher in a directive role rather than as a resource to be sought when needed. In half the classes (50.44 percent), children were characterized as contacting the teachers freely but mostly for routine requests and permissions. In addition, small percentages of classrooms were viewed as having child-teacher interactions in which the children contacted the teachers largely out of frustration (7.20 percent) and in which the children were hesitant to initiate contacts (6.30 percent). Only a third of the classes were designated as having child-teacher interactions whereby the children freely contacted the teachers as needed primarily as a resource and for enrichment.

A high degree of child-to-child interaction, with most of the children actively engaged with other children, was observed in 37.13 percent of the classrooms, and 47.23 percent were found to have a moderate degree, with considerable parallel play. Only 15.11 percent were described as low in the amount of child-child interactions, with most of the children rarely interacting with each other.

When the quality of these child-child interactions was examined, it was found that most take place in a socially acceptable form. A majority, 51.05 percent, were classified as being largely shared, cooperative, and positive, with another 10.26 percent definitely considered to be shared, cooperative, and positive. Only about a fifth of the children (20.14 percent) were judged as passive and docile in their interaction, while 9.84 percent of the interactions were evaluated as largely aggressive and negative, and 5.17 percent as decidedly aggressive and negative.

Grouping Patterns

Another factor investigated in attempting to determine the teacher's style and the amount of individualization in her classroom was the grouping patterns she used. Because of the variety of ways in which they were reported by the observers, classification of grouping patterns was difficult, though we were able to fit the responses into fairly loose categories. One-third of the classrooms utilized primarily small, self-selected groups. Such division into small groups might be an indication that individualization of instruction was taking place, but since the groups were "self-selected," it may be that the teacher was not diagnosing the child's needs and fitting him into the group where they could best be met. About one-fifth of the classes formed a single large group at all times during the observation. A variety of other patterns was noticed, but none in great numbers. Examples of these were age grouping, teacher-controlled and -directed groups, groups differentiated according to sex, and flexible, flowing, and spontaneous groups.

Parent Involvement

Another potent factor in many of the innovative preschool programs described earlier was the direct involvement of the parents in the education of their children. In many instances, they served as aides in the classroom, in others they participated in the learning program, and in still others they were equal partners with the academic staff in planning and implementing the program. We looked, then, at our sample of nursery schools to see if and how parents are involved in the education of their preschool children.

Directors were requested to indicate the extent to which parents took part in their school program. Over half the total sample responded that parents were encouraged to participate in the school program on a voluntary basis. Such participation ranged from acting as an assistant in the classroom or designing part of the program to driving students on a field trip or helping with a party. Though some schools affirmed that they welcomed parent involvement in any facet of the program, others reported that parents were encouraged to join in school activities but not to participate in the classroom. Where schools specified little or no parent involvement, a reason sometimes offered was that working parents simply were not available to help.

The majority of the sample insisting that parent participation was *required* was accounted for by the parent coop schools. Each one stated that it was mandatory that the parent take part in the school program. Over half the college labs and Montessori schools maintained that they encouraged parent participation only on a voluntary basis. It appeared that most of the activities in which the parents participated in these schools took place outside the classroom. Parent aides in the classroom were seen consistently only in parent coop schools.

Another index of the degree to which parents are involved in the school's program may be the number and kind of parent meetings convened by the school. No one type of meeting was specified by more than one-fifth of the directors in the sample. About 16 percent reported holding general parent meetings in which the focus of discussion was on the parents' concerns rather than on those involving the teachers and the parents. Just under 14 percent mentioned sponsoring discussion groups, and only slightly fewer said that PTA-type meetings were held. About 11 percent organized parties, classes, or social programs for the parents, and over 8 percent reported holding parent committees and club meetings. Nine percent organized no parent meetings of any kind. Other categories of responses each accounted for less than 5 percent of the total and included informal visits, orientation meetings, programs with speakers and discussion, work parties, workshops, fathers' meetings, community-type programs, mothers' meetings, special programs, seminars, and parent field trips. It is difficult to determine from the data how many of the meetings and events in question actually elicited discussion of the educational program of the school, its methods, and philosophy, and the progress of the students, but a picture of consistent parent involvement in aspects of the school such as these certainly does not emerge.

When administrators were asked how often parent meetings of any type were held in their school, the responses ranged from daily to yearly. Many directors said that such meetings were held on an informal, unscheduled basis.

A DAY IN NURSERY SCHOOL

In order to summarize some of the findings of our study, we have attempted to arrive at a synthesis of a typical nursery school day from the data gathered. In part, this is based on teachers' daily schedules which the observers were asked to obtain when they were in the classroom. Though these were difficult to procure in many cases, from those which were sent to us and from other data, a very obvious daily pattern of time and activity did emerge. The schedule would vary somewhat, of course, from school to school, but the following description appears to be typical for many nursery schools throughout the United States.

Upon arrival at school, children go directly to their classroom and immediately become occupied in largely unstructured activities. They remain so engaged for about half an hour. Although they are relatively free to change from activity to activity during this time, the teacher is very much the locus of decision making and authority. The activities and the room arrangement have been largely predetermined by the teacher in that some materials have been put out for use today and others not. A considerable variety and number of materials are available and in usable condition. These might include animals to observe, handle, and care for. Fish are by far the most likely to be on hand, but so might hamsters, gerbils, guinea pigs, turtles, and mice. Unit table blocks to build with, clay to mold, a phonograph with records to play, and a piano also usually are in evidence. Collage materials and easels and paints may be in use at this time, although these may also appear later in the day in more structured activities. Children usually have access during this period to crayons, dolls and accessories, dress-up clothes, housekeeping toys, puzzles, some science materials to explore, assorted table toys, and cars, trucks, and trains of various kinds. While engaged in these activities, children interact rather freely with each other and with the teachers in a warm, positive way. All are apparently quite happy. There is a reasonable amount of noise, and the classroom space seems to be used adequately. When instances of aggression occur between children, these are generally worked out in a constructive, non-threatening way. The teachers sometimes find it necessary to remind children of the rules and routines of the classroom but not in an overbearing fashion.

After approximately half an hour, the relatively unstructured situation gives way to a more structured one, which may take the form of actual lessons being taught by the teacher or of large or small group activity, such as plays, show and tell, singing songs, or instruction on a particular concept. The children might discuss or share an object or news item as an informal language lesson. Informal music might be the focus through singing songs or, less often, playing rhythm instruments. For those schools with a more academic orientation, the children will be occupied with lessons in arithmetic, reading readiness, social studies, or science. Some degree of individualization of the program may be apparent.

About an hour after arrival, the children have a break, with juice, milk, cookies, or crackers being served. The informal conversation at this juncture often forms an important part of the program. The snacks usually have been set up in advance by an aide or assistant, although the children have some responsibility in serving themselves and in cleaning up. If there are no toilets in the room for use as needed, all the children will be sent to the restroom at this time.

Two different patterns of activities are seen following snack time. One calls for the children to return to unstructured activities in the classroom in a manner similar to the first period in the morning. In other schools, the children are taken outdoors for play activities. This outside time is sometimes still referred to as recess, thus suggesting that it is more of a break than a continuation of learning activity.

The variety and quantity of equipment accessible to children on the outdoor playground is less than that in the classroom, though they do not usually have to wait long for turns to use it. The play yard may contain a climbing apparatus, some limited riding equipment such as tricycles or wagons, a sandbox and accessories, swings, and occasionally a slide and some balls. The children are apt to be quite free to choose their activities and change them at will. Group games may be organized for part of the fifteen to forty-five minutes that the children remain outdoors.

Outdoor play is generally followed by a half-hour period of more structured classroom activities. Art projects or individual work of a more regulated nature than the free play at the beginning of the day might fill this time. If the school is in session only in the mornings, this will form the final segment of the program. In such cases, children stay with these activities until called for by their parents.

The day care center program diverges somewhat from the foregoing description. Such centers may open as early as 6:30 or 7:00 A.M. with free, unstructured indoor play occurring as children are dropped off by their parents. Usually all the children have arrived at school by 9:00 A.M. The morning program is then quite close to the one described above. At the conclusion of the last block of rather structured activities, a hot lunch is served, which is followed by a nap lasting perhaps as long as two hours. Then the children are awakened for an afternoon snack not unlike that of the morning.

After this, the children may occupy themselves with free play either inside or out. The afternoon play session is somewhat longer than the morning's, with some groups even remaining outdoors until their mothers come for them. Generally, the afternoon activities appear to be less defined, less organized, and more variable than the morning activities.

The nursery school schedule on the whole is tentative and flexible. Teachers try to vary the classroom program so as to capitalize on a range of interests as much as possible. This may cause specific deviations in schedule from school to school or room to room, but it is probable that the typical day in the typical nursery school would proceed as we have described it.

What we have presented here as a picture of preschool practice in the United States has both encouraging and discouraging aspects. Our impression, however, of these preschools is that though they are comfortable places for children to be, they are at the same time pedestrian and unimpressive. We must ask ourselves if this is good enough. With all that we know about child development and with all that needs to be improved and that education can accomplish, can we afford to be satisfied with the placid and slow-changing water of the main river of early schooling?

THREE

NURSERY SCHOOLS
IN PERSPECTIVE

CHAPTER 6
CONCLUSIONS AND OBSERVATIONS

The preceding chapters have sought to do two things. Those of Part One portray the intense interest in the education of young children that emerged during the 1960s and the accompanying ideas, not necessarily new, that acquired considerable currency. Some people think that the "educational discovery of the young child" was the most significant educational development of the decade, if not the century to date. This interest spawned some federal funding, research, and imaginative laboratory-based experimental programs, as well as a general expansion in facilities for children too young to attend regular schools.

The chapters of Part Two describe 201 nursery schools thought to be representative of all those in nine major cities of the United States and assumed to be not unlike those found generally in our larger cities. The data pertaining to them were derived from the schools' directors and from observations carried out by persons considered to be specialists in the field. The result is an inventory of census-type data, a self-portrait painted by the directors, and a portrayal of what trained observers saw in schools and classrooms—in effect, a picture of the average urban nursery school in the United States, circa the early 1970s.

By juxtaposing the guidelines and innovations at the core of this interest with actual nursery school practices, a sense of congruity or incongruity may be gained. Since avoiding them seemed to us to be artificial, evaluative judgments were sometimes included in the data presentation. Consequently, the reader already should have a sense of incongruity between nursery schools as they exist and ideas and practices considered to be at the forefront of research and theory. Part Three explores this emerging sense of incongruity with a view toward delineating it and presenting some recommendations which, if acted upon, might accelerate the needed improvement of nursery schools in this country.

It will be recalled that, in order to get data on the schooling of four-year-olds, our sample necessarily included children from six months to six years, with our observations pertaining to the nursery school as a whole but directed particularly to the age group immediately preceding kindergarten. The pattern for five-year-olds already is established, even if not fully implemented, in the United States. Kindergarten is generally recognized as the first year of public school, even though many states and cities do not make clear-cut financial provision for it. An organizational structure for the schooling of four-year-olds is as yet quite nebulous.

AUTHORITY AND RESPONSIBILITY

One of the deficiencies confronting us regarding schools for young children is the apparent lack of systematic, comprehensive procedures for licensing and regulating them or even merely keeping track of statistics regarding their existence. This is true at federal, state, and local levels of the educational enterprise. Until a few years ago, writers referring to nursery school enrollments could present only rough estimates or would state that reliable figures were not available. Even today, the data prepared by government agencies lack an adequate breakdown into types of schools and periods of enrollment.

There is a considerable vacuum with regard to direction at the state level. The initiative has come primarily from the federal level (e.g., Headstart and the National Laboratory in Early Childhood Education). State regulations and procedures, with few exceptions, are geared to the past and assume primarily custodial rather than educative functions. Departments or offices of health and child welfare, more than of education, are involved, and licensing is based on factors of health conditions and sanitation in schools rather than qualifications of personnel and quality of programs. Recent insights and hypotheses about the *educational* importance of the preschool years seem not to have penetrated policies and actions of most state governments. There are some notable exceptions, of course and the situation may change rapidly. Nonetheless, most state governments are to be faulted, if not charged with outright neglect, with respect to the lack of a guiding framework for preschools now operating under their jurisdiction. The lack of plans for the future is also distressing.

The situation at the local level, as our experience clearly reveals, is equally chaotic. It is a sad reflection on the state of the art that the

Yellow Pages and a keen lookout for signs constitute the best means of finding preschools. We know that the most informal institutions—backyard playgroups and today's variety of the Dame School—simply escaped our net. No doubt, some of them have escaped the net of health and safety inspectors, too, and goodness knows what custodial and educative functions are being performed by them and at what cost.

If our data can be trusted, large numbers of nursery schools in urban areas are independent of *any* external controlling body. More than one-third of our sample of seven types is in this category. Even those preschools that are not fully independent are under rather remote control, quite unlike, for example, the control of a local school board. Church-controlled and Montessori schools receive only very general guidelines except pertaining to the teaching of religion in the case of the former and to the use of certain materials and accompanying methodologies in the latter. It would seem that whatever their affiliations, preschools are a rather independent lot.

There will not be ready agreement regarding the ideal framework of authority and responsibility for overseeing nursery schools. Clearly, the broad definition of education encompasses the whole of a child's development; agencies for health, education, and welfare all have an interest. Many specialists in child development are less than happy with the present primary school and desire to see the nursery school kept completely separate. Some specialists strongly resist for the four-year-old anything akin to school; others, distressed by the present situation, see inclusion of preschool responsibility in the framework of state and local public education as an imperfect but more desirable alternative. We will return to this problem following a review of other problems and needs in the field.

Before leaving the matter of authority and responsibility, we underscore the need for federal leadership in regard to comprehensive data collection and analysis and for financial assistance to states seeking definitive answers to their role and commitment in educating young children. Likewise, we urge states to move quickly from their general status of neglect through omission to a position of firm commission regarding the education of young children. Those not already waiting for reports of special task forces should commission such immediately, with instructions to consider the needs of young children (and their parents) from the prenatal stage to the primary years of schooling.

The Professionalization of Early Schooling

Before turning to more specific data, a few words are in order concerning one inescapable conclusion: Large numbers of nursery schools operate in professional and intellectual isolation—no more, perhaps, than do many elementary schools in this country—but isolation nonetheless. They do not, in general, reflect the surging interest that has characterized the scholarly frontiers; they do not reflect, for example, the urgency to utilize the early years fully that comes through in the writings of Bloom and Bruner referred to in Chapter 1. Directors and teachers have heard of these men and their ideas, yes, but these exciting streams of thought appear to have caused barely a ripple in the placid river of daily practice.

It is too much to expect congruence between the thinking of leaders in any field and the broad base of practice; nevertheless, there are some more insidious signs of intellectual and professional isolation, if not stagnation, growing partly out of a myopic commitment to the close-at-hand. For better or for worse, nursery schools do not belong to a system. Perhaps they gain from the absence of bureaucratic restraints, but they lose the opportunity of continuing exchange with other schools, the infusion of ideas into and through the system, and the opportunity to discuss ideas with supervisors and consultants employed by the system. Perhaps this isolation is why nursery school programs are so overwhelmingly dominated by the ideas of fifteen years ago.

Perhaps even more serious, within the schools there appeared to be no ongoing group intellectual process through which the staff looked at itself and the program, identified problems, and looked outside of itself for ideas and solutions. The data of Chapter 4 suggest directors' satisfaction with programs, rather than the restless, wholesome dissatisfaction one might expect or even hope for during a period of unusual ferment in a field such as that found now. Similarly, the data of Chapter 5 suggest an absence of hardheaded self-evaluation of commitment and effort on the part of nursery school staffs. Perhaps this picture of rather self-satisfied equanimity is good for the tranquillity of children, but it certainly runs counter to what usually are identified as the characteristics of a self-renewing process. This situation is not unlike that which we found also in elementary schools,[1] except that it seemed to be more severe, especially when coupled with the relative lack of opportunity for external peer-group socialization. Our impressions were reinforced by the apparent paucity of knowledge about their members on the part of preschool organizations, when indeed, those operating schools for young children even belonged to an organization.

This general condition of intellectual and professional isolation raises serious questions about staff qualifications. On paper, these appear to be at least as good as one might expect, given the lax control situation. Directors and senior teachers are college-educated for the most part, and many have had formal training in early childhood education. Nonetheless, the percentage not having had such training is large (see Table VII, Appendix A), strikingly so when this sample is compared with a sample of public school kindergarten teachers. Perhaps more critical than preservice preparation, however, is the question of what happens to personnel when neither the pressure of a well-organized profession nor opportunities for peer-group communication and socialization prevail. The data of Table VII suggest relatively little participation in formal in-service education, whether or not for degree purposes, on the part of those involved with the nursery schools of our study. One would expect, then, perseverance with, rather than questioning of, long-standing practices and rather myopic satisfaction and preoccupation with the immediate rather than concern with change. These are impressions that come through the data, hard and soft, in a variety of ways.

Those whose urgent concern with the importance of the early childhood years would lead them to immediate, rapid expansion of facilities must temper this urgency with realization that there is not "out there" a well-populated profession of early childhood educators waiting to be mobilized. There is, in fact, barely a professional core, the preparation of which, we fear, is largely outdated. A sudden expansion of interest in and funds for early schooling unaccompanied by extensive provision for solid preparatory programs might well result simply in compounding the already unsatisfactory conditions. In effect, the results could be comparable to suddenly expanding the demand for physicians without at the same time assuring both more places in medical schools and the necessary protection of the public against quacks and imposters.

In effect, when one assembles a general picture from the preceding three topics of analysis, the following emerges: This country's nursery schools appear to constitute a loose array of individual institutions about which relatively little is known, over which no governmental body exercises clear-cut authority, among which communication is minimal, and within which there are few signs of an intellectual enterprise of self-study and improvement.

The most responsible leaders indigenous to this amorphous body have cried out to authorities for years, seeking a place for the nursery school movement in the educational mainstream. They have met in groups, often at their own expense, preparing criteria both for the health and safety inspection of facilities and for the certification of personnel. More often than not, they have been ignored. Students desiring professional preparation often discovered, to their dismay, that university-level programs and state credential requirements in early schooling were almost nonexistent. They have had to prepare in primary or elementary education, securing a course or two in early childhood development and perhaps, thanks to a sympathetic adviser, bootlegging a student-teaching experience in a nursery school or kindergarten. Campus nursery schools, usually maintained by departments of home economics as laboratories in child care, had programs only indirectly related to schooling. It is not surprising, then, that the vast majority of today's practitioners, supportive of children and kind though they may be, lack both clear-cut perceptions of what nursery schools are for and the necessary repertoire of pedagogical skills for teaching effectively.

These conditions have changed in many places, and the pace of change is accelerating. Nonetheless, it is clear that there is little governmental awareness of the limited training of most preschool personnel, and this lack of awareness extends also to some specialists in the field. Unfortunately, not all the shortcomings in our educational system can be corrected through massive infusion of funds; in fact, as we have seen in the United States, support without full awareness of present conditions or plans for improvement accomplishes little. Clearly, extensive provision for the educational needs of young children will require a level of funding that far surpasses anything presently contemplated by federal and state governments, if we read the signs at all correctly. An impulsive, philanthropic response in the form of vast appropriations will be as unrewarding as some similar, previous responses for other levels of education. The situation must be carefully appraised, beginning with the kind of federal fact-finding and state assumption of authority and responsibility recommended earlier. Perhaps this report will provide some guidelines for the priority-directed efforts now required.

Therefore, we urge that expansion of early schooling and education proceed systematically, with the first priority being provision of resources for preparing personnel. However, it must be recognized that there is also an extreme shortage of "teachers of teachers." Universities and colleges presently fortunate enough to have even small staffs of professionals in early education should be supported in their efforts to expand. Part of this expansion should entail including on the faculty, part-time or for short terms, competent nursery school personnel who do not possess a doctorate but who could provide needed clinical skills. Again, the supply is limited, but almost every university mounting a program in early childhood education has access to a few, often self-trained, competent practitioners whose experience and insights would add much to the more academic and often less-experienced members of the regular faculty.

Likewise, states should exercise caution in regard to legislation mandating universal schooling for four-year-olds. As we shall see in succeeding pages, not all members of this age group stand to profit from it, and few stand to profit from a conception of preschool which is essentially a downward extension of primary school. In fact, the evidence as to the ineffectiveness or even detrimental aspects of early schooling so conceived appears to be at least as good as the evidence to support its benefits. As we shall see, there is need for diverse approaches to early education, including schooling, each having a unique role to play in relation to the varied needs of young children. Therefore, a panoply of alternative early childhood education programs should be supported, with none being compulsory and all being backed by adequate personnel-preparation programs and appropriate state regulatory procedures to protect children and parents alike from profit-seeking entrepreneurs.

School Atmosphere

In spite of this second-class citizenship for early schooling in the structure of our formal educational system, our data give relatively little evidence of irresponsibility and deliberate neglect of children by local nursery schools. There are shortsightedness regarding goals, a certain innocuousness of program, and a failure to take advantage of new-found insights into the capabilities of young children; but most practitioners in nursery schools are deeply concerned about the children in their care and often passionately committed to what they are doing. This is at once commendable and an obstacle to widespread change.

The physical settings of the schools in our sample were pleasant and healthful. Few were prototypes of the educational facilities recently designed and recommended for young children, but this is not surprising given the somewhat peripheral status of early schooling. Similarly, teachers tended to be pleasant to and supportive of the children, who appeared to be enjoying themselves. As we shall see, the provision of a pleasant place for play and socialization is a major goal of most nursery schools, and in this they seem to be succeeding. But in regard to children's enjoyment and apparently productive social activity, one must ask the question, "Compared with what?" Left to their own devices, children of this age appear to enjoy themselves in small groups.

One must ask—and we do not do so nearly often enough—in contemplating the effects of schooling, how much of what we consider "good" is in addition to what would be present without schools. There are, of course, no all-embracing answers, since what is superb for one child is somewhat positive for a second and questionable for a third. Children's individual differences call for more than merely separate progress through the same program.

What Nursery School for my Child?

When we begin to get into such evaluative comments as "The children appeared happy" and "Compared with what?" we come very close to the central controversy over the function of nursery schools. Likewise, we touch on parental concern with, "Should I send my child to nursery school and, if so, where?" The answer can only be, "It all depends." It all depends on what parents want for their children, what they can provide at home, and what alternatives are open to them. Our data already have suggested the choices likely to be available.

If parents want to "prepare their child for school" and have the financial means to purchase educational games, picture books, and manipulative materials, and if they provide relatively "good" language models and spend a considerable amount of time speaking, playing, reading, and storytelling with their children, it is unlikely that a nursery school will add much. On the other hand, given these same family conditions and the unavailability of other young children in the vicinity, a half-day nursery school may very well provide peer-group play and socialization and is probably available at low cost.

On the other hand, if parents provide these learning resources but also want some kind of relatively rigorous intellectual structuring for their children, the chances of finding it in a nursery school are rather remote. A few schools providing it exist, and a great many more *claiming* to provide such opportunity are available, but their ingredients frequently do not match the label. Although the deliberate development of cognitive styles and problem-solving abilities is widely recommended by some specialists in the field, general practice lags far behind. Few well-developed examples of cognitively oriented nursery schools exist apart from special research and development projects.

In situations where both parents are working or impoverished, the problem is quite different. The child may be getting ample opportunity, at least quantitatively, for play and peer-group socialization but little of the intellectual stimulation recommended by cognitive psychologists. Many of the nursery schools included in our sample could provide the rhythm of play, rest, and modest intellectual stimulation that would be beneficial for these children. They would be of greatest benefit if accompanied by close parent involvement so as to buttress in the home the goals and approaches of the nursery school. It would be exceedingly important for these children, too, to enjoy a range of activities carefully planned for cognitive structuring and stimulation. In effect, large numbers of urban children require both what "good" nursery schools traditionally have sought to provide and what emerges as desirable from the recent upsurge of interest in educating the young. Ironically, little of either is available to them because of the general inaccessibility of existing nursery schools, a paucity of free ones, inadequate programs in those attended, the inability of parents to participate, and often, a failure of parents to be aware of and to seek out what is required.

These conditions usually are accentuated for minority-group families, and certain other problems are added. One of these only recently has received serious attention and is surrounded by considerable controversy: Habits and language patterns in low-income, minority-group homes differ from those in most white, middle-class homes and schools. This discrepancy is very evident when a language other than English is spoken, but even the English spoken often is in some way different. Children attending a nursery school where teachers are not sensitive to the problem or see the deviation as undesirable may suffer a variety of negative repercussions. Spanish-speaking parents and those seeking to develop a sense of "black is beautiful" in their children reject schools which deliberately or thoughtlessly contribute to emasculation of their cultural characteristics. Attendance at a nursery school seeking to develop the child's positive awareness of his cultural heritage may be the most desirable step prior to attendance at a school with a more diverse range of goals.

It becomes apparent that providing early schooling for children of such different needs is a momentous task. One approach to this problem is to encourage diversity in nursery school types. Some parents want a religious orientation for their children and seek out church-affiliated schools. Some want the relatively ordered regimen they associate with Montessori schools. Some want emphasis on manners and morals ("it is good to share, to help the teacher, and not to take something that someone else has"), which are stressed in most nursery schools.

Another approach is to encourage comprehensive nursery schools having a broad range of goals and activities. In the succeeding section, we turn to the range of goals espoused in the schools of our sample, as stated by the directors and, sometimes, the teachers. Of course, there is not necessarily a congruence between stated goals and existing programs.

Before leaving the topic of "What nursery school for my child?" we wish to sound a few warnings. First, there appears to be no correlation between the fees charged and the excellence of the schools, even when one is very eclectic in defining "excellence." Those with the highest fees did not stand out as exemplary in our sample. Second, the relationship between the stated philosophy, function, and goals and the actual programs appeared to be no closer for high-fee than for low- or no-fee schools. The former were able to offer a more fully developed and articulated rhetoric to exhort their virtues but, as stated earlier, the ingredients of most schools failed to match the labels they attached to themselves. Third, there appeared to be rather limited involvement of parents in the high-fee schools. Frequently, the parents were informed (usually in print) about what presumably was going on, commonly in terms and tones of "what a good school you have" or "how lucky you are to have your child at the Crestview School," but true parental involvement and home-school collaboration or interchange appeared minimal.

In the light of our data on this problem, admittedly limited, we think it appropriate to caution parents prepared to pay sizable fees and travel considerable distances for the "right" nursery school, sometimes at considerable sacrifice. One simply cannot conclude from either the high fees or the inviting promotional literature that such-and-such a nursery school is the right one. Nor can one accept the criterion that "all the right families send their children." One must go behind school and classroom door, perhaps several times, to see what goes on there, and one must make a judgment about whether the nursery school to be selected provides an important element in the child's life that is not provided adequately in the home. Since many parents are reluctant or unable to do this and since many lack a basis for judging nursery school programs, it would appear that some general protection against exploitation is desirable. At least part of this would be provided if nursery schools were required to meet more rigorous educational criteria, especially in regard to the pre-service and in-service education of teachers.

Philosophy, Function, and Goals

The directors of the nursery schools composing our sample endorsed most of the emphases possible in early schooling, both traditional ones and those more recently recommended. In effect, by responding to our list of eleven possibilities as they did (with an opportunity to add others), they were saying to us that all aspects of child development should be fostered through an array of program possibilities. They opted for a comprehensive school designed to be virtually all things to all children.

Nonetheless, within the directors' general position of eclecticism, there were some clear and occasionally sharp gradations of choice. It is not surprising that, given the traditional, middle-class, and elitist raison d'être for nursery schools discussed earlier, the affective and social realms of development should rank high in the sample as a whole. Emotional development, social-interpersonal skills, and the arts and creative expression were ranked first, second, and third in the total sample. Likewise, it is not too surprising that the categories worded "language skills, reading and vocabulary development," and "academic skills" ranked at the bottom of the list. The low rating accorded language and academic skills should not be interpreted as a rejection of recent interest in cognitive development, since "concept and intellectual development" received substantial recognition by the nursery school directors. To use the rhetoric of an earlier era, they were committed to "the whole child"—social, emotional, physical, and intellectual development.

It is not surprising, either, that the directors of our sample of parent cooperatives revealed an accentuation of this general pattern: an even stronger commitment to emotional and social development, and scant recognition of "language skills, reading, and vocabulary development" and "academic skills." The parent cooperative was created in large measure to provide for the daily social and emotional needs of the child, to be a kind of collective mother. On the other hand, the markedly greater commitment to both academic and language arts skills on the part of Montessori schools also is predictable. In fact, our data support the dichotomous history of interest in early childhood education: the acquisition of simple skills and orderly work habits for the indigent and deprived (who caught Dr. Montessori's attention) and happy social play for the middle and upper classes.[2] Of course, the modern Montessori school has come a long way since those early beginnings, catering now to those who can manage the fees and incorporating the whole range of possible emphases in early schooling. The Montessori schools constituted the most comprehensive in our sample, judging from commitments expressed by directors.

When we look at data obtained from our effort to get beyond general commitment to the more precise goals of directors, the same eclectic picture emerges. However, the questions regarding functions and goals were more open-ended, and perhaps this is why a certain inconsistency begins to emerge. Although the concept of the "whole child" still comes through as top priority, preparation for school moves up into an almost parallel position of importance, ahead of child care. Part of this interest probably can be attributed to intellectual development in general, but it is clear that specific skills seen as part of emphasis on later schooling also were clearly intended. Although a large proportion of our group eschewed preparation for school as a basic, philosophical commitment, children's success in primary school became much more important as our probing got closer to actual functions of the 201 nursery schools.

It will be recalled from Chapter 4 that the nursery school directors were not heavily preoccupied with curricular problems and that, in general, they viewed their *programs* as successful or even unique. What comes through as an overall impression of directors' views, then, is commitment to most of the major goals variously cited as desirable for nursery schools and satisfaction with the ongoing programs designed for their attainment. Our data raise serious questions, however, about what these goals mean specifically for school staffs, about the "fit" of program to goals, and about the ability of nursery school personnel to design curricula and to teach for the ends implied by stated philosophical commitments. These same questions have been raised also about elementary school staffs—who receive somewhat more extensive and sustained preparation—and answered frequently in the negative, and so it should not be considered inappropriate to entertain them in seeking to evaluate nursery school staffs. However, negative answers should not be interpreted as a conclusion that such schools are bad places for children. On the contrary, the overall impact of many schools is probably positive, especially given the liking for and positive support of children that appeared to characterize so many of the directors, teachers, and aides whom we observed and with whom we talked during our visits.

Program

A major conclusion emerging from our data is that the overwhelming majority of the nursery schools studied conduct a rather narrowly prescribed traditional program. The children draw and paint, listen to music, play with blocks and toys, listen to and discuss stories, and play together outdoors every day, except when the weather is discouraging. They extend their association with stories and words into what usually is regarded as reading readiness; they combine nature walks, care of pets, and the like into informal explorations in science. Cooking usually is included as a form of organized play, and the children participate in some role playing and rhythms. Throughout, they talk in small groups, run and jump, and observe a set of rules pertaining to respect for one another, the teacher, and things in their environment. The college laboratory schools and Montessori schools appeared to offer somewhat richer programs, with the latter including a higher proportion of more formal academic activity.

Our first conclusion about the program is that most of the schools in our sample were providing approximately the same thing, demonstrating a narrower range of schooling than was implied by their stated goals. It will be recalled from the preceding chapter that there was an enormous, not just a slight, discrepancy between the list of activities appearing regularly in most nursery schools observed and the list of desired activities compiled by our group of specialists. Our data show (see Table 5-1 in Chapter 5 and Table IX in Appendix A) that the former not only was much shorter but also contained very nearly the same activities regardless of the school's type, according to our classification, or its emphases as articulated by the director.

This conclusion leads to a second; namely, that certain well-established, traditional means initially establish, if not justify, the ends. There are some things that nursery schools "just do." It is relatively easy to develop a kind of goal-oriented, semi- or pseudophilosophical rhetoric to lend credence to these means. This rhetoric then lends itself readily to revision and the accommodation of new concepts, largely through accretion rather than deletion and substitution, giving the appearance of change by minor changes.

The writer is reminded of his first encounters with a nursery school/kindergarten faculty—a sophisticated group, incidentally—with whom he was to have a long and gratifying association. He asked, not at all innocently, why the environment included blocks, sand boxes, ducks, bantams, wheeled toys, and the like. These queries produced an incredulous silence. To ask such questions was to be a disbeliever in church. Ultimately, this staff came to ask itself such questions and to inquire into the well-known and widely accepted artifacts of nursery school life. The resulting process of self-examination was arduous and healthy. To put the matter gently, we found a paucity of such critical self-appraisal in the schools we visited. Rather, we were exposed again and again to an all-embracing, confident rhetoric of nursery schools directed to the whole child and to a range of activities falling far short of the implications of this rhetoric.

Our data suggest a third conclusion regarding nursery school programs, one for which directors and teachers must not be faulted too severely. In our sample there was no fit between ends and means, even though justification for the former appeared to emerge largely from the latter. There was no clear correspondence between emphases implied in goals and emphases realized in programs, except in a very gross way. For example, except in Montessori schools, which ranked academic goals as highly important, the amount of time spent on "academic, preschool, or school-type" activities was in excess of that implied by the relatively low ranking of this category of goals. A more precise study in this area is needed. It is our hypothesis that such a study would reveal a considerable looseness of fit between, for example, the amount of attention to a given developmental area implied in the goals and the amount actually devoted to it on a day-to-day basis. At this rather general level of the relationship between ends and means the schools and their directors should, indeed, be faulted.

At a more refined level of fit, however, the fault is with the state of the art generally regarding early childhood education. Many specialists agree that deliberate intervention in cognitive development is desirable, but there is sharp disagreement over the most desirable or efficient means. Experts even disagree on the desirability of efficiency. Likewise, the development of motor coordination is deemed desirable but, as yet, relatively little is known about sequences of motor development and when and how to intervene productively—certainly not enough to guide the practitioner confidently. Intensity of disagreement on such matters among specialists in research and development adds zest to the ongoing ferment but provides little help or security to practitioners, and probably reinforces their reluctance to depart from traditional ways of doing things.

Given the state of the art, it is not at all surprising that we found scarcely any instances where teachers of young children were proceeding with a rather precise, sequenced curriculum designed to develop specific behaviors clearly envisioned by these teachers. Few of the school environments provided much in the way of balancing devices to be used by children in refining their motor coordination. Likewise, we rarely found teachers appraising a child's eye-hand coordination and, as a result of diagnosis, rearranging the immediate environment to provide materials more suited to that child's present stage of development. Nor were there materials selected and arranged so as to provide for all areas of development (as articulated in statements of goals) and so as to facilitate productive choices by children proceeding on some schedule of at least partial self-determination. The obvious exceptions were some of the university-based laboratory schools with embryonic experimental programs and some aspects of the Montessori schools.

It is clear that the school staffs in our sample—which we believe to be reasonably representative of nursery schools in cities of the United States—either do not know what constitutes well-conceived programs designed to foster development in the areas to which they claim to be dedicated or simply lack the skills to implement such programs. This appears to be the case in the social and affective realms, to which nursery schools have long been committed, as well as in the cognitive realm, which has more recently drawn attention. Since teachers are not being precise about what they are trying to do or how to do it, it follows as an expectation that evaluations by teachers would be primitive or nonexistent, and this is, indeed, our finding.

These interrelated findings suggest caution in current efforts to hold teachers—and often only teachers—accountable for producing by their instruction certain effects in children. The techniques of precise definition of behavioral objectives and operant conditioning briefly discussed in Chapter 2 have a certain rational attractiveness and are readily learned. It is easy next to conclude that teachers must state clearly their aims, teach for these ends using pedagogical techniques which, in turn, can be prescribed and learned, and then be held accountable for the end results. But this is to obfuscate a fact of more than passing import: We are not yet agreed on what nursery schools are for. Further, we are not agreed on the means—especially of substance—most disposed to the attainment of general ends. Therefore, to elevate certainty what are at best hypotheses is to engage in misleading scientism. It is the wise man who knows the degree of scientific rigor to apply to a particular situation.

The rapidly growing body of literature on early childhood education reveals an increasing number of experimental programs designed with clear goals in mind and with built-in evaluation procedures regarding the appropriateness and effectiveness of various means for achieving them. It is reasonable to assume, with Gordon,[3] that such programs, originating from rather precise theoretical points of view, should be amenable to an analysis based on specification of goals, pupil characteristics, instructional settings, and the relationships among them. In concluding his analysis of six relatively influential and fully developed programs, Gordon notes both the difficulties inherent in the process of making these relationships precise and the fact that we are a long way from a scientific theory of instruction conceived in these broader-than-pedagogical terms. Nonetheless, he goes on to point out the substantial contribution of these innovators to a better understanding of the nature of learning and the mechanics of schooling.

In work of the kind reported by Gordon, there are both sharp and subtle differences in theoretical position that frequently reflect differing views of the child. As we mentioned earlier, these differences produce intensive study and are useful in cautioning us against overcommitment to positions which are at best only tentative. Especially useful in this work is the effort to make assumptions clear and programs consistent with them. As this endeavor continues, nursery schools will be able to select among alternative positions and move forward with appropriate curricula and teaching methods. It is clear, however, that there is still a paucity of exemplary programs defined in this fashion. It is also clear, and of at least equal import, that the links between this frontier work and the actual procedures of nursery schools generally are fragile or nonexistent. Strengthening or creating these links is a task of formidable proportions for which strategies are either primitive or lacking.

There are certain salutary checks and balances in the lag between research and development and ongoing practice. Certainly, it is a good thing that nursery school teachers, by and large, are not trying out every new trend or fad. On the other hand, it is most regrettable that the staffs of nursery schools appear not to be constructively self-critical and busily engaged, as best they can, in analyzing and reconstructing their own programs so as to improve continuously the fit among assumptions, goals, characteristics of children enrolled, and ongoing activities. The process of internal problem solving calling for sustained dialogue, decisions, actions, and evaluation was missing in the schools we visited, as was, unfortunately, any substantial participation in the external ferment now characterizing the field of early childhood education.

Relationships Between Goals or Philosophy and Program

We already have said a good deal about the apparent lack of fit between stated goals and emphases in the program, but one concluding observation on this matter is called for. Even though the nursery school directors placed academic emphases and preparation for school low on their list of priorities (except for the Montessori schools, as mentioned earlier), the impression gained from miscellaneous comments on our observation forms is that the children's imminence of entry into primary school loomed large in the minds and practices of directors and teachers alike. The hard data pertaining to classroom practices, already discussed, support this impression. Many of these nursery schools, protestations by their staffs to the contrary, simply are a first rung on the tall ladder of schooling. They spend somewhat more time than the kindergarten on play-oriented activities and less on school-readiness activities, but "school as a presence" is much more evident than the rhetoric about philosophy and goals would suggest.

This observation emerges also from our studies of early schooling in England, Israel, and selected countries of Asia. We gathered together in Bangkok a group of specialists in early childhood education, and their comments confirmed what we already had concluded tentatively about most of the eight countries studied (although there were some interesting differences among them): that a head start for school is a major parental motivation for sending children to nursery school and that school personnel are aware of this and cater to a considerable degree to school expectations, even though their rhetoric stresses emotional and social development as in the United States.

Our observation here is not intended to be pejorative, except with respect to the lack of fit betwen rhetoric and practice. The notion of nursery school as the beginning of school is not necessarily a bad thing (see Chapter 7). In fact, our analyses of proposals for early education in both Israel and the United States reveal a considerable preoccupation with school readiness for disadvantaged children. What does bother us is the unimaginative and stereotyped program in the academic realm. Most of it is a kind of watered-down kindergarten and early first-grade curriculum, emphasizing the alphabet, numbers, and other specifics of content. This is a far cry from the emphases on language and perceptual and cognitive development recommended by Bloom, Bruner, Hunt, and others (see Chapter 2) and often found at the core of the kinds of programs described by Gordon and referred to earlier in this chapter.

Those who are cautious about the benefits of early schooling or who are against any further expansion and expenditures for schools frequently point out that the effects of nursery school and kindergarten attendance wash out by at least ages eight or nine. Even if we push aside the fact that few good, carefully controlled, longitudinal studies have been conducted, taking the total research output into account, the only reasonable assumption is that the results are inconclusive. However, we still are confronted with the fact that such studies as have been conducted measure the effects of the kinds of nursery schools described in preceding chapters. It is clear that these schools lack a clear sense of direction, do not envision how to attain their goals, and lack in their staffs more than a marginal level of expertise. Most of them appear to provide a pleasant environment, but it is misleading to think that their unfocused programs of play, music, stories, and passes at the alphabet and numbers will distinguish their products several years later on tests sharply focused on what regular schools have been teaching for two or three years.

What is surprising is that some presumably intelligent persons—sharply differentiated in their intent from those who seek to reduce public support for schooling—conclude that the lack of identifiable benefits from nursery schools, as defined by academic achievement, constitutes adequate argument against institutionalized education. Stacked against such conclusions is the growing body of evidence regarding the importance of educational intervention in the development of the young child, the incapability of many parents—however well-meaning—to provide for this at even very rudimentary levels, and the possibility of creating productive group environments (call them schools, if you wish) deliberately focused on the development of skills and abilities otherwise not likely to be provided for adequately. This is what the educational discovery of the young child is about.

Research, Development, and Evaluation in Nursery Schools

We have referred in sections of this report to research on the education of young children, an expected corollary of the educational discovery of the young. A small number of centers and projects across the country, funded by the federal government and philanthropic foundations, conduct such inquiry and also move beyond into the program development and training presumably related to it. It is obvious from our conclusions regarding the conduct of 201 nursery schools that practice is widely separated from such centers, many of which receive considerable attention and are regarded as pacesetters. It is obvious, also, that nursery schools have plenty to do as caretakers and show little or no inclination to engage in either experimentation or research. This is to be expected.

Nursery schools operating as part of laboratory schools in universities, however, tend to justify their existence in part as centers for inquiry into the field. Our data suggest that this, too, is more the rhetoric of stated goals and functions than a description of reality. The nursery schools in this classification visited by our staff devoted almost all their time and energy to "keeping school." There was little evidence of research either into alternative patterns or modes of practice or regarding the consequences of existing, monolithic programs. In effect, then, so-called laboratory nursery schools are not providing us with evidence regarding the merits of various approaches to early schooling, nor are they providing the research feedback that might be used for systematic revision of ongoing practice.

Many of the university-based nursery schools did report some research studies, but these were almost exclusively within the classic design of studies in child development and learning. They were predominantly psychological in character, frequently measuring the effects of rewards, classifying neurological disorders, or exploring characteristics of transfer in learning situations. What was disappointing in regard to these was their scattered, noncumulative character; more often than not, they simply replicated similar studies done elsewhere, adding no new knowledge. Studies on the effects of rewards usually re-created laboratory tests, using contrived rewards rather than studying the effects of ongoing reward systems in the context of classroom reality. The nursery schools merely provided a convenient, accessible research setting for the researchers; they did not benefit from the results, which were usually published but not fed back into the schools. Had there been such feedback, little could have been done with it.

The foregoing description of research activity in university-based laboratory schools applies equally to evaluation for our entire sample of 201 nursery schools. We already have seen that teachers were not engaged in any systematic evaluation of their children. They were not using observation scales or other instruments in order to obtain a comprehensive picture of each child from which to project emphases in instruction designed to strengthen aspects of emotional, social, motor, or cognitive development. In addition, school staffs were not meeting together for purposes of examining goals, activities, needs, and the like regarding current emphases and future revisions. As we have seen, they were at once both pleased with and complacent about their existing curricula. Just as there appeared to be little or no internal evaluation, there was no evidence, either, of external evaluation of programs or practices.

We have come full circle in this chapter. Most of the nursery schools in cities of the United States are, apparently, rather sublimely isolated educational enclaves, each following passively a relatively traditional and narrow set of activities which constitutes both means and justification for ends. They operate quite apart from though not entirely unaware of arenas of intense inquiry into the educational potentialities of young children. They have no lines of direct communication with this research nor do they communicate much with one another. Until this study, we have had no comprehensive descriptions of nursery school activities, and we do not yet know much about the effects of what they do. Effects do not seem to show up in school-based, standardized tests administered several years later, and we do not know why. Nursery school directors firmly believe that what they are doing is good for children and that those who attend have an advantage over those who do not. We have a lot to learn.

NOTES

1 John I. Goodlad, M. Frances Klein, and Associates, *Behind the Classroom Door*, revised edition, Charles A. Jones, Worthington, Ohio, 1973.
2 Norma J. Feshbach, John I. Goodlad, and Avima Lombard, *Early Schooling in England and Israel,* |I|D|E|A| Reports on Schooling, Early Schooling Series, McGraw-Hill, New York, 1973.
3 Ira J. Gordon, "An Instructional Theory Approach to the Analysis of Selected Early Childhood Programs," *Early Childhood Education*, Seventy-first Yearbook of the National Society for the Study of Education, Part II, University of Chicago Press, Chicago, 1972, pp. 203–204.
4 Ibid., p. 225.

CHAPTER 7

RECOMMENDATIONS

A number of recommendations for the improvement of early child-hood schooling were implied in the preceding chapter. In this chapter we will make these explicit and add to them.

It is generally assumed that educational recommendations are most effective if directed precisely at those who should execute them. Though some of our recommendations are so directed, we have seen that nursery schools in this country constitute an amorphous array of scattered entities, largely divorced from any educational channels of authority and responsibility. In seeking reform, one cannot point the finger, in Nader-like fashion, at management, labor unions, or special-purpose government agencies. Therefore, some of our recommendations are "for whom it may concern"—legislators, parents, child development specialists, researchers, and nursery school directors and teachers—in a spirit of "if the shoe fits, wear it." In addition, many suggestions are presented in the form of needs or desirable directions for change.

DATA AND STATISTICS

One of the most frustrating findings of this study is the paucity of data regarding the whole field of preschool activity. Even to have reliable enrollment figures would help, but this is not enough. *We recommend that there be a federal effort to develop definitions and classifications of facilities for infants and young children and to maintain a comprehensive body of data regarding groups of children enrolled (socio-economic status, geographic location, and the like), periods of enrollment, education of teachers, per pupil costs, source of support, etc.* If these data are gathered best state by state, then uniformity of instruments, collection, and interpretation must be assured.

In addition, we very much need more dynamic data banks to be used for longitudinal research and for analyzing trends over a period of years. *Therefore, we recommend that an appropriate federal agency conduct, at intervals of perhaps five years, in-depth analyses of a nation-wide sample of nursery schools in regard to curriculum, pedagogy, education of teachers, evaluation procedures, and the like.* Thus, the kinds of data presented in this study would be made available regularly and in a consistent format. Such data are essential to longitudinal studies designed to test inferences regarding cause-and-effect relationships. Simply to know children have attended nursery schools is virtually useless in seeking to appraise the effects of such attendance. We must know of what their school experience consisted and, knowing it, we have some chance of ferreting out what may or may not make a difference in relation to selected criteria of effectiveness and data pertaining to these criteria. The present lack of such information leaves legislators, for example, in a quandary regarding proposed legislation on schools for young children.

AUTHORITY AND RESPONSIBILITY

We have noted the general vacuum with respect to state leadership for early schooling. We cannot assume that a preference for the present state of ad hoc development rather than intervention has led to a deliberate decision not to act. Certainly, many legislators have been influenced by their concern for rising taxes—and by those lobbyists who do not wish further expenditures for public education. We are inclined, however, to place more credence on the argument that legislators are, as yet, unaware of research pertaining to early childhood development and the recent educational discovery of the young. If this were not so, there would be far more legislative proposals for cutting from the upper years and adding to the early years as a means of responding to this discovery without adding to the costs of schooling. If this were not so, there would be more state interest in the present conduct of preschools. Some states pay more attention to regulating nominally satisfactory practices regarding automobile repairs than to regulating nursery schools, many of which are little more than baby-sitting way stations for children dropped off each day for a few hours of custodial care.

Most of our state governments must be faulted sharply and severely for omissions regarding early schooling that amount literally to neglect through inertia. As a case in point, one of the best states in regard to its record on educating the young child and one of the first to make kindergarten available to all five-year-olds, has marked time unduly in regard to four-year-olds. In the early 1960s, a well-known educator was approached by the governor regarding the desirability of providing schooling at state expense for all four-year-olds. The consultant advised against such a plan on the grounds that we lacked an adequate corps of trained personnel, programs for their training, and pedagogical know-how. He recommended, however, that exploratory programs be financed, especially for the economically disadvantaged; that university-based programs in early education be enlarged and enhanced through state appropriations; and that linkages between such programs, facilities designated for experimentation, and a network of demonstration schools be forged. Had such been done at that time, this state would now have a firm base for legislative decisions regarding early schooling. Instead, in the 1970s, the legislature failed to support proposals somewhat similar to those recommended in the 1960s put forward by a task force commissioned by the chief state school officer, in part, legislators claimed, because of uncertainty about the benefits of schooling for four-year-olds. An intervening period of exploration and research might well have provided some of the necessary data.

Our recommendations for state intervention suggest two parallel and simultaneous courses of action. *First, states should develop criteria for the licensing and conduct of nursery schools to assure appropriate education in child development, curriculum planning, and evaluation on the part of director/operators; adequacy of facilities, materials, and equipment from an educational as well as hygienic point of view; honesty in regard to claims and information contained in promotional brochures; and periodic submission of data regarding enrollment, preparation of personnel, fees, etc.*

Second, states should provide public facilities for optional attendance of four-year-olds in school, special appropriations for preparing personnel, laboratory facilities for development of alternative programs, and a variety of communications and disseminating networks for extending information about frontier work to the variety of nursery schools which now exist. In effect, we are not proposing restraints on and the elimination of private ventures but, rather, the upgrading of preschools generally through the development of both standards and exemplary practices, the latter under public auspices. Much of what exists is moribund and must be shaken loose through insistence on higher standards and stimulation by example.

TOWARD IMPROVED PROFESSIONALIZATION

We have pointed out the intellectual isolation of nursery schools. They do not exist as part of a professional "press," as the sociologist might put it. We know something of the power of such a press, whether it is in the expectations for creative scholarship at Harvard, the University of Chicago, the University of California, and other great universities; or in the peer-group review of scholarly manuscripts; or in the socialization of medical interns. If there is any press exerting its influence on nursery schools, it is exceedingly weak and reinforces largely outmoded behaviors. There seem not to be communications networks, associations, or expectations demanding enlightened response to the educational discovery of the young child. Each little school goes its own independent but surprisingly uniform way, not aware, sad to say, of its anachronistic character.

Correcting this condition will not be easy. We have no ready solutions, but at least three directions offer promise. *First, we recommend the requirement of continuous internal self-evaluation and periodic external review for licensing purposes.* This should be designed to stimulate a process of self-study, to get nursery school staffs to escape from their present disquieting state of contentment and satisfaction. The initiation of some serious dialogue among nursery school faculties regarding ends and means just might lead some to reach out for new ideas. The external review process should be nonpunitive, designed to relate effectively to the internal process and move it along. Extant facilities for children need to be improved, not destroyed. Ultimately, more demanding, rigorous processes of review may be appropriate.

Second, there need to be lines of communication established between nursery schools and centers or projects in early education and schooling operating out of universities, community enterprises, etc. A nursery school operating in intellectual isolation cannot pull itself up by its own bootstraps but could profit greatly by affiliation with such projects. A university-based center might make use of a dozen private nursery schools for observation, apprentice teaching, and research, providing in return in-service workshops, annotated reading lists, access to campus seminars and conferences, etc. The intent is to agitate nursery school staffs a little—to upset their equilibrium and to provide constructive input. Although some staffs will be defensive, many will welcome just being noticed.

Third, clusters of nursery schools surrounding centers of research, development, and training in early education need to be linked together into peer-group consortia, communicating with each other as well as with such centers. It is particularly through these ties that a sense of collegial professionalism will begin to grow. This can be cultivated in many ways, at first by initiating a center or hub. An association of directors can be formed, with monthly meetings and agenda directed to preparing them for program improvement. There can be a newsletter for sharing ongoing experiences, reviewing articles and books, suggesting new instructional materials, etc.—at first prepared primarily by professional personnel of the experimental center or project but increasingly taken over by the nursery school staffs. There can be peer-taught seminars and workshops in which nursery school teachers demonstrate to colleagues some of their newer procedures. There can be interschool visits and analyses of what is observed.

All the above can be done at relatively little cost. That centers of research, development, and training supported frequently by government funds often would be facilitating, at least indirectly, private schooling should not be allowed to become a deterrent. There are not sufficient funds to provide public educational programs for all four-year-olds, but redeploying a small portion of public money devoted to early childhood education in order to help private nursery schools help themselves would be money well spent at this particular time in history.

TOWARD IMPROVED PROGRAMS AND TEACHING

Preceding pages have suggested a framework with which to create a new set of expectations for those who operate nursery schools and within which to provide opportunities for ideas, interschool communication, intraschool self-study, in-service activities conducted by peers, and the like. The plan calls for a central group engaged continuously in research, program development, coordination of communication and training, provision of guidance toward higher goals, and so on. The ultimate purpose, of course, is to upgrade curriculum and instruction generally in early education and schooling.

Three of our major findings in this report are central to any serious plan for such upgrading: (1) the lack of fit between stated philosophy or goals and the provision of program; (2) the narrow array of program offerings; and (3) the lack of pedagogical sophistication on the part of teachers. There is little hope that existing nursery schools will be able to improve markedly by themselves in these three critical realms, even with the infusion of newly trained teachers. New teachers tend to adjust to the extant circumstances, becoming part of the condition rather than agents for change. Our research to date on educational change suggests the potential power and role of an external agency, provided that agency has prestige, resources, and the view that institutions must learn to help themselves.[1] To provide only consultation is not adequate; such an agency must be a true partner. Though separate, it must be "one of us," so to speak, from the viewpoint of affiliated or collaborating nursery schools. A federally funded Research and Development Center for Early Education serving as the hub for the St. Louis League of Nursery Schools, for example, might satisfy such criteria.

We strongly recommend the creation of several such centers in each state, preferably in connection with major universities having a corps of first-rate personnel in early childhood education and schooling. Federal and state funds would serve initially to build up such staffs with both research and clinical personnel. It is essential that each of these centers maintains exemplary programs undergoing continuous revision. These should be in all areas of nursery school commitment: cognitive, psychomotor, affective, and social-personal development. It is in lack of imagination regarding program development that nursery schools are most deficient. What they need is to be shown how to do better what they claim to be doing now and to have their sights lifted in regard to the importance of and possibilities for cognitive development as at least a parallel commitment to emotional development. Directors and teachers must come to see what well-developed programs in each realm look like and then have opportunities for guided implementation of similar programs in their own settings.

The proposed research and development centers must be firmly restrained from turning only to research and preparation of new personnel, important as these are. Likewise, they must be restrained from building up large consulting staffs, which are expensive and can be both wasteful and nonproductive. To repeat, the purpose is to develop several exemplary programs for the guidance and stimulation of an affiliated consortium of nursery schools and to foster this consortium as a social system for peer-group help and socialization. The center shows the way and acts as a catalyst, but it is the schools that help themselves and each other.

At first, it will be necessary for the hub also to provide brief workshops, preferably in the schools, in pedagogical techniques regarding the stimulation, motivation, and reinforcement of children in whatever is included in programs. Much of this must be done by outstanding teachers added temporarily to the center's regular staff. Increasingly, however, as talent is refined in the cooperating schools, the directors and teachers will begin to set up temporary "pedagogical service stations" for helping each other, and ultimately, this activity will extend beyond the initial consortium to include neighboring schools. As the press for improvement increases, creative new approaches to helping one another will emerge.[2]

The centers, or hubs, proposed here are not intended to be of temporary duration, however—they always will be needed for research, curriculum development, the production of materials, and the training of personnel. It is to be hoped that a practical relationship to the field always will be of prime importance. It is the necessity of permanence and continuity that suggests the desirability of such centers being established within universities, especially since a nucleus of needed resources already is available in many.

We reiterate, then, the concept of seeking to improve existing nursery schools as the most promising way to improve quickly the education of an existing cohort of young children. The exemplary center is proposed as the vanguard of the more comprehensive commitment to public education for young children recommended subsequently.

TOWARD A CHILDHOOD PHASE OF SCHOOLING

In this concluding section of our report, we draw inferences from an earlier study of elementary schools reported elsewhere.[3] The essence of these final pages is refinement of our major recommendation: *There should be provided at public expense an early childhood phase of schooling embracing children ranging in age from 4 to 7 or 8.* It is to be nongraded; classes are to be multiage; and it may or may not be located physically with the next phase of schooling. Admission should be voluntary and available on the fourth birthday or at any appropriate time thereafter. Transfer or entry to the next phase should be available at any time after age 6 if the match between child and the general character of the program in this next phase appears, according to professional judgment, to be closer than the match between the child and the early phase.

The writers came to this conclusion somewhat hesitatingly at first but with increasing firmness as the data of this study were analyzed and juxtaposed with the findings of the earlier study of elementary schools referred to above. We were hesitant to include with a school unit that has been so criticized, the elementary school, the nursery segment of schooling which, to date, has remained free of bureaucratic entanglements. Nevertheless, it became increasingly clear to us that the quality of programs and instruction we had observed a few years earlier in 32 kindergarten classrooms in urban and suburban schools was significantly better than that observed generally in the 201 nursery schools. These kindergarten classes, in our judgment, were also significantly better on all our criteria than the first-, second-, and third-grade classes in the same schools.

It appears to us that kindergartens have been influenced most by what we have identified with the most enlightened thrusts of early childhood schooling. They tend to provide programs that can be identified with the most frequently articulated goals of nursery schools—namely, emotional and social development. Like nursery schools, however, they are deficient in programs for cognitive development and, too frequently, often under pressure from parents, school boards, or unenlightened superintendents, present a watered-down program in academic skills patterned after that provided in most first-grade classes. Nonetheless, they appear usually to operate with a good deal of freedom from prescribed curriculum restraints and with considerable attention to the characteristics of five-year-old children. They offer the best hope for the good education of children within the organized school system. It appears that more than just the rhetoric surrounding the educational discovery of the young child has gotten through to a number of our kindergartens.

Unlike kindergartens, nursery schools are isolated from the educational mainstream, as stressed in this and the preceding chapter. Their staffs usually miss out on the conferences, workshops, in-service education activities, and professional journals which kindergarten teachers share. Unlike kindergartens, nursery schools lack assurance that incoming teachers have been prepared in child growth and development, curriculum planning, appropriate materials, and pedagogy.

It seems to us, therefore, that it might be possible to keep some of the apparent benefits enjoyed by five-year-olds while securing them also for four-year-olds on the one hand and six- and seven-year-olds on the other if all these ages were brought into a first or primary phase of schooling. This proposal obviously parallels certain elements of the British Infant School,[4] but it is modeled somewhat more closely after the *Report of the Task Force in Early Childhood Education* in California on which one of the authors served.[5]

In regard to program emphases, we lean more heavily toward cognitive development than was apparent in the British Infant Schools visited by one of the authors and somewhat less heavily toward the academic skills stressed so strongly in the curriculum section of the task force report. We see the latter as more appropriate for terminal behaviors in an early childhood phase of schooling. In fact, one of our major reasons for including six- and seven-year-olds in this early phase is to remove them from some of the pressure of expectations imposed upon them at the beginning of their schooling. Instead, in the proposed plan they would move into reading and other skills developmentally and individually rather than encountering them as the first selective hurdle in the school's relentless processes of sorting children.

In regard to a general perspective for this early childhood phase of schooling, we identify closely with several statements in the California report:

> ... Since it is clear that early diagnosis, intervention, and prevention are dependent upon a close liaison among educational, social, and health services, a cooperative working relationship among persons in these fields is vital. ... In order to make the early years of learning truly effective, assessment of appropriate and significant developmental levels must be the basis for planning the educational program for each child. If and when needed, corrective social, medical, and psychological facilities must be made accessible to permit the young individual to reach his full potential. ... There must be encouragement of local autonomy and creativity in program development, with provision for maximum flexibility within broad state guidelines. School districts and other agencies involved in the programs must be allowed freedom to experiment and individualize to meet the needs of the children they serve.[6]

Likewise, we endorse in that report the recommendations for parent education and involvement, for this early school to be a community educational center, and for extensive attention to teacher education. In addition, we support the substance of discussions among task force members pertaining to the health, education, and general welfare of the very young child, discussions which took into account the importance of prenatal parental education. The group envisioned the provision of physical, social, and psychological services, coordinated close to the home in what sometimes is labeled "Home Start." For some four-year-olds encompassed by such a Home Start effort, it is conceivable that entry into the early phase of schooling described here might not be appropriate. This is one of several reasons for our recommendation that entry into school on the child's fourth birthday be an available option but not a mandatory provision. In effect, then, we see the Home Start effort preceding and overlapping the first phase of school, with both educational measures designed to assure an optimum beginning in life for each child, regardless of place of abode, socioeconomic background, or educational status of parents.

Implicit and explicit in our recommendations is commitment to a kind of double-barreled approach to development in early childhood schooling: an effort to upgrade existing nursery schools on the one hand and the creation of a public, tax-supported early childhood unit of schooling on the other. With perhaps 30 to 40 percent of our four-year-olds enrolled in the former and with these programs operating generally at what we believe to be an unsatisfactory level, the chance to upgrade the educational opportunities for so many children at relatively low cost is too good to pass by. This can be done without state and local provision for buildings, supplies, and teachers, the items consuming almost all dollars spent on schooling. By creating a number of research and development centers and then holding them responsible for upgrading these nursery schools, as recommended on preceding pages, advances in knowledge, program development, and training for the whole of early education and schooling are simultaneously assured.

But there remains some 60 to 70 percent of the four-year-old population for whom no such opportunities exist, and a large proportion of these come from those segments which have the most to gain and are the least able to afford the luxury of schooling in the private sector. Consequently, public support for the private sector without attention to the public sector would be discriminating, even though constructive for those benefiting from it. Therefore, we have recommended the public intervention earlier described. We urge, in the spirit of the California task force, that this be done in stages, earliest provisions being in geographic areas where the need is greatest, for experimental and exemplary program development, and for the preparation of personnel, this last being critically urgent.

WHAT ARE NURSERY SCHOOLS FOR?

The California report disappoints us most as a guide to other states in the emphases and narrowness of the proposed curriculum, except for its treatment of language development. Other modes of expression are taken care of in only a sentence or two, and the importance of imagery, fantasy, and the superego as they might be developed through drama, play, and fairy tales are omitted. Although forward-looking and well-conceived, then, the California report, like so many others, does not quite come to grips with the vital question of what early education and schooling are for. The more the report gets into specifics, the more we see the seemingly inescapable academically oriented activities of an early school preparing for a later school instead of activities designed with the goal of each child's discovering and expanding himself as a person. Why are we so incapable of envisioning more than a real-life version of "Sesame Street"?

There is no way of translating into specific recommendations our central concern about the most fundamental shortcomings of programs in early education. We have had the benefits of extensive observation of nursery school classrooms and discussions with directors, teachers, and early childhood specialists in the United States, England, Israel, and Asia. We have investigated the relevant literature of many lands. What comes through overwhelmingly is a desire to "do good": to keep children safely and happily engaged, to compensate for handicap or disadvantage, to develop the traits of the whole child, and to prepare for school. *What is missing is a sense of what the child is trying to do—perhaps must do—during these formative years and a sense of the scar tissue he will carry with him throughout life if his early strivings for identity are frustrated by neglect or inept intervention.*

This is not to suggest for a moment that the child, left to his own devices, will mature in a wholesome fashion. If this were the case, there would be no need for education and certainly none for schooling. Even if there were a built-in mechanism for only good unfolding —which is not the case—society is not sufficiently benign to assure unswerving adherence to a positive shaping subsequently. The environment must be shaped.

The essential elements in this shaping are never-failing adult support and a set of guiding values infused into every activity. For the early phase of schooling, the values to be supported are that the child achieve a sense of personal well-being expressed in his self-confident relationship with objects, peers, and adults; his lack of fear; his confrontations with his occasionally angry, hating, antisocial self; his ability to move in and out of an imaginary world in which knights fight battles with serpents and dragons and win; and his transition from narcissistic contemplation of self to interaction with an increasingly expanding environment. These are the marks of the child successfully using his early years, not his level of performance on school-oriented tests. These are the emerging attributes for which he must have unfaltering adult support. These are the goals for the first phase of schooling.

Reading, numbers, and the like are meaningful to the degree they help the child achieve these goals—and very meaningful, indeed, they can be, because they are the tools of the human race that extend self-transcendence in limitless ways. But they are not the goals of early schooling. Unfortunately, it is mistaking these mundane means for the ends of education that has corrupted schooling at all levels. Early schools have the best opportunity and the most serious responsibility for maintaining at all times the necessary distinction.

NOTES

1   John I. Goodlad, "Staff Development: The League Model," *Theory Into Practice*, Oct. 1972, pp. 205–214; and Mary M. Bentzen and Kenneth A. Tye, "Effecting Change in Elementary Schools," *The Elementary School in the United States*, Seventy-second Yearbook of the National Society for the Study of Education, Part II, University of Chicago Press, Chicago, 1973.

2   Our experience with this phenomenon is documented in a series of special film reports on |I|D|E|A|'s Study of Educational Change and School Improvement: *The League*, 4 parts, |I|D|E|A|, P.O. Box 446, Melbourne, Fla. 32901. The study is also reported in the volumes of the |I|D|E|A| Reports on Schooling, Series on Educational Change, McGraw-Hill, New York, in press.

3   John I. Goodlad, M. Frances Klein, and Associates, *Behind the Classroom Door*, revised edition, Charles A. Jones, Worthington, Ohio, 1973.

4   For a discussion of the British Infant School, see Lillian Weber, *The English Infant School and Informal Education*, Prentice-Hall, Englewood Cliffs, N.J., 1971.

5   Report of the Task Force on Early Childhood Education, *Early Childhood Education*, California State Department of Education, Sacramento, 1972.

6   Ibid., p. 4.

APPENDIX A
DATA TABLES

TABLE I   AREAS OF EMPHASIS IN PROGRAM

Areas of Emphasis	Total Sample						College Labs			
	N	Percent of Responses				N	Percent of Responses			
		High	Medium	Low	No Tally and Other		High	Medium	Low	No Tally and Other
Academic Skills	203	31.53	33.97	36.96	3.8	17	29.41	35.29	23.52	11.76
Arts and Creative Expression	200	75.0	20.5	3.0	1.5		82.35	11.76		5.88
Cognitive-Intellectual Development	201	61.18	30.33	3.97	2.97		70.58	17.64		11.76
Concept Acquisition	200	67.0	26.0	5.5	1.5		88.23	11.76		
Emotional Development	200	85.5	10.5	3.00	1.00		88.23	5.88	5.88	
Language Skills: Oral Development	200	70.0	23.5	4.5	2.0		100.00			
Language Skills: Reading and Vocabulary Development	201	32.32	32.35	18.87	8.34		41.17	5.88	5.88	47.05
Motor Skills	197	62.93	20.29	8.11	0.5		94.11	5.88		
Sensory Awareness	199	71.84	19.09	4.52	4.52		100.00			
Sensory-Motor Skills	199	65.30	27.13	4.51	2.51		100.00			
Social-Inter-personal Skills	201	76.10	20.38	0.98	2.98		82.35	5.88	5.88	5.88
Verbalizing Feelings	198	67.68	21.20	6.55	1.51		88.23		5.88	5.88
Other	64									

| | Montessori | | | | | Parent Coops | | | | |
| | Percent of Responses | | | | | Percent of Responses | | | | X^2 |
N	High	Medium	Low	No Tally and Other	N	High	Medium	Low	No Tally and Other	
24	62.50	16.66	8.33	12.50	20	5.00	30.00	60.00	5.00	0.01
	58.33	37.50		4.16		75.00	15.00	5.00	5.00	0.98–0.95
	87.50	8.33		4.16		35.00	50.00	10.00	5.00	0.01
	87.50	4.16	4.16	4.16		50.00	40.00	5.00	5.00	0.05–0.02
	87.50	8.33	4.16			90.00	5.00		5.00	
	70.83	12.50	4.16	12.50		50.00	35.00	10.00	5.00	0.05–0.02
	62.50	29.16		8.33		10.00	35.00	40.00	15.00	0.01
	75.00	12.50	12.50			50.00	35.00	10.00	5.00	0.05
	91.66	4.16		4.16		55.00	25.00	5.00	15.00	0.02–0.01
	79.16	16.66		4.16		55.00	25.00	10.00	10.00	0.05–0.02
	75.00	16.66	4.16	4.16		80.00	15.00		5.00	
	70.83	20.83	8.33			70.00	20.00	5.00	5.00	0.99–0.98

TABLE II   FUNCTIONS OF SCHOOL

Functions	Total Sample		College Labs		Montessori		Parent Coops	
	N	Percent of Responses	N	Percent of Responses	N	Percent of Responses	N	Percent of Responses
General Child Development	98	29.5	12	40.00	15	39.47	13	40.62
Education and Readiness for School (General and Specific Skills)	89	26.8	4	13.33	11	28.94	8	25.00
Child Care	47	14.2	1	3.33				
Development of Aspects of Self	27	8.1	1	3.33	4	10.52		
Socialization	20	6.0	1	3.33	1	2.63	2	6.25
Miscellaneous	13	3.9	2	6.66	2	5.26	1	3.12
Parent Education	9	2.71	2	6.66	1	2.63	5	15.62
Preparation of Personnel	9	2.71	4	13.33	3	7.89		
Research and Program Development	6	1.8	3	10.00	1	2.63		
Religious Development (Christian and Hebrew)	5	1.5						
Development of Creativity	3	0.9					2	6.25
No Tally	6	1.8					1	3.12
Totals	332		30		38		32	

TABLE III   SPECIFIC OBJECTIVES OF SCHOOLS

Objectives	Total Sample		College Labs		Montessori		Parent Coops	
	N	Percent of Responses	N	Percent of Responses	N	Percent of Responses	N	Percent of Responses
Development of Self, Personality Traits, and Attitudes	68	17.6	4	13.33	1	12.50	5	13.51
Schooling Readiness and Specific Skills	62	16.1	6	20.00	2	25.00	6	16.21
Child Development	52	13.5	6	20.00	3	37.50	6	16.21
Socialization	36	9.35	3	10.00			8	21.62
Child Care	22	5.71						
Parent Education and Participation	21	5.45	3	10.00			4	10.81
Training of Personnel	14	3.63	6	20.00				
Learning Skills, Attitudes, and General Atmosphere	12	3.11						
Religious Education	12	3.11						
Cognition and Concept Development	11	2.85						
Research and Program Development	11	2.85	2	6.66	1	12.50	1	2.70
Preparation for Living	9	2.33						
Compensatory Education	7	1.81						
Development of Creativity	6	1.55					4	10.81
Broadening Experiences from the Home	6	1.55						
Cultural Programs	6	1.55						
List of Previously Printed Objectives	6	1.55						
Bilingual Programs	3	0.77						
Service to Community or Church	2	0.51					1	2.70
Miscellaneous	16	4.15					2	5.40
No Tally	5	0.77			1	12.50		
Totals	385		30		8		37	

TABLE IV PROGRAM EVALUATION PROCEDURES

Evaluation Procedures	Total Sample		College Labs		Montessori		Parent Coops	
	N	Percent of Responses	N	Percent of Responses	N	Percent of Responses	N	Percent of Responses
Staff Evaluations	80	27.97	9	39.13	1	11.11	5	20.83
State, County, City Evaluations	48	16.78	1	4.34	1	11.11	1	4.16
Evaluation by Funding or Sponsoring Agency	43	15.03	1	4.34			2	8.33
None	27	9.44	1	4.34	1	11.11	5	20.83
Parent Involvement in Evaluation	19	6.64	1	4.34			5	20.83
Independent Associations	14	4.89			3	33.33		
Owners, Directors	13	4.54			1	11.11		
Questionable Procedures	11	3.84						
University or Professional People	8	2.79	5	21.73			5	20.83
Standardized Tests	5	1.74						
Visitors	4	1.39	1	4.34				
Evaluation by Student-Trainees	4	1.39	4	17.39				
Evaluation Occurs, No Identified Process	3	1.04					1	4.16
Follow-up Studies (Formal and Informal)	3	1.04						
Formal Research	2	0.69						
No Tally	2	0.69			2	22.22		
Totals	286		23		9		24	

TABLE V   EVALUATION OF STUDENT PROGRESS

Procedures	Total Sample		College Labs		Montessori		Parent Coops	
	N	Percent of Responses	N	Percent of Responses	N	Percent of Responses	N	Percent of Responses
Teacher Observation and Evaluation	153	45.67	12	44.44	4	44.44	17	58.62
Records and Observation (not specified by whom)	64	19.10	3	11.11	3	33.33		
Use of Tests	58	17.31	7	25.92	1	11.11	2	6.89
None	13	3.88			1	11.11	1	3.44
Miscellaneous	12	3.58						
Staff Evaluations	10	2.98					1	3.44
Sociometric Data	7	2.08	1	3.70				
Parent Observations	7	2.08	1	3.70			7	24.13
Specialist Evaluations	4	1.19	1	3.70			1	3.44
Student-Trainee Evaluations	4	1.19	2	7.40				
Testing Used Prior to Enrollment	3	0.89						
Totals	335		27		9		29	

TABLE VI   PROCEDURES USED FOR REPORTING TO PARENTS

Procedures	Total Sample		College Labs		Montessori		Parent Coops	
	N	Percent of Responses	N	Percent of Responses	N	Percent of Responses	N	Percent of Responses
Conferences: Teachers, Directors, Social Workers	146	28.91	15	30.61	6	50.00	10	25.00
Informal Contacts with Parents	113	22.37	10	20.40	1	8.33	13	32.50
Phone Calls	75	14.85	7	14.28	1	8.33	5	12.50
Written Reports	54	10.69	6	12.24	3	25.00	4	10.00
Parent Group Meetings and Programs	50	9.90	5	10.20			7	17.50
Home Visits	24	4.75	2	4.08				
Reporting Indicated; Process Unspecified	11	2.17						
Newsletters and Impersonal Notes	10	1.98	1	2.04				
Miscellaneous	6	1.18						
Parent Observation	5	0.99	3	6.12	1	8.33		
None	5	0.99						
Casework, Consultation	3	.59						
No Tally	3	.59						
Totals	505		49		12		40	

TABLE VII A   NURSERY SCHOOL PERSONNEL, PROFESSIONAL PREPARATION

Level of Preparation	Directors	Teachers	Assistant Teachers	Aides Not Related to Children
No High School		1		1
Some High School		1	4	50
High School Graduate	6	42	42	22
Some College	40	143	100	7
College Degree	99	359		
Some Graduate Work		7		
Graduate Degree	60	38	2	
Formal Training in Early Childhood Education	104	221	44	10
Montessori	10	31	12	1
Inservice or Workshops		1	1	3

TABLE VII B   NURSERY SCHOOL PERSONNEL, YEARS OF EXPERIENCE

Years of Experience in Nursery Education	Directors	Assistant Teachers	Teachers	Aides Not Related to Children
6 months or less	2	5	19	1
1 year	10		9	11
2 years	11	37	9	2
3 years	15	19	9	1
4 years	13	19	8	1
5 years	14	31	17	
6 years	15	11	1	
7 years	17	8	1	1
8 years	13	9	1	
9 years	4	1		1
10 years	8	11		2
11 years	3			
12 years	6	2	Others reported in range of years	
13 years	4	1		
14 years	1			
15 years	8	4		
16 years +	27	Others reported in range of years		

TABLE VIII   SHARING OF FACILITIES

Type of Sharing Arrangement	Total Sample		College Labs		Montessori		Parent Coops	
	N	Percent of Responses	N	Percent of Responses	N	Percent of Responses	N	Percent of Response
None	89	41.39	10	55.55	15	62.50	8	40.00
Church or Temple	66	30.69	2	11.11	5	20.83	7	35.00
Community Services and Groups (Adults and Children)	25	11.62			1	4.16	1	5.00
Sharing with Other Schools or Other Groups within the School	14	6.51	3	16.66	3	12.50	3	15.00
Facilities Used for Medical or Training Purposes	8	3.72	3	16.66				
No Tally	7	3.25					1	5.00
Private Facilities Used for School and Other Purposes	3	1.39						
Miscellaneous	3	1.39						
Totals	215		18		24		20	

TABLE IX FREQUENCY OF CURRICULAR AREAS AND ACTIVITIES IN PROGRAM

Curricular Area or Activity	Totals N	Daily		Frequently		Occasionally		Rarely or Never		No Tally	
		N	Percent of Responses	N	Percent of Responses	N	Percent of Responses	N	Percent of Responses	N	Percent of Responses
Informal Arithmetic	203	99	50.22	56	27.57	25	12.30	16	7.87	5	2.45
Formal Arithmetic	198	33	17.26	20	10.09	14	7.06	77	38.88	54	27.27
Art	200	165	82.50	23	11.50	4	2.00	2	1.00	5	2.50
Foreign Languages	201	18	8.95	10	4.96	20	9.93	118	58.69	31	15.40
Informal Language	197	134	68.02	21	10.65	8	4.06	9	4.56	25	12.69
Formal Language	199	41	20.60	21	10.55	10	5.02	69	34.67	58	29.14
Informal Music	202	156	77.22	32	15.84	6	2.97	2	0.99	6	2.97
Formal Music	199	39	19.58	36	18.07	15	7.52	61	30.63	48	24.11
Musical Instrument Instruction	197	11	5.58	25	12.69	42	21.31	87	44.16	26	13.19
Informal Reading Readiness	201	125	62.18	32	15.91	11	5.47	14	6.96	17	8.44
Formal Reading Readiness	198	43	21.71	22	11.11	14	7.06	74	37.36	45	22.71
Reading	196	31	15.81	7	3.57	15	7.65	105	53.56	34	17.34
Informal Science	198	101	50.99	52	26.25	28	14.13	9	4.54	8	4.03
Formal Science	199	20	10.04	26	13.04	30	15.05	74	37.16	49	24.60
Informal Social Studies	198	73	36.86	54	27.25	32	16.15	25	12.61	13	6.56
Formal Social Studies	197	12	6.08	24	13.16	20	10.13	84	42.63	56	28.41
Blocks	198	161	81.30	18	9.08	5	2.52	7	3.53	6	3.02
Carpentry	200	40	20.00	42	21.00	43	21.50	62	31.00	10	5.00
Cooking	198	14	7.06	46	23.21	87	43.93	42	21.20	8	4.04
Dramatization and Role Playing	201	66	32.82	72	35.81	38	18.69	16	7.94	6	2.97
Organized Group Games	202	72	35.64	59	29.20	39	19.30	26	12.87	5	2.47
Informal Rest	198	91	45.95	8	4.02	22	11.10	58	29.28	15	7.57
Naps	200	86	43.00	1	0.50	4	2.00	94	47.00	12	6.00
Nature Walks	199	9	4.51	89	44.71	78	39.18	16	8.00	5	2.51
Outdoor Play	198	164	82.82	22	11.10	5	2.52	4	2.02	3	1.51
Rhythms	199	77	38.69	94	47.23	22	11.05	2	1.00	3	1.50
Story Time	198	169	85.34	20	10.10	4	2.01	2	1.01	2	1.01
Trips	198	66	33.32	66	33.32	99	49.98	29	14.64	4	2.02

TABLE IX   FREQUENCY OF CURRICULAR AREAS AND ACTIVITIES
IN PROGRAM (Continued)

Curricular Area or Activity	College Laboratories (N = 17)									
	Daily		Frequently		Occasionally		Rarely or Never		No Tally	
	N	Percent of Responses	N	Percent of Responses	N	Percent of Responses	N	Percent of Responses	N	Percent of Responses
Informal Arithmetic	13	76.47	2	11.76	1	5.88	0	0.00	1	5.88
Formal Arithmetic	4	23.52	2	11.76	3	17.64	6	35.29	2	11.76
Art	15	88.23	0	0.00	0	0.00	0	0.00	2	11.76
Foreign Languages	0	0.00	2	11.76	3	17.64	9	52.94	3	17.64
Informal Language	15	88.23	1	5.88	0	0.00	0	0.00	1	5.88
Formal Language	6	35.29	2	11.76	0	0.00	6	35.29	3	17.64
Informal Music	16	94.11	1	5.88	0	0.00	0	0.00	0	0.00
Formal Music	4	23.52	1	5.88	4	23.52	6	35.29	2	11.76
Musical Instrument Instruction	2	11.76	1	5.88	3	17.64	9	52.94	2	11.76
Informal Reading Readiness	14	82.35	1	5.88	0	0.00	0	0.00	2	11.76
Formal Reading Readiness	6	35.29	2	11.76	2	11.76	6	35.29	1	5.88
Reading	3	17.64	3	17.64	1	5.88	5	29.41	5	29.41
Informal Science	13	76.47	4	23.52	0	0.00	0	0.00	0	0.00
Formal Science	3	17.64	3	17.64	2	11.76	6	35.29	3	17.64
Informal Social Studies	10	58.82	5	29.41	2	11.76	0	0.00	0	0.00
Formal Social Studies	2	11.76	2	11.76	2	11.76	8	47.05	3	17.64
Blocks	15	88.23	1	5.88	0	0.00	0	0.00	1	5.88
Carpentry	8	47.05	6	35.29	1	5.88	2	11.76	0	0.00
Cooking	3	17.64	11	64.70	2	11.76	1	5.88	0	0.00
Dramatization and Role-Playing	11	64.70	4	23.52	1	5.88	1	5.88	0	0.00
Organized Group Games	2	11.76	7	41.17	2	11.76	6	35.29	0	0.00
Informal Rest	11	64.70	1	5.88	1	5.88	3	17.64	1	5.88
Naps	4	23.52	0	0.00	1	5.88	12	70.58	0	0.00
Nature Walks	1	5.88	12	70.58	2	11.76	1	5.88	1	5.88
Outdoor Play	15	88.23	1	5.88	0	0.00	1	5.88	0	0.00
Rhythms	9	52.94	6	35.29	2	11.76	0	0.00	0	0.00
Story Time	14	82.35	2	11.76	1	5.88	0	0.00	0	0.00
Trips	0	0.00	7	41.17	7	41.17	3	17.64	0	0.00

TABLE IX   FREQUENCY OF CURRICULAR AREAS AND ACTIVITIES IN PROGRAM (Continued)

Curricular Area or Activity	Montessori (N = 24)									
	Daily		Frequently		Occasionally		Rarely or Never		No Tally	
	N	Percent of Responses	N	Percent of Responses	N	Percent of Responses	N	Percent of Responses	N	Percent of Responses
Informal Arithmetic	19	79.16	4	16.67	0	0.00	1	4.17	0	0.00
Formal Arithmetic	11	45.83	3	12.50	2	8.33	4	16.67	4	16.67
Art	20	83.33	3	12.50	1	4.17	0	0.00	0	0.00
Foreign Languages	4	16.66	7	29.16	3	12.50	9	37.50	1	4.17
Informal Language	18	75.00	2	8.33	1	4.17	0	0.00	3	12.50
Formal Language	11	45.83	5	20.83	0	0.00	5	20.83	3	12.50
Informal Music	15	62.50	6	25.00	1	4.17	1	4.17	1	4.17
Formal Music	7	29.16	6	25.00	3	12.50	3	12.50	5	20.83
Musical Instrument Instruction	3	12.50	4	16.66	6	25.00	8	33.33	3	12.50
Informal Reading Readiness	22	91.66	0	0.00	0	0.00	0	0.00	2	8.33
Formal Reading Readiness	12	50.00	4	16.67	1	4.17	4	16.67	3	12.50
Reading	13	54.16	2	8.33	4	16.67	4	16.67	1	4.17
Informal Science	15	62.50	5	20.83	3	12.50	0	0.00	1	4.17
Formal Science	5	20.83	6	25.00	6	25.00	4	16.67	3	12.50
Informal Social Studies	12	50.00	7	29.16	2	8.33	1	4.17	2	8.33
Formal Social Studies	2	8.33	8	33.33	5	20.83	6	25.00	3	12.50
Blocks	15	62.50	0	0.00	2	8.33	6	25.00	1	4.17
Carpentry	6	25.00	2	8.33	4	16.67	11	45.83	1	4.17
Cooking	6	25.00	1	4.17	10	41.66	7	29.16	0	0.00
Dramatization and Role-Playing	4	16.67	7	29.16	7	29.16	6	25.00	0	0.00
Organized Group Games	12	50.00	3	12.50	6	25.00	3	12.50	0	0.00
Informal Rest	6	25.00	1	4.17	2	8.33	12	50.00	3	12.50
Naps	6	25.00	0	0.00	0	0.00	13	54.16	5	20.83
Nature Walks	2	8.34	8	33.33	10	41.66	2	8.33	2	8.33
Outdoor Play	21	87.50	2	8.33	0	0.00	0	0.00	1	4.17
Rhythms	11	45.83	11	45.83	2	8.33	0	0.00	0	0.00
Story Time	19	79.16	2	8.33	1	4.17	2	8.33	0	0.00
Trips	0	0.00	4	16.16	12	50.00	7	29.16	1	4.17

TABLE IX   FREQUENCY OF CURRICULAR AREAS AND ACTIVITIES IN PROGRAM (Continued)

Curricular Area or Activity	Parent Cooperatives (N = 20)									
	Daily		Frequently		Occasionally		Rarely or Never		No Tally	
	N	Percent of Responses	N	Percent of Responses	N	Percent of Responses	N	Percent of Responses	N	Percent of Responses
Informal Arithmetic	6	30.00	8	40.00	3	15.00	2	10.00	1	5.00
Formal Arithmetic	0	0.00	0	0.00	1	5.00	10	50.00	9	45.00
Art	17	85.00	2	10.00	0	0.00	0	0.00	1	5.00
Foreign Languages	0	0.00	0	0.00	1	5.00	15	75.00	4	20.00
Informal Language	11	55.00	5	25.00	0	0.00	1	5.00	3	15.00
Formal Language	0	0.00	2	10.00	3	15.00	7	35.00	8	40.00
Informal Music	12	60.00	6	30.00	1	5.00	0	0.00	1	5.00
Formal Music	3	15.00	2	10.00	3	15.00	6	30.00	6	30.00
Musical Instrument Instruction	1	5.00	3	15.00	6	30.00	8	40.00	2	10.00
Informal Reading Readiness	9	45.00	3	15.00	3	15.00	3	15.00	2	10.00
Formal Reading Readiness	1	5.00	2	10.00	1	5.00	9	45.00	7	35.00
Reading	1	5.00	0	0.00	3	15.00	14	70.00	2	10.00
Informal Science	9	45.00	5	25.00	4	20.00	0	0.00	2	10.00
Informal Social Studies	6	30.00	5	25.00	3	15.00	3	15.00	3	15.00
Formal Social Studies	0	0.00	1	5.00	3	15.00	8	40.00	8	40.00
Blocks	14	70.00	4	20.00	1	5.00	0	0.00	1	5.00
Carpentry	5	25.00	9	45.00	4	20.00	1	5.00	1	5.00
Cooking	1	5.00	5	25.00	11	55.00	2	10.00	1	5.00
Dramatization and Role-Playing	6	30.00	6	30.00	4	20.00	2	10.00	2	10.00
Organized Group Games	5	25.00	6	30.00	4	20.00	4	20.00	1	5.00
Informal Rest	6	30.00	1	5.00	2	10.00	9	45.00	2	10.00
Naps	1	5.00	0	0.00	0	0.00	17	85.00	2	10.00
Nature Walks	1	5.00	3	15.00	14	70.00	1	5.00	1	5.00
Outdoor Play	14	70.00	4	20.00	0	0.00	1	5.00	1	5.00
Rhythms	6	30.00	9	45.00	3	15.00	1	5.00	1	5.00
Story Time	17	85.00	2	10.00	0	0.00	0	0.00	1	5.00
Trips	0	0.00	5	25.00	13	65.00	0	0.00	2	10.00

TABLE IX FREQUENCY OF CURRICULAR AREAS AND ACTIVITIES IN PROGRAM (Continued)

	Chi Square for Three Separate Programs		
Area or Activity	X^2	Area or Activity	X^2
Informal Arithmetic	14.60*	Informal Social Studies	5.75
Formal Arithmetic	19.14*	Formal Social Studies	8.48
Art		Blocks	
Foreign Languages	16.30*	Carpentry	18.23*
Informal Language		Cooking	24.36*
Formal Language	17.75*	Dramatization and Role Playing	12.17
Informal Music		Organized Group Games	11.45
Formal Music	6.59	Informal Rest	7.55
Musical Instrument Instruction		Naps	
Informal Reading Readiness	15.51*	Nature Walks	15.27*
Formal Reading Readiness	11.08	Outdoor Play	
Reading	22.18*	Rhythms	3.97
Informal Science	4.74	Story Time	
Formal Science	7.52	Trips	9.00

* Significant at the 0.05 level of confidence.

TABLE X EXTENT OF PARENT PARTICIPATION

Type of Participation	Total Sample		College Labs		Montessori		Parent Coops	
	N	Percent of Responses	N	Percent of Responses	N	Percent of Responses	N	Percent of Responses
Encouraged, Voluntary	109	55.05	10	58.82	12	50.00		
Required	25	12.62	1	5.88			19	100.00
None-Never	24	12.12	2	11.76	2	8.33		
Very Limited Voluntary Participation	17	8.58	3	17.64	4	16.66		
Discouraged	14	7.07			4	16.66		
No Tally	7	3.53			1	4.16		
Not Encouraged, but Limited Participation	2	1.01	1	5.88	1	4.16		
Totals	198		17		24		19	

TABLE XI   TYPES OF PARENT MEETINGS

Type of Meeting	Total Sample		College Labs		Montessori		Parent Coops	
	N	Percent of Responses	N	Percent of Responses	N	Percent of Responses	N	Percent of Responses
General Parent Meetings	52	16.82	5	14.70	4	14.28	10	30.30
Discussion Groups	43	13.91	7	20.58	7	25.00	8	24.24
PTA	41	13.26	5	14.70	7	25.00	2	6.06
Parties, Classes, Programs, Social Groups	35	11.32	2	5.88	2	7.14	1	3.03
None	28	9.06	1	2.94				
Parent Committees and Club Meetings	27	8.73						
Informal Visits	14	4.53					1	3.03
Work Parties	13	4.20	3	8.82	3	10.71	3	9.09
Orientation Meetings	13	4.20	3	8.82	2	7.14	1	3.03
Speaker and Discussions	13	4.20	5	14.70	1	3.57	2	6.06
Workshops	8	2.58			1	3.57	1	3.03
Fathers' Meetings	7	2.26	1	2.94			1	3.03
Community-type Programs	5	1.61						
Mothers' Meetings	4	1.29	2	5.88	1	3.57	3	9.09
Special Programs	3	0.97						
Seminars	2	0.64						
Parent Field Trips	1	0.32						
Totals	309		34		28		33	

TABLE XII   PROCEDURES USED TO OBTAIN DATA ABOUT
CHILD AND FAMILY AT REGISTRATION

Procedure	Total Sample		College Labs		Montessori		Parent Coops	
	N	Percent of Responses	N	Percent of Responses	N	Percent of Responses	N	Percent of Responses
Written Forms	216	60.5	15	60.00	20	57.14	14	58.33
Interviews or Conferences	102	28.57	7	28.00	12	34.28	5	20.83
Home-School Visits	23	6.44	1	4.00			3	12.50
Procedure Used, but Unidentified	6	1.68			3	8.57	1	4.16
None	4	1.12	1	4.00			1	4.16
Miscellaneous	3	0.84	1	4.00				
No Tally	3	0.84						
Totals	357		25		35		24	

TABLE XIII   ENTRANCE REQUIREMENTS

Requirement	Total Sample		College Labs		Montessori		Parent Coops	
	N	Percent of Responses	N	Percent of Responses	N	Percent of Responses	N	Percent of Responses
Medical-Physical	82	30.48	7	35.00	9	31.03	10	37.03
Special Needs	43	15.98			1	3.44		
Emphasis on Normality or Ability to Function in Group	23	8.55	2	10.00	5	17.24	1	3.70
Age-Maturity	21	7.80	2	10.00	3	10.34	2	7.40
Limited Membership Restriction	16	5.94	3	15.00	1	3.44	5	18.51
Racial-Ethnic Composition	15	5.57	3	15.00			1	3.70
Toilet-Trained	14	5.20			8	27.58		
Parent Participation	5	1.85					4	14.81
High Financial Status	4	1.48	1	5.00	2	6.89		
Interview or School Visits	4	1.48						
Probationary Period	1	0.37						
Miscellaneous	4	1.48	1	5.00			1	3.70 (sex balance)
None	20	7.43	1	5.00			3	11.11
No Tally	17	6.31						
Totals	269		20		29		27	

TABLE XIV   PROBLEMS OF THE SCHOOL

Problem Area	Total Sample		College Labs		Montessori		Parent Coops	
	N	Percent of Responses	N	Percent of Responses	N	Percent of Responses	N	Percent of Responses
Program or Curricular Difficulties	51	17.77	8	29.62	2	5.88	1	3.70
Physical Facilities and Equipment	50	17.42	4	14.81	2	5.88	3	11.11
Personnel Problems	48	16.72	7	25.92	8	23.52	2	7.40
Funding	34	11.84	3	11.10	3	8.82	4	14.81
Parental Problems, Dissatisfaction, Unrest	29	10.10			3	8.82	4	14.81
Parent Participation, Parent Education	22	7.66	1	3.70	7	20.58	6	22.22
Neighborhood Problems	14	4.87	1	3.70	1	2.94		
Transportation of Children	9	3.13			5	14.70	2	7.40
Racial-Ethnic Composition	5	1.74						
Interpersonal Relationships, School-Other Groups	4	1.39	1	3.70			3	11.11
Maintaining Discipline	4	1.39						
Sporadic Attendance	3	1.04			1	2.94		
Miscellaneous	14	4.87	1	3.70	1	2.94	1	3.70
No Tally*			1	3.70			1	3.70
None*					1	2.94		
Totals	287		27		34		27	

* These categories were not counted as problem categories for the total sample.

TABLE XV   UNIQUENESS OR SUCCESS AREAS OF THE SCHOOL

Unique Aspect or Success Area	Total Sample		College Labs		Montessori		Parent Coops	
	N	Percent of Responses	N	Percent of Responses	N	Percent of Responses	N	Percent of Responses
Program Emphasis or Curricular Aims	112	31.11	16	40.00	13	37.41	5	15.62
Qualifications and Attributes of Staff	54	15.00	6	15.00	5	14.28	4	12.50
Parent Education or Involvement	38	10.55	2	5.00	1	2.85	7	21.87
General Atmosphere of School	30	8.33			5	14.28	2	6.25
Facilities and Equipment	22	6.11	3	7.50	5	14.28		
Interpersonal Relationships within School and with Other Groups	14	3.88	1	2.50	1	2.85	6	18.75
Freedom of the School	12	3.33	1	2.50			1	3.12
Community Involvement, Relationships and Support	12	3.33	1	2.50				
Staff and Paraprofessional Training Programs	11	3.05						
Socioeconomic, Ethnic, Racial Integration	11	3.05	3	7.50	2	5.71	3	9.37
Staff Relations with Parents	11	3.05	3	7.50			2	6.25
Miscellaneous	9	2.50					1	3.12
Miscellaneous Offerings or Attributes of School (Non-Program)	7	1.94	4	10.00				
Organization of School	4	1.11			1	2.85		
Funding	4	1.11			1	2.85		
No Tally	3	0.83					1	3.12
Problems of Teachers	2	0.55						
Other Resources Available to School	2	0.55						
None	2	0.55			1	2.85		
Totals	**360**		**40**		**35**		**32**	

TABLE XVI   DEGREE OF STRUCTURE OBSERVED IN CURRICULAR AREAS AND ACTIVITIES

Curricular Area or Activity	Total Sample—Percentage of Responses*									
	Highly Regulated		Some Structure		Unstructured		Not Observed		No Tally	
	N	Percent of Responses	N	Percent of Responses	N	Percent of Responses	N	Percent of Responses	N	Percent of Responses
Informal Arithmetic	16	13.11	63	51.63	43	35.24	70		30	
Formal Arithmetic	22	59.45	14	37.83	1	2.70	115		64	
Art	31	13.57	92	47.91	69	35.93	23		13	
Foreign Languages	6	30.00	13	65.00	1	5.00	136		46	
Informal Language	16	9.93	75	46.58	70	43.47	35		30	
Formal Language	28	58.33	18	37.50	2	4.16	108		58	
Informal Music	20	13.42	92	61.74	37	24.83	50		21	
Formal Music	20	46.51	23	53.48	0		110		61	
Musical Instrument Instruction	4	16.66	13	54.16	7	29.16	139		51	
Informal Reading Readiness	13	10.65	65	53.27	44	36.06	56		37	
Formal Reading Readiness	24	52.17	19	41.30	3	6.52	111		60	
Reading	8	22.85	16	45.71	11	31.42	125		52	
Informal Science	7	6.14	53	46.49	54	47.36	75		30	
Formal Science	6	26.08	14	60.86	3	13.04	123		69	
Informal Social Studies	10	11.76	36	42.35	39	45.88	95		36	
Formal Social Studies	10	47.61	10	47.61	1	4.76	132		61	
Blocks	9	6.04	36	24.16	104	69.79	50		18	
Carpentry	5	12.82	8	20.51	26	66.66	130		40	
Cooking	11	23.40	31	65.95	5	10.63	129		40	
Dramatization and Role-Playing	4	3.36	32	26.89	83	69.74	66		29	
Organized Group Games	25	28.40	51	57.95	12	13.63	90		35	
Informal Rest	16	25.00	28	43.75	20	31.25	103		41	
Naps	27	55.10	22	44.89	0		112		42	
Nature Walks	5	12.82	27	69.23	7	17.94	135		40	
Outdoor Play	4	2.68	46	30.87	99	66.44	54		20	
Rhythms	25	26.04	61	63.54	10	10.41	90		31	
Story Time	41	27.51	92	61.74	16	10.73	50		16	
Trips	8	20.51	26	66.66	5	12.82	137		35	

* Percentages based on only those cases observed. Cases observed for each area = N for columns of Highly Regulated, Some Structure, and Unstructured.

TABLE XVI   DEGREE OF STRUCTURE OBSERVED IN CURRICULAR AREAS AND ACTIVITIES (Continued)

Curricular Area or Activity	College Laboratories (Total N = 20)*									
	Highly Regulated		Some Structure		Unstructured		Not Observed		No Tally	
	N	Percent of Responses	N	Percent of Responses	N	Percent of Responses	N	Percent of Responses	N	Percent of Responses
Informal Arithmetic	2	18.18	3	27.27	6	54.54	6		3	
Formal Arithmetic	3	75.00	1	25.00	0		10		6	
Art	1	5.26	7	36.84	11	57.89	0		1	
Foreign Languages	1	100.00	0		0		17		2	
Informal Language	3	17.64	3	17.64	11	64.70	2		1	
Formal Language										
Informal Music	1	6.25	8	50.00	7	43.75	4		0	
Formal Music	1	100.00	0		0		14		5	
Musical Instrument Instruction	1	100.00	0		0		18		1	
Informal Reading Readiness	2	13.33	4	26.66	9	60.00	2		3	
Formal Reading Readiness	8	62.50	3	37.50	0		9		3	
Reading	0		3	75.00	1	25.00	12		4	
Informal Science	0		3	30.00	7	70.00	7		3	
Formal Science	0		1	100.00	0		14		5	
Informal Social Studies	1	11.11	2	22.22	6	66.66	9		2	
Formal Social Studies	1	100.00	0		0		14		5	
Blocks	1	7.14	3	21.42	10	71.42	5		1	
Carpentry	1	16.66	1	16.66	4	66.66	12		2	
Cooking	0		3	75.00	1	25.00	14		2	
Dramatization and Role-Playing	0		2	14.28	12	85.71	5		1	
Organized Group Games	2	33.33	2	33.33	2	33.33	13		1	
Informal Rest	1	20.00	0		4	80.00	11		4	
Naps	2	100.00	0		0		16		2	
Nature Walks	1	33.33	2	66.66	0		15		2	
Outdoor Play	0		3	20.00	12	80.00	4		1	
Rhythms**	2	22.22	1	11.11	6	66.66	7		4	
Story Time	3	25.00	5	41.66	4	33.33	6		2	
Trips	0		4	80.00	1	20.00	14		1	

* Percentages based on only those cases observed. Cases observed for each area = N for columns of Highly Regulated, Some Structure, and Unstructured.
** Chi square significant at 0.01 level of confidence.

TABLE XVI   DEGREE OF STRUCTURE OBSERVED IN CURRICULAR
AREAS AND ACTIVITIES (Continued)

Curricular Area or Activity	Montessori (Total N=26)*									
	Highly Regulated		Some Structure		Unstructured		Not Observed		No Tally	
	N	Percent of Responses	N	Percent of Responses	N	Percent of Responses	N	Percent of Responses	N	Percent of Responses
Informal Arithmetic	5	21.73	13	56.52	5	21.73	2		1	
Formal Arithmetic	7	50.00	7	50.00	0		8		4	
Art	3	12.50	11	45.83	10	41.66	1		1	
Foreign Languages	3	37.50	5	62.50	0		12		6	
Informal Language	3	17.64	8	47.05	6	35.29	5		4	
Formal Language	3	21.42	9	64.28	2	14.28	4		8	
Informal Music										
Formal Music	6	60.00	4	40.00	0		10		6	
Musical Instrument Instruction	1	20.00	4	80.00	0		15		6	
Informal Reading Readiness	2	12.50	12	75.00	2	12.50	2		8	
Formal Reading Readiness	5	45.45	6	54.54	0		8		7	
Reading	3	33.33	4	44.44	2	22.22	10		7	
Informal Science	3	20.00	6	40.00	6	40.00	8		3	
Formal Science	2	40.00	2	40.00	1	20.00	14		7	
Informal Social Studies	4	36.36	4	36.36	3	27.27	10		5	
Formal Social Studies	3	50.00	3	50.00	0		15		5	
Blocks	3	25.00	4	33.33	5	41.66	7		7	
Carpentry	1	25.00	1	25.00	2	50.00	14		8	
Cooking	4	44.44	5	55.55	0		13		4	
Dramatization and Role-Playing	0		2	33.33	4	66.66	11		9	
Organized Group Games	5	45.45	6	54.54	0		12		3	
Informal Rest	1	20.00	3	60.00	1	20.00	13		8	
Naps	2	50.00	2	50.00	0		14		8	
Nature Walks	0		3	75.00	1	25.00	17		5	
Outdoor Play	0		5	38.46	8	61.53	10		3	
Rhythms**	3	27.27	8	72.72	0		12		3	
Story Time	4	44.44	4	44.44	1	11.11	15		2	
Trips	0		2	100.00	0		18		6	

* Percentages based on only those cases observed. Cases observed for each area = N for columns of Highly Regulated, Some Structure, and Unstructured.
** Chi square significant at 0.01 level of confidence.

TABLE XVI DEGREE OF STRUCTURE OBSERVED IN CURRICULAR AREAS AND ACTIVITIES (Continued)

Curricular Area or Activity	Parent Cooperatives (N=20)*									
	Highly Regulated		Some Structure		Unstructured		Not Observed		No Tally	
	N	Percent of Responses	N	Percent of Responses	N	Percent of Responses	N	Percent of Responses	N	Percent of Responses
Informal Arithmetic	2	16.66	5	41.67	5	41.67	6		2	
Formal Arithmetic	1	100.00	0		0		10		9	
Art	1	5.55	10	55.56	7	38.89	1		1	
Foreign Languages	0		0		0		12		8	
Informal Language	2	15.38	6	46.15	5	38.46	4		3	
Formal Language	3	75.00	1	25.00	0		10		6	
Informal Music	2	13.33	8	53.33	5	33.33	3		2	
Formal Music	1	33.33	2	66.66	0		10		7	
Musical Instrument Instruction	0		1	100.00	0		9		10	
Informal Reading Readiness	1	8.33	6	50.00	5	41.66	5		3	
Formal Reading Readiness	1	100.00	0		0		9		10	
Reading	1	25.00	3	75.00	0		12		4	
Informal Science	1	7.69	3	23.07	9	69.23	2		5	
Formal Science	0		2	66.66	1	33.33	8		9	
Informal Social Studies	1	16.66	0		5	83.33	7		7	
Formal Social Studies	1	100.00	0		0		10		9	
Blocks	0		3	17.64	14	82.35	2		1	
Carpentry	0		2	22.22	7	77.77	6		5	
Cooking	0		4	80.00	1	20.00	10		5	
Dramatization and Role-Playing	0		3	20.00	12	80.00	2		3	
Organized Group Games	0		1	50.00	1	50.00	10		8	
Informal Rest	1	33.33	0		2	66.66	10		7	
Naps	0		0		0		11		9	
Nature Walks	0		2	66.66	1	33.33	12		5	
Outdoor Play	1	7.14	4	28.57	9	64.28	2		4	
Rhythms**	2	22.22	6	66.66	1	11.11	7		4	
Story Time	5	31.25	9	56.25	2	12.50	2		2	
Trips	0		2	66.66	1	33.33	7		10	

* Percentages based on only those cases observed. Cases observed for each area = N for columns of Highly Regulated, Some Structure, and Unstructured.
** Chi square significant at 0.01 level of confidence.

TABLE XVII   MATERIALS AND EQUIPMENT, PERCENT BY TYPE OF PRESCHOOL CLASSROOM AND BY ALL CLASSROOMS

Equipment	Indoors				Outdoors			
	All N=216	P N=20	CL N=20	Mont. N=26	All N=216	P N=20	CL N=20	Mont. N=26
Bulletin Boards	56.94	75.00	70.00	61.53	1.38		10.00	
Adult Chairs	61.11	35.00	70.00	50.00	3.70	5.00		
Comfortable Chairs	10.18	15.00	10.00	15.38	0.46			
Child-size Straight Chairs	94.90	90.00	95.00	15.38	4.16		20.00	
Child-size Rockers	33.79	25.00	50.00	84.61	0.46			
Chalk Board	70.37	50.00	55.00	11.53				
Cots	37.96	5.00	25.00	11.53				
Cubby or Lockers	69.90	50.00	90.00	76.93	0.46			
Desks for Working	14.35	5.00	15.00	26.92				
Mats for Resting	25.00	25.00	20.00	34.61				
Phonograph	83.33	90.00	75.00	50.00				
Piano (organ)	57.87	50.00	80.00	46.15				
Running Water	77.77	90.00	95.00	65.38	11.11	20.00	35.00	
Tables for Working	96.29	90.00	90.00	84.61	5.55	5.00	30.00	
Television	30.55	10.00	15.00	15.38				
Toilets	93.05	90.00	100.00	57.69	2.31			
Animals (real)	76.85	35.00	75.00	100.00	14.35			19.23
Balls	37.96	40.00	20.00	26.92	24.53	20.00	35.00	15.38
Blocks (unit/table)	84.25	85.00	90.00	61.53	3.70	5.00	10.00	
Blocks, Crates (floor)	55.55	65.00	55.00	15.38	11.11		35.00	
Books: Texts—Primers, Pre-primers	24.53	50.00	25.00	38.46				
Books: Library (picture)	93.51	100.00	90.00	88.46	0.46			
Carriages, Buggies	37.03	55.00	40.00	7.69	4.62		5.00	
Clay	57.40	55.00	55.00	30.76	0.92		5.00	
Climbing Apparatus	21.75	45.00	25.00	3.84	63.88	60.00	80.00	50.00
Collage Materials	62.96	70.00	65.00	53.84				
Cooking Materials (toy & real)	37.96	45.00	40.00	46.15				
Crayons	87.96	85.00	90.00	84.61				
Dolls & Accessories	82.87	95.00	95.00	19.23	0.92		5.00	
Dress-up Clothes	63.42	80.00	70.00	15.38	1.85		5.00	
Easels/paints	74.53	80.00	75.00	57.69	7.40	10.00	20.00	7.69
Filmstrips & Projector	12.96	5.00	10.00	3.84				
Finger Paints	43.98	65.00	35.00	23.07	0.46		5.00	
Housekeeping Toys	88.88	95.00	85.00	69.23	0.92	5.00	10.00	

TABLE XVII MATERIALS AND EQUIPMENT, PERCENT BY TYPE OF PRESCHOOL CLASSROOM AND BY ALL CLASSROOMS (Continued)

Equipment	Indoors				Outdoors			
	All N=216	P N=20	CL N=20	Mont. N=26	All N=216	P N=20	CL N=20	Mont. N=26
Jump Ropes	19.44	20.00	10.00	7.69	10.64		35.00	11.53
Math Materials	63.88	60.00	70.00	92.30				
Mats for Working	22.22	15.00	30.00	69.23	0.46			
Mechanical Toys	47.68	30.00	60.00	30.76				
Movies	9.72		20.00	7.69				
Music Listening	76.85	85.00	75.00	34.61				
Programmed Materials	39.81	35.00	50.00	50.00				
Puppets	32.40	45.00	40.00	11.53				
Puzzles (wood inlay)	81.94	80.00	85.00	76.92				
Puzzles (cardboard)	37.50	40.00	45.00	26.92				
Riding Equipment: Bicycles	4.62				10.18	10.00	35.00	7.69
Riding Equipment: Tricycles	13.88	15.00	20.00	3.84	31.48	50.00	65.00	7.69
Riding Equipment: Scooters	4.16	5.00			7.87	5.00	35.00	3.84
Riding Equipment: Wagons	16.20	25.00	15.00	3.84	27.77	45.00	65.00	7.69
Riding Equipment: Cars	14.81	5.00	5.00	3.84	11.11	10.00	40.00	7.69
Rhythm Instruments	62.96	50.00	85.00	53.84				
Sand & Accessories (and substitutes)	16.66	15.00	25.00	7.69	46.29	50.00	65.00	23.07
Science Materials & Corner	70.37	85.00	80.00	69.23	4.16	5.00	20.00	
Slides	9.25	10.00	15.00	3.84	30.09	20.00	60.00	26.93
Store Equipment	27.77	40.00	45.00	11.53	3.24		10.00	
Stuffed Animals	48.14	35.00	50.00	19.53	0.92			
Swings	5.09	5.00			47.68	40.00	60.00	34.61
Table Toys	80.09	80.00	85.00	42.30	1.85		5.00	3.84
Tools	5.55	5.00		7.69	18.98	20.00	50.00	15.38
Trucks/Cars/Trains (highly defined)	59.25	55.00	55.00	30.76	8.79	15.00	20.00	7.69
Trucks/Cars/Trains (creative play)	56.48	75.00	65.00	23.07	8.33		20.00	11.53
Water Play Area	33.33	40.00	50.00	50.00	12.96	30.00	30.00	7.69
Water Toys	27.77	35.00	35.00	46.15	8.33	30.00	20.00	3.84
Woodworking Materials	31.48	55.00	40.00	19.23	8.33	45.00	35.00	
Workbooks (Non-Programmed)	10.18		5.00	23.07	0.46		5.00	

TABLE XVIII   UNIQUE ASPECTS OF INDIVIDUAL CLASSROOM PRACTICES

Unique Aspect	Total Sample		College Labs		Montessori		Parent Coops	
	N	Percent of Responses	N	Percent of Responses	N	Percent of Responses	N	Percent of Responses
General Program Emphasis	79	24.45	3	9.37	6	17.64	1	3.70
Facilities and Equipment	51	15.78	4	12.50	7	20.58	2	7.40
Unusual Program Offerings or Learning Opportunities	35	10.83	6	18.75	5	14.70	5	18.51
Parent Involvement and Education	22	6.81	1	3.12			9	33.33
Individualization or Freedom of Program	19	5.88	2	6.25	3	8.82	2	7.40
Group Composition	17	5.26	3	9.37	1	2.94	4	14.81
Research, Program Development Emphasis or Preparation of Staff	17	5.26	2	6.25	1	2.94	1	3.70
Interpersonal Relations	16	4.95	1	3.12	4	11.76		
No Tally	15	4.64	1	3.12	4	11.76		
Miscellaneous	11	3.40	3	9.37				
Teacher Performance	9	2.78						
Staff Uniqueness	9	2.78	1	3.12				
Funding	6	1.85			1	2.94		
Nothing	6	1.85						
Staff Development, Utilization and Qualifications	5	1.54	2	6.25			3	11.11
Availability of Resources Beyond School	4	1.23	3	9.37	1	2.94		
Nongrading of School	2	.61			1	2.94		
Totals	323		32		34		27	

APPENDIX B
INSTRUMENTS

DIRECTOR INTERVIEW FORM
Director, Administrator, Teacher Interview
(Circle which person is interviewed)
One for each school

1. Descriptive Data (order of items may be varied to fit the situation)

    a. School _____

    b. City and state _____

    c. Age range of school _____

    d. Number of children in school _____

    e. Number of classes/groups _____

    f. Control of school:

    College laboratory _____

    Headstart _____

    Independent _____

    Parent cooperative _____

    Parochial or church-controlled _____

    Public (federal, state- or city-controlled) _____

    Other _____

    g. Program emphases: (Check as many as apply. Star main emphasis.)

    Behavior modification _____

    Compensatory education _____

    Custodial or day care _____

    Exceptional children's center _____

    Infant centers _____

    Montessori _____

    Parent education _____

    Preparation of paraprofessionals _____

    Program development & research _____

    Teacher training _____

    Other _____

    h. Size of town where school is located: (Locate and mark location of school on map.) Metropolitan (100,000 or more).

    (1) Central city (city limits) _____

    (2) Old suburb _____

    (3 New suburb _____

    Large-medium city (over 25,000) _____ small town_____

    i. Range of socioeconomic status of parents _____

    j. Primary source(s) of funds _____

    k. Amount of tuition charged _____

    l. How much of a waiting period before child may enter _____

    m. How often director on site _____

2. How important, in your opinion, are the following areas to your program?

	Low	Medium	High
1. Academic skills (reading, writing, drawing, arithmetic)			
2. Arts and creative expression			
3. Cognitive-intellectual development			
4. Concept acquisition (training in concepts of time, color, size)			
5. Emotional development (confidence, self-esteem)			
6. Language skills: oral development			
reading and vocabulary development			
7. Motor skills (large muscle)			
8. Sensory awareness			
9. Sensory-motor skills (visual, auditory, muscle training)			
10. Social-interpersonal skills (cooperation, rules)			
11. Verbalizing feelings			
12. (Other: specify)			

3. What do you consider to be the primary function(s) of your school? (Child care, readiness for school, child development program, etc.)

4. What are the specific objectives of your program?

5. Is your program evaluated? If so, how?

6. What forms of evaluation of student growth are used by the school and/or teachers? (Teacher observation, standardized tests, sociometric data, etc.)

7. Is any reporting done by the school and/or teacher to parents? (Conferences, written reports, phone calls, informal talks, etc.) If so, how often?

8. Teaching Personnel

	Number	High school graduate	Some college	College degree	Graduate degree	Formal training in early childhood ed.	Years experience in nursery ed.	Other teaching experience
Director, head teacher								
Teachers								
Assistant teachers								
Aides								
A. Aides not related to children								
B. Parent aides								
Specialists								
Consultants								
(For remainder, record only pertinent information)								
Nutritionist								
Housekeeper								
Custodian								
Others								

9. Are your facilities and materials shared by other groups? If so, what other groups use them and how often?

10. The following items are possible curricular areas and activities which might be found in programs for young children. We would like to have an indication of how frequently they occur in your program.

Curricular Area and Activity	Frequency			
	Daily	Frequently	Occasionally	Rarely or Never
Curricular Areas:				
Arithmetic				
Informal				
Formal				
Art				
Foreign Languages				
Language				
Informal				
Formal				
Music				
Informal				
Formal				
Musical Instrument Instruction				
Reading Readiness				
Informal				
Formal				
Reading				
Science				
Informal				
Formal				
Social Studies				
Informal				
Formal				

10. (Continued)

Curricular Area and Activity	Frequency			
	Daily	Frequently	Occasionally	Rarely or Never
Other (specify)				
Activities: Blocks				
Carpentry (woodwork)				
Cooking				
Dramatization and Role-Playing				
Group Games (organized)				
Informal Rest				
Naps				
Nature Walks				
Outdoor Play				
Rhythms				
Story Time				
Trips				
Other (specify)				

11. To what extent do parents participate in the daily activities? (Required, encouraged, resources, discouraged, etc.)

12. Do you organize any parent meetings? If so, what types (PTA, work parties, discussion groups)? How often are they held? What is your average attendance?

Type	How often held	Average Attendance

13. Do you attempt to obtain any information about the child and/or his family when he registers? If so, how (written forms, administrator interview, teacher conference, etc.)? (If possible please obtain a sample of any forms they have for admission.)

14. Are there entrance requirements or criteria students or parents must meet (medical, racial, intellectual, etc.)? If so, what are they?

15. What are the approximate percentages of children who attend your school on varying days?
    _____ all day every day
    _____ half-day every day   _____ other (specify)
    _____ Monday, Wednesday, & Friday half-day _____
    _____ Tuesday and Thursday half-day   _____
    _____ other (specify)

    _____

16. What is the average adult per child ratio for the school? _____

17. Describe facility of school
    a. Indoor (size of room, appearance, restroom facilities, sinks)
    b. Outdoor (appearance, apparatus, materials, size, safety)
    c. Overall physical facilities

18. What are the major problems or issues which your school and/or teachers face?

19. What would you consider to be unique about and/or particularly successful in your school?

CLASSROOM OBSERVATION FORM

(1 per teacher observed)

I. Descriptive Data

Date _____

1. School _____

2. City and state _____

3. Teacher _____

4. Age range of this group _____

5. Time period this group in session _____

6. Number of children in group: Girls _____ Boys _____

7. Adult/Child ratio _____

8. Number of Aides/Other personnel _____

9. Teacher preparation _____

Observer name _____

II. Observation Time
   A. Length of observation
   B. Time of day observed

III. Collect daily schedule of teacher—note variability in program

IV. Curricular Activities
   (Please rate all activities observed)

	Structure			
Curricular Area and Activity	**Highly regulated** R	**Some structure** S	**Unstructured** U	**Not observed** O
Curricular Areas:				
Arithmetic				
Informal				
Formal				
Art				
Foreign Languages				
Language				
Informal				
Formal				
Music				
Informal				
Formal				
Musical Instrument Instruction				

IV. Curricular Activities (Continued)

Curricular Area and Activity	Structure			
	Highly regulated R	Some structure S	Unstructured U	Not observed O
Reading Readiness Informal				
Formal				
Reading				
Science Informal				
Formal				
Social Studies Informal				
Formal				
Other (specify)				
Activities: Blocks				
Carpentry (woodwork)				
Cooking				
Dramatization and Role-Playing				
Group Games (organized)				
Informal Rest				
Naps				
Nature Walks				
Outdoor Play				
Rhythms				
Story Time				
Trips				
Other (specify)				

V. Materials and Equipment

	(Check everything which is in sight)	
	Present Indoors	**Present Outdoors**
Furniture and Facilities: Bulletin boards		
Chairs: A. adult		
B. comfortable, stuffed, rocker		
C. child-size straight chairs		
D. child-size rockers		
Chalkboard		
Cots		
Cubby or locker for personal items		
Desks for working		
Mats for resting		
Phonograph		
Piano		
Running water		
Tables for working		
Television		
Toilets		
Materials: Animals (real) (Note what:)		
Balls		
Blocks (unit, table)		

V. Materials and Equipment (Continued)

	(Check everything which is in sight)	
	Present Indoors	**Present Outdoors**
Blocks, crates (floor)		
Books: a. texts (pre-primers, primers)		
b. library (picture)		
Carriages & buggies		
Clay		
Climbing apparatus (jungle gym, bars)		
Collage materials		
Cooking materials		
Crayons		
Dolls & accessories		
Dress-up clothes & accessories		
Easels (& all materials used with easels), paints		
Filmstrips		
Finger paints		
Housekeeping toys (materials for dramatic play, e.g., dishes)		
Jump ropes		
Math materials (abacus, clocks, ruler, number games)		
Mats for working		
Mechanical toys (take-apart toys)		
Movies		
Music listening (records, etc.)		
Programmed materials (learning games) language, math, reading		
Puppets		
Puzzles: A. wood inlay		
B. cardboard		
Riding equipment: A. bicycles		
B. tricycles		
C. scooters		

V. Materials and Equipment (Continued)

	(Check everything which is in sight)	
	Present Indoors	Present Outdoors
D. wagons		
E. cars		
F. other (specify)		
Rhythm instruments (e.g., bells, castanets, cymbals, drums, maracas, rhythm sticks)		
Running water		
Sand (all toys & accessories)		
Science materials & corner (e.g., battery, flower boxes, prism, seeds, globe, magnifier)		
Slides		
Store equipment		
Stuffed animals		
Swings		
Table toys (blocks, games, Bingo, Lego)		
Tools (hoes, rakes, shovels)		
Trucks, cars, trains, boats (small—not rideable) A. highly defined toys		
B. creative play equipment		
Water play area		
Water toys		
Woodworking materials (bench, clamp, hammer, etc.)		
Workbooks (non-programmed materials)		

VI. Overall Ratings
 Facilities and Equipment   **Indoor Outdoor**

  1. Variety of equipment and materials

   Minimum equipment & materials: sparse

   Some equipment & materials: somewhat
    below average

   Moderate amount of equipment & materials:
    adequate

   Ample materials, wide breadth of materials

   Very well equipped, rich array of materials

  2. Quantity of equipment and materials

   Very limited, insufficient for number of
    children

   Adequate amount, turns for children re-
    quired, but not unduly frustrating

   Ample amount for number of children in
    the group

  3. Space within school and classrooms
   _____ Cramped, crowded, much too little
   _____ Insufficient for program and number of children
   _____ Adequate, but not spacious
   _____ Large, open, spacious

  4. Ventilation of classrooms
   _____ Inadequate, close, stuffy
   _____ Adequate, comfortable classrooms
   _____ Drafty, too open and airy

  5. Physical surroundings in classroom (location, decoration, color, etc.)
   _____ Dingy and depressing
   _____ Neither dingy nor cheerful
   _____ Cheerful and sunny

  6. Organization of room
   _____ No obvious organization, chaotic
   _____ Rigid organization, little flexibility
   _____ Organized, but inefficient/ineffective (interferes with move-
    ment)
   _____ Allows for freedom of movement with little disruption to
    others

7. Condition of equipment in classroom
   _____ Poor: in need of repairs and paint, dirty
   _____ Adequate: usable, patched
   _____ Good: has been repaired, kept up
   _____ Excellent: new equipment

8. Safety of classroom
   _____ Very unsafe: disrepair, fire hazards
   _____ Meets minimum safety standards
   _____ Adequate safety precautions
   _____ High safety standards in operation

9. Access to outdoors
   _____ Rarely (because of weather, space, etc.)
   _____ Daily walks, but outdoors not readily available
   _____ At specified times during week/month
   _____ Daily, but scheduled and routine
   _____ Daily, whenever desired

10. Outdoor area
    _____ None attached to school
    _____ Some space attached to school, somewhat crowded
    _____ Large, open, accessible

Classroom Activities

1. Noise level
   _____ Of a chaotic nature, noisy to the point of discomfort
   _____ Reasonable amount of noise
   _____ Unnaturally quiet for preschool

2. Routines and rules
   _____ High emphasis on routines (proper toileting, manners, frequent verbalization by teacher on procedures and rules)
   _____ Some emphasis on routines, but fairly casual attitudes
   _____ Little or no emphasis on routines, rules rarely mentioned; very casual

3. Emphasis on academic preparation and academic skills
   _____ Academic skills main goal and activity of the program
   _____ Materials and curricula-type projects are an important part of the program (i.e., most Headstart programs)
   _____ Some emphasis on academic preparation, other goals important
   _____ Academic materials and activities quite secondary
   _____ Academic, educational activities are absent or discouraged

4. Degree of integration and organization

_____ Disorganized, program seems unplanned

_____ Moderate organization and planning

_____ Coherent, directed, smooth transitions and implementation of program

5. Variety of activities available to children in the program

_____ Few activities

_____ Moderate number of activities

_____ Many activities

6. Children's use of space

_____ Hampered, restricted

_____ Use most areas appropriately

_____ Use every amount available

7. Individualization of program

_____ No evidence of individualization; entirely group-oriented

_____ Individuals recognized, but used to forward group activity primarily; no diagnosis and prescription of individual needs occurring

_____ Limited individualization; little diagnosis and prescription for individual needs

_____ Much individualization evident; diagnosis and prescription for children's needs evident

Interaction

1. Degree of teacher-child interaction

_____ Very little interaction although physical proximity may be high (i.e., teacher passes out food but does not interact with children)

_____ Some degree of physical or verbal interaction (pats on head, body, some individual verbal recognition of children)

_____ A high degree of either physical or verbal interaction present (i.e., holds child on lap; talks intimately with child)

_____ Little interaction, but teacher readily available and active when needed

2. Quality of teacher-child interaction

_____ Cold, critical, disinterested, punitive

_____ Moderately warm and interested in children

_____ Very warm, supportive and accepting

3. Degree of child-child interaction

_____ Low: most children rarely interact with each other (parallel rather than interactive play)

_____ Moderate amount of child-child interaction, considerable parallel play

_____ High: most children actively engaged with other children

4. Quality of child-child interaction

_____ Aggressive, negative interaction

_____ Largely aggressive, negative interaction

_____ Passive, docile in interaction

_____ Largely shared, cooperative, positive interaction

_____ Shared, cooperative, positive interaction

5. Degree of child-teacher interaction

_____ Low: children rarely or never initiate contact with teacher

_____ Moderate amount

_____ High: many children initiate contact with teacher

6. Quality of child-teacher interaction

_____ Children hesitate to initiate contacts

_____ Children contact largely out of frustration

_____ Children freely contact teacher as needed, primarily for routine requests and permission

_____ Children freely contact teacher as needed, primarily for resource and enrichment

7. Interpersonal aggression

_____ Aggression strongly inhibited

_____ Moderately disapproved of

_____ Reasoned and discussed

_____ Ignored

_____ Permitted

8. Interest, activity, and engagement of children

_____ Very little activity, lethargy

_____ Children generally busy, not greatly involved

_____ Children busily engaged, involved in task

9.	Little involvement with children or program	Busy with routines, etc., but little engagement with children	Moderately engaged with children & program	Highly engaged with children & program	Unobtrusiv with childr but engage in observati
Interest, activity & engagement of teachers					
10. Interest, activity & engagement of aides					

	Subdued, detached emotionally	Moderately happy, enthusiastic	Very enthusiastic, cheerful, eager
11. Mood & morale of children			
12. Mood & morale of teacher			
13. Mood & morale of teacher aides			

Teacher Behavior

1. Locus of control and decision-making
   _____ Group and class teacher-controlled
   _____ Children have opportunities to make decisions but teacher directs most of the time
   _____ Children have many opportunities to make decisions

2. Role of teacher
   _____ Authority in charge, highly directive
   _____ Directive, but unobtrusively
   _____ Resource for children to use
   _____ Little direction or interaction with children unless necessary

3. Type of reinforcement used most frequently by teacher (May check more than one)
   _____ Group pressure
   _____ Loss of privilege
   _____ Scolding, warning, threatening
   _____ Punitive isolation within or outside of classroom
   _____ Physical punishment
   _____ Teacher ignored situation
   _____ Verbal praise
   _____ Physical rewards (smile, pats, nods of head)
   _____ Tangible rewards (candy, toy)
   _____ Diverting child to new activity
   _____ Talking to the child (reasoning)
   _____ Planned time out (temporary withdrawal)
   _____ No occasion for discipline occurred or no basis for judgment
   _____
   _____
   _____
   _____
   _____
   _____

VII. Describe grouping of children observed. Note size, frequency, and structure of groups.

VIII. Cross-cultural ethnic composition

IX. Please collect any materials which look promising. Note why you consider them to be promising.

X. Uniqueness of program. Note anything of unusual interest (problem areas or success areas).

XI. Observations. (Additional observations and impressions may be recorded on reverse side of printed pages.)

APPENDIX C
ANNOTATED BIBLIOGRAPHY

The materials listed here are addressed to a wide range of readers, all of whom are concerned with the education of the very young child. Readers are individual in their tastes and needs despite their overarching concern for and interest in the preschool child. The arrangement of the list, therefore, was made to best serve the purposes of readers at various stages in their thinking.

The following groupings have been used: Part I, "Scanning the American Scene," introduces "the play and the players," in an easy-to-read collection of writings which nevertheless gives a clear picture of what is happening in a fast-growing field. The selections in Part II, "Delving More Deeply," on the other hand, are directed toward those already knowledgeable who wish added information about research findings, experimental programs, and future trends. "Theory and Thrusts," Part III, is for the even more serious student who wishes to probe the social, psychological, and pedagogical underpinnings of the movement toward earlier education for children. Part IV, "Practices and Programs," emphasizes the "development" aspects, offering many descriptions of programs in action testing out research implications. The final section, Part V, "Informative Texts and Practical Pamphlets," is for the practitioner: the teacher in the classroom, the parent in the school, the parent at home, the paraprofessional, and the administrator.

Obviously, there is a great deal of overlapping from one group to another. Hopefully, the detailed commentaries and annotations will provide the reader with the necessary clues to find and bridge those crossings.

Lillian K. Drag
Specialist in Curriculum Materials
Research Division
|I|D|E|A|
July, 1972

PART I. SCANNING THE AMERICAN SCENE

Overview materials listed below indicate basic considerations for parents, teachers, and administrators who wish to become informed in a highly volatile field. They indicate the forces at work, the general trends, and crucial issues. The treatment is brief and readable, intended to introduce the reader to the field.

Anderson, Robert H., and Harold G. Shane, eds: *As the Twig Is Bent: Readings in Early Childhood Education.* Boston: Houghton Mifflin, 1971.
Selected articles discuss the history of early childhood education, its traditional approaches, and its current controversies. Readings provided in areas of administrative and program concerns, curriculum theory, practice and evaluation.

Association for Childhood Education International: *Basic Propositions for Early Childhood Education.* Washington, D.C.: The Association, 1967.
A position paper by 1965–67 Association for Childhood Education International Nursery School Education Committee.

————: *Housing for Early Childhood Education: Centers for Growing and Learning.* Washington, D. C.: The Association, 1968.
Educators, architects, school administrators discuss interaction of program and facilities in planning, building anew, or remodeling early childhood learning centers. Replete with illustrations and examples of actual programs.

Association for Supervision and Curriculum Development, NEA: *Early Childhood Education Today.* Edited by Alexander Frazier. Washington, D.C.: The Association, 1968.
Guidelines to the development of programs. Deals with significant issues: nature and needs of the young learner, organizing sound education for the very young, parent involvement, and personnel for staffing.

Biber, Barbara: *Young Deprived Children and Their Educational Needs.* Washington, D.C.: Association for Childhood Education International, 1967.
Discusses the basic life deficits of deprived children: innovative language and thinking, lack of close relationships, and physical and psychological uncertainties. Suggests educational practices: emphasizing order, teaching how to play, teaching how to relate to teachers and others. Explores the kinds of experiences required to provide for those needs.

Childhood Education: "Learning from Parents." Vol. 48, No. 3, December 1971. Washington, D.C.: Association for Childhood Education International, 1971.
This issue describes briefly the development of new teacher-parent

roles and relationships, programs using parents as teachers, and re-lated research.

Commission on Mental Health: *Crisis in Child Mental Health: Challenge of the 1970's,* Report of the Commission, New York: Harper & Row, 1970.
Evidence denies that we are a child-centered society and indicates our stinginess when it comes to providing the wherewithal for adequate services to children.

Cook, Ann, and Herbert Mack: "Business in Education: The Discovery Center Hustle," *Social Policy,* vol. 1, pp. 4–11, September/October 1970.
"The preschool market is expanding, and businesses are cashing in on child-minding, child-testing and child-teaching."

Education Commission of the States: Task Force on Early Childhood Education, *Early Childhood Development: Alternatives for Program Implementation in the States,* Denver: Education Commission of the States, 1971.
A report based on a nationwide study, which calls for a centralized state plan for early childhood services. It defines directions and objectives for such programs with suggested alternative program approaches including realistic cost figures and possible methods of funding.

Education U.S.A.: *Preschool Breakthrough: What Works in Early Childhood Education,* Washington, D.C.: National School Public Relations Association, 1970.
Includes a review of the new philosophies and old controversies of early childhood education. Reviews research results, explains some of the federal arrangements for supporting innovations, and describes current experimental studies.

Educational Facilities Laboratories: *Schools for Early Childhood* by Paul Abramson, New York: Educational Facilities Laboratories, 1970. (Profiles of Significant Schools)
Focus is on the creation of facilities in which early learning can take place. Illustrates new centers specifically built for early education and old facilities that have been successfully remodeled. Also includes a nonschool approach. Program objectives, varying widely, are spelled out for each facility. Profusely illustrated. See also Educational Facilities Laboratories' *Early Learning Center,* 1970.

Educational Leadership: vol. 28, no. 8, May 1971, Washington, D.C.: Association for Supervision and Curriculum Development, NEA, 1971. Titled: "Early Childhood Education: a Perspective." Articles in Part 4, "Guidelines for Analyzing Early Childhood Education Programs" are elaborated in Part 3 which deals with Aims and Objectives, Program Procedures, Administrative Features, and Evaluation. June Patterson, Dave Elliott, Joe Frost, et al., contribute.

Educational Policies Commission: *Universal Opportunity for Early Childhood Education,* Washington, D.C.: National Education Association, 1966.
A brief statement of belief that all children should have the opportunity to attend school at public expense beginning at the age of four. Explains why this extension of education is advocated and includes a brief description of the type of program envisioned.

ERIC Clearinghouse on Early Childhood Education: *Childhood Resources Information Bulletin,* vol. 1, no. 2, Fall 1969. Urbana, Ill.: ERIC Clearinghouse, 1969.
In question and answer format this bulletin deals briefly with preschool programs, research, program guides, and other selected topics. Sources for further information are listed.

————: *Early Childhood Selected Bibliographies Series.* Urbana, Illinois: ERIC Clearinghouse, 1968.
Six bibliographies available on microfiche or hard copy from ERIC: No. 1, Physical; No. 2, Language; No. 3, Education; No. 4, Cognition; No. 5, Social; and No. 6, Personality. More recent issue: Parent Participation in Education.

Featherstone, Joseph. "The Day Care Problem: Kentucky Fried Children," *The New Republic,* vol. 163, pp. 12–16, Sept. 12, 1970.
A survey of day care centers for profit reveals inadequate programs. Discusses the marketing of franchises for child care and the obvious lack of effective standards for the services.

Hechinger, Fred M. (ed.): *Pre-School Education Today: New Approaches to Teaching Three-, Four-, and Five-Year-Olds,* New York: Doubleday, 1966.
Brings together the best (and still useful) thinking up to 1966, including: Martin Deutsch, "Early Social Environment: Its Influence on School Adaptation," Chapter 2, and "Facilitating Development in the Pre-School Child: Social and Psychological Perspectives," Chapter 4. J. McVicker Hunt, "The Psychological Basis for Using Pre-School Enrichment as an Antidote for Cultural Deprivation," Chapter 3. Shirley Feldmann, "A Pre-School Enrichment Program for Disadvantaged Children," Chapter 5. Carl Bereiter et al., "An Academically Oriented Pre-School for Culturally Deprived Children," Chapter 6.

Hurd, Gordon E.: *Preprimary Enrollment Trends of Children Under Six: 1964–1968.* National Center for Educational Statistics, Washington, D.C.: U.S. Government Printing Office, 1970.
Enrollment patterns are analyzed by age, color, level, type of control, family income level, occupation of household head, place of residence, and region.

Katz, Lilian G.: *Four Questions on Early Childhood Education,* Urbana, Ill.: ERIC Clearinghouse on Early Childhood Education, 1970. (Paper based on a speech given September 1970.)

Briefly sketches educational effort in United States during fifties and sixties, with special reference to early childhood education. Questions raised are

1   What kinds of goals make sense? Academic? Intellectual?
2   What do we have to do to make these things happen? Qualities of programs need "open" classroom using subject matter as tools; getting satisfaction versus fun; a dynamic view of behavior and development.
3   What qualities must teachers have to realize goals? Material model, therapeutic model, instructional, and facilitating modes are presented.
4   What qualities of the system or administration must be brought into existence in order to achieve goals?

McLure, William P., and Audra M. Pence: *Early Childhood and Basic Elementary and Secondary Education: Needs, Programs, Demands, Costs,* Special Study No. 1, National Educational Finance Project. Urbana-Champaign: University of Illinois, 1970.
Pp. 11–30, "Early Childhood Education" gives overview of developments, status of enrollments, needs from birth to age six, and six basic types of alternative programs. Defines some dimensions for concrete action in the next decade.

National Association for the Education of Young Children: *Open Education: The Legacy of the Progressive Movement,* Washington, D.C.: NAEYC, 1970.
Proceedings of a conference: David Elkind, "Experience and Cognitive Growth"; James B. Macdonald, "The Open School: Curriculum Concepts"; Roma Gans, "The Progressive Era: Its Relation to the Contemporary Scene"; Vincent Rogers, "English and American Primary Schools"; Bernard Spodek, "Extending Open Education in the U.S."; and selected bibliography.

National Council of State Consultants in Elementary Education: *Education for Children Under Six,* The Council, 1968.
A pamphlet which presents a point of view and basic considerations in dealing with such problems as goals and values in nursery schools; providing appropriate experiences; legal questions; housing, facilities and equipment, personnel; financing programs; answering frequently asked questions.

National Elementary Principal, vol. 51, no. 1, September 1971. Washington, D.C.: National Association for Elementary School Principals, NEA, 1971.
Title: "Early Childhood Education." This issue discusses trends, issues, and implications for elementary school educators. Earl Schaefer offers the research basis for a new perspective; Ira Gordon discusses parent involvement; David Elkind describes a Piagetian perspective; M. Frances Klein and Jerrold Novotney, "American

Nursery Schools—Help, Hindrance, or Enigma?" report a national survey.

Novotney, Jerrold M., and M. Frances Klein: "Preschool Education: As the Crow Flies," *National Elementary Principal,* vol. 51, pp. 30–39, January 1972.
A brief account of an investigation of the state of early childhood education in England, Israel, and selected countries of Asia. See also *National Elementary Principal,* vol. 51, no. 1 (annotated above) for related article.

Phi Delta Kappan, vol. 50, no. 7, March 1969. Bloomington, Ind.: Phi Delta Kappa, 1969.
A special issue on "Early Childhood Education" with articles by Harold Shane, Ira Gordon, Frank Estvan, Robert Anderson, James Macdonald, Bernard Spodek, and others dealing with cultural, environmental, physical, organizational, curricular, instructional, social and individual aspects.

Pines, Maya: *Revolution in Learning: the Years from Birth to Six,* New York: Harper & Row, 1966.
A layman, believing we can produce more intelligent as well as happier human beings by stimulating children to learn more during early years, reports on the work and programs of Jean Piaget, J. McV. Hunt, Lev Vygotsky, Jerome Bruner, O. K. Moore, Montessori, Bereiter and Engelmann, Benjamin Bloom, Martin Deutsch, Susan Gray, and others.

Powledge, Fred: *To Change a Child: a Report on the Institute for Developmental Studies,* Chicago: Quadrangle Books in cooperation with Anti-Defamation League of B'nai B'rith, 1967.
An account of the Institute and aspects of its program in early childhood education, with many direct references to the works of Martin Deutsch. Examples of practice are highlighted by sensitive photographs.

Stanley, Julian C., ed. *Preschool Programs for the Disadvantaged: Five Experimental Approaches to Early Childhood Education.* Proceedings of the 1st Annual Hyman Blumberg Symposium on Research in Early Childhood Education. Baltimore, Md.: Johns Hopkins University Press, 1972.
Includes: Bereiter, Carl, "An Academic Preschool for Disadvantaged Children: Conclusions from Evaluation Studies"; Weikart, David P., "Relationship of Curriculum, Teaching and Learning in Preschool Education"; McAfee, Oralie, "An Integrated Approach to Early Childhood Education"; Risley, Todd, "Spontaneous Langauge and the Preschool Environment"; and Blank, Marion, "The Treatment of Personality Variables—a Preschool Cognitive Program." Discussion follows on status and future of preschool compensatory education and variables in evaluating day care.

U.S. House of Representatives, Committee on Education and Labor: *Needs of Elementary and Secondary Education for the Seventies,* Washington, D.C.: The Committee, 1970.

Includes U. Bronfenbrenner, "Motivational and Social Components in Compensatory Education Programs—Suggested Principles, Practices and Research Designs"; A. Gartner and F. Reissman, "The Paraprofessional and Educational Needs of the Seventies"; E. W. Gordon, "Problems in the Determination of Educability in Populations with Differential Characteristics"; G. Lesser, "The Need for Educational Diversity"; J. O. Miller, "Early Childhood Education: the Need and the Challenge"; and R. Peck, "Personalized Education: An Attainable Goal in the Seventies."

White House Conference on Children, 1970: *Profiles of Children.* Washington, D.C.: U.S. Government Printing Office, 1971.

A statistical chart book to accompany the Report of the White House Conference on Children gives a picture of some of the societal conditions children find themselves in. Preschool years are documented on pp. 56–67.

PART II. DELVING MORE DEEPLY

There seems to be a "current awareness" of the value of early childhood education by the profession, governmental agencies, and the public at large. Up to the present time, the physical health, welfare, socialization, and emotional development of the child have been major considerations. Suddenly, the intellectual development of the child has emerged as the burning issue. The potential of early learning, especially for the disadvantaged child, has sparked a rash of research projects and experimental programs. Are they well founded? Are they doing more good than harm? Are they effective? Do they, indeed, maximize intellectual growth? These are the questions which the research reports listed below attempt to answer. Whether their source is university-based, federally or foundation-supported, from the practitioner, or from the scientist, they serve a common goal: to reinforce effective educational innovations.

Almy, Millie: "New Views on Intellectual Development in Early Childhood Education," *Intellectual Development: Another Look,* Washington, D.C.: ASCD, NEA, 1964, p. 24.

It seems doubtful to this investigator ". . . that early childhood education programs that are narrowly focused or designed primarily for acceleration in a particular area will have much beneficial effect on later intellectual development."

——— et al.: *Young Children's Thinking: Studies of Some Aspects of Piaget's Theory,* New York: Teachers College Press, 1966.

This monograph presents two studies, one cross-sectional, another longitudinal, dealing with the thought processes children evidence when faced with problems involving the concepts of quantity and number. Examines the relation of "conservation" to other intellectual abilities and to school readiness and achievement.

Athey, I. J., and D. O. Rubadau (eds.): *Educational Implications of Piaget's Theory: A Book of Readings,* Waltham, Mass.: Blaisdell Publishing Company, 1970.

Includes recent exploratory efforts to design preschool programs directly based upon Piagetian theory, such as the Ypsilanti, Michigan Preschool Program. This program is described in two chapters: Constance Kamii and Norma Radin, "A Framework for a Preschool Curriculum Based on Piaget's Theory"; and Hanne Sonquist, Constance Kamii, and Louise Berman, "A Piaget-Derived Pre-School Curriculum."

Baratz, Stephen S., and Joan C.: "Early Childhood Intervention: The Social Science Base of Institutional Racism," *Harvard Educational Review,* vol. 40, pp. 29–50, Winter 1970.

Maintain that compensatory education has been devised to prevent cognitive deficiencies that do not exist. Rather, the problems encountered by ghetto children (mostly black) are thought to derive from a different, nonetheless distinctly well-developed and "functionally adequate" cultural and linguistic system. Educators should adapt instruction to these children, rather than the other way around. However, economically disadvantaged children need to learn standard English, too.

Bernbaum, Marcia, comp.: *Early Childhood Programs for Non-English Speaking Children,* Urbana: ERIC Clearinghouse on Early Childhood Education, University of Illinois, 1971.

Summary of research on the bilingual preschool child and programs for him. Discusses practical guidelines to use in the classroom and the community. Describes existing models and lists sources of information.

Biber, Barbara: *Challenges Ahead for Early Childhood Education,* Washington, D.C.: National Association for the Education of Young Children, 1969.

———, E. Shapiro, and D. Wickens: *Promoting Cognitive Growth from a Developmental-Interaction Point of View,* Washington, D.C.: NAEYC, 1971.

Bronfenbrenner, Urie: *Motivational and Social Components in Compensatory Education Programs: Suggested Principles, Practices, and Research Designs,* Ithaca, N. Y.: Cornell University, 1968.

Discusses motivating processes: modeling, reinforcement, group commitment, involvement in superordinate goals, etc. Applies these to role of teacher, school, family, neighborhood, and larger community. Indicates that a good intervention program should include "employing the superordinate goal of concern for young children as a means for involving the entire community in the examination of opportunities it offers to its children. . . ."

Butler, Annie L.: *Current Research in Early Childhood Education: A Compilation and Analysis for Program Planners,* Washington, D.C.: American Association of Elementary-Kindergarten-Nursery Education, NEA, 1970.
Describes the current scene, delineating its conflicts. Reviews studies in intellectual growth research, later school research, teacher role, potency of models, early stimulation, parent involvement, etc. Concludes with an analysis of the diversity in findings. Comprehensive bibliography.

Caldwell, Bettye M.: "The Rationale for Early Intervention," *Exceptional Children,* vol. 36, pp. 717–726, Summer 1970.
Draws support from animal studies, descriptive surveys contrasting development in children reared in different social environments, and major conceptual analyses of early stimulation for development. Guidelines for research and action programs are included.

————: "What is the Optimal Learning Environment for the Young Child?" *American Journal of Orthopsychiatry,* vol. 37, pp. 8–21, January 1967.
Answer given: When (a) a young child is cared for in his own home (b) in the context of a warm and nurturant emotional relationship (c) with his mother (or a reasonable facimile of) under conditions of (d) varied sensory and cognitive input. Where not available in natural environment of the child, a carefully prepared learning environment is called for.

De Hirsch, Katrina: "Preschool Intervention," in National Institute of Neurological Diseases and Stroke, *Reading Forum,* monograph 11. Washington, D.C.: U.S. Government Printing Office, 1971.
Outlines an ideal intervention program based on current findings. Proposes early-as-possible "intervention" involving mothers, paraprofessionals, and child-family center workers in an intimate and trusting relationship.

Durkin, Dolores: *Children Who Read Early; Two Longitudinal Studies,* New York: Teachers College Press, 1966.
In these studies (one in California, the other in New York), differences between the preschool lives of the early readers and those of other children were analyzed with a view to guiding future school practice. Answers were sought to questions: What is the effect of an earlier start on later achievement in reading? What kinds of children tend to be early readers? From what kinds of families do early readers come? How do children learn to read at home?

Fowler, William: "The Design of Early Developmental Learning Programs for Disadvantaged Young Children," Supplement to the *IRCD Bulletin,* vol. III, 1A, 1966.

Suggests, first, psychocognitive diagnosis on a continuing basis. Other principles follow: importance of order and coherence in providing developmental stimulation; early incorporation of symbolic manipulation; necessity of sequencing and selection of content; assessment of progress; active, physical manipulation of materials through play; a social psychological setting emphasizing cooperation in small group learning situations.

Gordon, Ira J: On Early Learning: The Modifiability of Human Potential, Washington, D.C.: Association for Supervision of Curriculum Development, 1971.

States a philosophical position about the goals of development, indicating the data and new understanding currently available on the nature of development. Stresses the importance of involving the parents and the general community much more, especially in providing models of adults who speak with the child.

————: Parent Involvement in Compensatory Education. Urbana, Ill.: University of Illinois Press, 1970.

Early compensatory education projects under survey are described in light of locus of control, location of service, purposes and goals, and use of personnel. Parent participation and program content for parental involvement with emphasis on home visitation programs are discussed.

Grotberg, Edith (ed.): Critical Issues in Research Related to Disadvantaged Children, Princeton, N.J.: Educational Testing Service, 1969.

Proceedings of six Headstart research seminars designed to bring together experts in the general and specific research areas in early childhood. Papers were presented on motivation, the teacher and classroom management, Headstart populations, health and nutrition in early childhood, intervention in family life, and the teacher in intervention programs.

Hartup, Willard W.: "Early Childhood Education and Research—Significance and Needs," Journal of Teacher Education, vol. 21, pp. 23–33, Spring 1970.

"Research may be more valuable as a source of educational innovations than of educational prescriptions." Teacher's role in research is examined.

Hess, Robert, et al.: The Cognitive Development of Urban Preschool Children, Report to the Children's Bureau, Washington, D.C.: U.S. HEW, 1968.

Found mother's use of home resources, personal-subjective control strategies, facile and complex standard English, and affective behavior were highly associated with school performance.

Hess, Robert, and Roberta M. Bear (eds.): Early Education: Current Theory, Research, and Action, Chicago: Aldine Publishing Company, 1968.

Outstanding spokesmen in the field attack these central issues: At what age should formal education begin? What effect does the timing of education have on the child's later social and educational development? Do preschool years indeed deserve the support, financially and professionally, now bestowed on them? Can socially and economically disadvantaged children be successfully educated without involving families and community? What are the relative roles of man and machine in the early education process? Provides information on theories and existing programs of early learning.

Hodges, Walter L., B. R. McCandless, and H. H. Spicker: "The Development and Evaluation of a Diagnostically Based Curriculum for Preschool Psycho-socially Deprived Children." U.S. Office of Education Project Report, 1967. *Exceptional Children Monographs,* 1970.
Shows the debilitating effect of "managerial" teachers on preschool children.

Hodges, Walter L., and H. H. Spicker: "The Effects of Preschool Experiences on Culturally Deprived Children," *Young Children,* vol. 23, pp. 23–43, October 1967.
Describes some of the intervention programs which may have implications for future Headstart efforts. Much statistical information provides basis for organization, content, and effectiveness.

Hunt, J. McVicker: *The Challenge of Incompetence and Poverty: Papers on the Role of Early Education,* Urbana, Ill.: University of Illinois Press, 1969.

————: "Toward a Theory of Guided Learning in Development," in *Giving Emphasis to Guided Learning,* ed. by R. H. Ojemann and K. Pritchett. Cleveland: Educational Research Council, 1966.
Develops further the issues raised in *Intelligence and Experience.*

————: "Parent and Child Centers: Their Basis in the Behavioral and Educational Sciences," *American Journal of Orthopsychiatry,* vol. 41, pp. 13–38, January 1971.

Ilg, Frances and Louise Ames: *School Readiness: Behavior Tests Used at the Gesell Institute,* New York: Harper & Row, 1965.

Interchange: "Early Learning," vol. 2, no. 2, 1971. Canada: The Ontario Institute for Studies in Education, 1971.
Burton White analyzes excellent early educational practices; Jerome Kagan writes on preschool enrichment and learning; Karnes et al. develop a new professional role in early childhood education; others discuss logic, early reading, Australian and Canadian preschools, and a review of recent Montessori research.

Isaacs, Susan: *Intellectual Growth in Young Children* (1930), New York: Schocken Books, 1963.
Reflects Piaget's influence on the author and her differences with him based on her observations of children working and playing together. Reveals the eagerness with which children seek information and understanding. She records the children's excitement about

learning and the way affect permeates their cognition. Companion volume: *Social Development in Young Children.*

————: *The Nursery Years: The Mind of the Child from Birth to Six Years,* (1929), New York: Schocken Books, 1968.

Clear explanation of the principles of child guidance, based on the established facts of physical and mental growth. Characterized by concern with the child's point of view as well as the adult's offering help in understanding his fears, hostilities, and jealousy. Suggests how play may reveal concerns and serve as a tool for learning. Concerned with the match of new experience to the child's present understanding, with faith in the child's ability to learn in his own way. Considers the cognitive, the emotional, and the physical in understanding and developing the child. Reissued as a useful reference for parents as well as teachers and researchers.

John, Vera P., and Vivian M. Horner: *Early Childhood Bilingual Education,* New York: Modern Language Association, 1971.

Includes demographic information on minority language groups, discussion of psychological and educational issues, and description of 43 early childhood bilingual programs. Available curriculum materials for Spanish and Indian groups and related tests are listed.

————, and Sarah Moskovitz: "Language Acquisition and Development in Early Childhood," in the National Society for the Study of Education, *Linguistics in School Programs,* 69th Yearbook, part II, edited by Albert H. Marckwardt. Chicago: University of Chicago Press, 1970, pp. 167–214.

A thorough review of the literature which discusses the differences in language skills as a function of social class; explores the role of language in learning and thought; and describes various preschool programs with a language focus. Exhaustive bibliography.

Journal of Research and Development in Education: vol. 1, no. 3, Spring 1968, Athens, Ga.: College of Education, University of Georgia, 1968.

This issue reports the proceedings of the 21st Georgia Teacher Education Conference, "The World of the Child," Jan. 17–19, 1968. Papers include those of Willard Hartup, Warren Findley, James Hymes, Jr., Carl Bereiter et al., E. Paul Torrance, and others.

Katz, Lilian G.: "Early Childhood Education as a Discipline," *Young Children,* vol. 26, pp. 82–89, December 1970.

"A study of the variables and their interaction in the field of early childhood can aid in analyzing problems, reviewing research and expanding our knowledge." This article presents a useful plan to assist in this analysis. Defines early childhood education, describes parameters and develops a matrix for early childhood education. Parameters are: characteristics of clients (children and parents), characteristics of teachers and other assisting adults, program organization (curriculum), philosophical orientation and historical factors,

parent power, administrative factors and sponsorship, length of program, and physical plant and climate (regional).

Kohlberg, Lawrence A.: "Early Education: A Cognitive-Developmental
View," *Child Development,* vol. 39, pp. 1013–1062, December 1968.
A perceptive review of cognitive-developmental theories (Dewey,
Piaget, Vygotsky, and Baldwin) and their implications for preschool
education. Intellectual stimulation strategies support the critical role
of play. He concludes that for cognitive growth, specific forms of
stimulation or content are subordinate to a *systematic* formulation
of activities traditionally associated with nursery schools, including
play, aesthetics, and social activities.

————, and R. S. Mayer: *Preschool Research and Preschool Educational
Objectives: A Critique and a Proposal,* Cambridge, Mass.: Harvard
University, 1970. Mimeographed.

La Crosse, E. Robert, Jr., et al.: *The First Six Years of Life: a Report on
Current Research and Educational Practice,* Cambridge, Mass.: Harvard Graduate School of Education, 1968.
A report on the Preschool Project, Laboratory of Human Development, Harvard Graduate School of Education.

Lavatelli, Celia Stendler (ed.): *Language Training in Early Childhood Education,* Urbana, Ill.: University of Illinois Press, 1971.
Papers present what appear to be promising practices in language
training derived from current "psycho-linguistic" thought. Donald
Moore offers a thorough survey of the literature. Part II deals with
training procedures, including a description of the Tucson method
of language teaching, the tutorial program in infant training, and
Courtney Cazden's notes from England and Wales. Part III contains
some useful evaluation measures.

National Education Association: Elementary-Kindergarten-Nursery Department, *Values in Early Childhood Education,* Washington, D.C.: EKNE,
NEA, 1965.
Implications of Piaget's work for early childhood education:
1 Importance of sensorimotor experience is stressed.
2 Language, especially that which relates to labeling, categorizing,
   and expressing, is intimately tied to developing greater facility in
   thinking.
3 New experiences are more readily assimilated when built on the
   familiar.
4 Repeated exposure to a thing or idea in different contexts contributes to the clarity and flexibility of a growing concept of the
   thing or idea.
5 Accelerating learning of abstract concepts without sufficient related direct experiences may result in symbols without meaning.

National Education Association, Research Division:
Kindergarten Education in Public Schools, 1967–1968. Research Report 1969–R6. Washington, D.C.: NEA, 1969.

Head Start Programs Operated by Public School Systems, 1966–1967. Research Report 1968–R3. Washington, D.C.: NEA, 1968.
Nursery School Education, 1966–1967. Research Report 1968–R6. Washington, D.C.: NEA, 1968.

National Society for the Study of Education: *Early Childhood Education,* 71st Yearbook, Part II, edited by Ira J. Gordon, Chicago: University of Chicago Press, 1972.

An authoritative summation of the state of the field including the following contributions: Irving Sigel, "Developmental Theory and Preschool Education"; Ira Gordon, "An Instructional Theory Approach to the Analysis of Selected Early Childhood Programs"; Nancy and Halbert Robinson, "A Cross-Cultural View of Early Education"; Edith Grotberg, "Institutional Responsibilities for Early Childhood Education"; and Robert Anderson and Harold Shane, "Implications of Early Childhood Education for Lifelong Learning," and others.

The Ontario Institute for Studies in Education: *Problems in the Teaching of Young Children,* edited by Andrew J. Biemiller, monograph series no. 9, Toronto: The Institute, 1970.

Report of a conference containing seven papers attempting to gain a perspective on the specific technology available to the preschool teacher. The "problems" concern direct teaching approaches aimed at fostering intellectual development as an added dimension to current less structured programs. Emphasis is given to disadvantaged children.

Painter, Genevieve: *Infant Education,* San Rafael, Calif.: Dimensions Publications, 1968.

Describes a study on the effect of a tutorial program on the intellectual development of disadvantaged children. Gives assessment procedures, full reviews of the literature, the rationale of the training program, logistics of tutoring in the home, and complete analysis of the data. See also G. Painter, Part V.

Robinson, Halbert B.: "A Summary of the Problem of Timing in Preschool Education," Supplement to the *IRCD Bulletin,* vol. III, no. 2A, 1966.

Considers long-range goals of early education, the stability of early learning, hazards in beginning too early or too late. Concludes that the very early years of childhood constitute the optimum time for initiating educational intervention, though what patterns one should encourage or how to go about it are not clear.

Rowe, Richard R.: *Early Education and Child Care,* Cambridge, Mass.: Massachusetts Early Education Project, Harvard University, 1971. (Mimeographed)

Programs designed to overcome deficits in poor children are found to be used increasingly, although most early childhood programs offer developmental care. Finds no evidence that one type is more effective than another. Quality care seems to be most highly related to the staff/child ratio and to the quality of the director.

Schaefer, Earl S.: "Learning from Each Other," *Childhood Education,* vol. 48, pp. 3–7, October 1971.
Sees the professional educator as "teacher who supports and supplements the role of the parent educator rather than supplants them" from birth through school years. Cites family-centered approaches here and abroad to support author's thesis.

———: "Need for Early and Continuing Education," in Victor Denenberg (ed.), *Education of the Infant and Young Child,* New York: Academic Press, 1970.

Scott, Myrtle, Susan J. Eklund, and James O. Miller: *An Analysis of Early Childhood Education Research and Development,* Urbana, Ill.: National Laboratory on Early Childhood Education, 1970.
A study to provide data from which planning of the early childhood education research and development work funded by Office of Education could be implemented. Following programs of the Bureau of Research of Office of Education are reviewed: National Laboratory on Early Childhood Education; the Research and Development Centers; the Regional Education Laboratories; regular Cooperative Research Projects funded at above $10,000 for fiscal year 1969. Major programs are described, visitations made, data analyzed. Goals and objectives of 77 programs and projects; implementation strategies, organizational factors, problems encountered; conclusions and implications; and references are listed.

Sears, Pauline S., and Edith M. Dowley: "Research on Teaching in the Nursery School," in N. L. Gage (ed.) *Handbook of Research on Teaching,* Chicago: Rand McNally, 1963, pp. 814–864.
History of objectives in nursery school teaching precedes a review of teaching methods. Studies cited deal with warmth, nurturance, giving attention; dominative and integrative behavior of teachers; active guidance of children; discipline techniques; frustration of the child by adults or environments; small-group training procedures; effects of nursery school attendance. Discussion of teaching materials and environment and the teacher's personality and characteristics follow.

Smilansky, Sarah: *The Effects of Sociodramatic Play on Disadvantaged Preschool Children,* New York: John Wiley, 1968.
Describes one of the methods believed to have high potential for the promotion of the culturally deprived child: sociodramatic play corrects lack of sequence in activities and conversation, and relates scattered experiences and isolated concepts, using them in a lifelike situation and converting them into new conceptual schemes. Seems to develop the ability of positive social interaction, enrich the child's language, and broaden concepts through the interaction with co-players, peers, and adults.

————: *Progress Report on a Program to Demonstrate Ways of Using a Year of Kindergarten to Promote Cognitive Abilities,* Jerusalem: Henrietta Szold Institute for Child and Youth Welfare, 1964.
A guided intellectual development program worked out for a group of Oriental kindergartners. Teachers were actively to prepare the children for first grade.

Spodek, Bernard: "What Are the Sources of Early Childhood Curriculum?" *Young Children,* vol. 26, pp. 48–58, October 1970.
Reviews psychological theory, testing procedures, content of later schooling, and children themselves as possible sources of curriculum. Concludes none of the above are adequate in themselves. Instead gives priority to the goals of early education: "personal autonomy based on reason."

Wann, Kenneth, and others: *Fostering Intellectual Development in Young Children,* New York: Teachers College Press, 1962.
An early research study directed toward stronger emphasis on intellectual development of preschoolers. Presents conclusions about the nature of intellectual development, the present experiences and needs of these children, and implications for curriculum and teaching methods.

Weber, Evelyn: *Early Childhood Education: Perspectives on Change,* Worthington, Ohio: Charles A. Jones Publishing Company, 1970.
First-hand observations of innovative programs spurred the author to place new developments into a meaningful framework and to recommend changes for early childhood education. Mentions current theoretical bases for programs; some of the constraints and constants that cannot be ignored when working with young children; and new directions required by society today. Chapter 1, "General Trends," is followed by "Forces Propelling Change," offering equivalent of a foundations course in early childhood education: philosophical bases, impact of child psychology, theories of learning, sociological impact, and the process of change—with a comprehensive bibliography attached. Describes programs including infants and toddlers, those for children from ages two to five, and for children in the primary grades. Concludes with a chapter on "Directions for Change" with specific challenges to early childhood education. Rational, balanced (affective + intellectual) approach to achieving a humanistic school for early childhood. Good for all levels of education.

White, Burton L., et al.: *Early Education: Diagnosis and Partial Prescription,* Cambridge, Mass.: Harvard University, 1970. (mimeographed)
A paper reporting on the Harvard Preschool Project, a large-scale study analyzing the elements in the early experience of able first-grade children which helped them to develop their competencies. Introduction offers excellent summary of the "state of the field."

PART III. THEORY AND THRUSTS

Below is a very small selection from the voluminous body of work in the areas of learning theories, children's competencies, and early childhood development. The titles listed indicate the position of major theories which have influenced the movements and major impetus in the field of early education.

Auleta, Michael S.: *Foundations of Early Childhood Education: Readings,* New York: Random House, 1969.
Readings treat historical, psychological, and sociological data; curriculum resources; and educational innovations.

Beard, Ruth M.: *An Outline of Piaget's Developmental Psychology for Students and Teachers,* New York: Basic Books, 1969.
Deals with the sensorimotor, preconceptual, intuitive, concrete operations, and formal operations periods. Includes a glossary of Piagetian terminology.

Bloom, Benjamin: *Stability and Change in Human Characteristics,* New York: John C. Wiley, 1964.
In an analysis of 1,000 longitudinal studies of growth, Bloom found that for each human trait there is a characteristic growth curve, and that half an individual's intellectual potential has been realized by age four. The environment, he says, will have maximum impact on a specific trait during that trait's period of most rapid growth. By the age of six, a child has developed as much as two-thirds of the intelligence he will have at maturity. At least one-third of the development at age eighteen has taken place prior to entrance into school.

Brearley, Molly, and Elizabeth Hitchfield: *A Guide to Reading Piaget,* New York: Schocken Books, 1966.
Presents a selection of Piaget's normative findings in these areas: number and spatial-geometric concepts, moral judgment, and development during infancy. Samples of children's response protocols for each content area exemplify Piaget's clinical-type assessment procedures.

Bronfenbrenner, Urie, et al.: *Two Worlds of Childhood: U.S. and U.S.S.R.,* New York: Russell Sage Foundation, 1970.
In contrasting the upbringing of children in the two countries, the author brings into focus the untenable position in which we place children from their earliest years. Chapter 5, "Principles and Possibilities" draws the implications from studies cited, followed by Chapter 6 in which needed action in classroom, school, family, neighborhood, and larger community are suggested.

Carmichael, Leonard: *Manual of Child Psychology,* Paul Mussen (ed.), 3d edition, New York: John Wiley, 1970, 2 vols.

A basic reference source which includes an extensive bibliography on infancy.

Erikson, Erik H. *Childhood and Society.* Revised edition. New York: W. W. Norton, 1964.
Describes the critical stages or "central themes" of emotional development through which the individual passes from infancy to adulthood. The first developmental task during infancy is to focus on the "sense of trust," necessary for a solid basis for all future relationships. The second developmental task is that of acquiring a "sense of autonomy," a sense of asserting one's self, a major task during preschool age as well as in late infancy.

Fowler, William: *Infant Stimulation and the Etiology of Cognitive Processes,* Toronto: Ontario Institute for Studies in Education, 1971.
Overview of problems and concepts related to stimulation in human development. Reviews major features and biases of various theories of child development. See also Fowler's "Concept Learning in Early Childhood," *Young Children,* vol. 21, pp. 81–91, November 1965.

Hartley, Ruth E., Lawrence K. Frank, and Robert M. Goldenson: *Understanding Children's Play,* New York: Columbia University Press, 1952.
"Helps to acquire insight into the child's emotional needs and the exigencies of his adjustment to life. . . . Provides a fuller understanding of the *significance* of children's play and offers valuable aids in fostering the development of productive, well-integrated human beings" (Preface).

Hartup, Willard W., and N. Smothergill (eds.): *The Young Child: Reviews of Research,* Washington, D.C.: NAEYC, 1967.
A source for supplementary information.

Herron, R. E., and Brian Sutton-Smith (eds.): *Child's Play,* New York: John Wiley, 1971.
Readings on play in its cognitive and noncognitive dimensions reporting findings, developmental and normative. Piaget and Sutton-Smith debate the function of play in the development of the child.

Hess, Robert D., and Virginia C. Shipman: "Maternal Attitudes Toward the School and the Role of the Pupil: Some Class Comparisons," in A. Harry Passow, *Developing Programs for the Educationally Handicapped,* New York: Teachers College Press, 1968, pp. 109–129.
Describes some of the significant aspects of the attitudes that mothers of young children hold toward public school and how they are reflected in the child's performance. The feeling of power or powerlessness was found to be particularly important. Suggests that parents be involved in school more meaningfully. See also R. Hess in Edith Grotberg (ed.), *Critical Issues in Research Related to Disadvantaged Children,* Educational Testing Service, 1969.

Hoffman, Martin L., and Lois W. Hoffman (eds.): *Review of Child Development Research,* New York: Russell Sage Foundation, vol. I, 1964; vol. II, 1967.

A useful compilation of significant work up to 1967, with many reviews from the field of early childhood education.

Hunt, J. McVicker: *Intelligence and Experience,* New York: Ronald Press, 1961.
A basic work which relates the rate of intellectual development to environment: The greater the variety of situations the child faces, the more likely he is to be able to cope with them; the more he has seen and heard, the more things he is interested in seeing and hearing. Sees the problem as one of finding out how to govern the encounters that children have with their environments to foster optimal intellectual development, what he calls "the problem of the match."

International Review of Education: vol. 16, 1970 (Special number), "Preschool Education: Aspects and Problems."

Isaacs, Susan: *Childhood and After: Some Essays and Clinical Studies* (1948), New York: Agathon Press, 1970.
A selection of the many articles written for the educational and clinical world by a renowned child psychologist and educator. Especially pertinent: "The Educational Value of the Nursery School," and "Essential Needs of Children" in the essay on "Children in Institutions."

Murphy, Lois B.: *The Widening World of Childhood,* New York: Basic Books, 1962.
When issued, this publication offered a fresh look at the child in today's culture. Especially helpful: Part 1, The New and the Strange; Part 3, Aspects of Mastery; Part 4, Coping and Development.

Piaget, Jean: *The Psychology of Intelligence,* Patterson, N.J.: Littlefield, Adams & Co., 1963.
A theoretical explanation of Piaget's ideas. Further readings (more comprehensible) describing Piaget's work:
Piaget, Jean: *Six Psychological Studies,* edited by David Elkind, New York: Random House, 1967.
Almy, Millie, et al.: *Young Children's Thinking,* see Part II for annotation.
Brearley, Molly, and Elizabeth Hitchfield: *A Guide to Reading Piaget,* see above for annotation.
Flavell, J. H.: *The Developmental Psychology of Jean Piaget,* Princeton, N.J.: Van Nostrand, 1963.
Furth, Hans G.: *Piaget for Teachers,* Englewood Cliffs, N.J.: Prentice-Hall, 1970.
Isaacs, Nathan: *The Growth of Understanding in the Young Child: A Brief Introduction to Piaget's Work,* London: Educational Supply Assn., 1961.
Piaget, Jean: *The Language and Thought of the Child,* New York: Appleton-Century-Crofts, 1963.
————, and Barbara Inhelder: *The Psychology of the Child,* New York: Basic Books, 1969.

Sigel, Irving E., and F. H. Hooper: *Logical Thinking in Children,* see below for annotation. All the above contribute insights about the thought processes of children: how they learn and the meanings they attribute to everyday phenomena. Piaget details the transitions from intuitive to logical thinking. He insists on the need for providing opportunities for direct experience and for recognizing the child's level of maturation and readiness for the experience.

Scott, John P.: *Early Experience and the Organization of Behavior,* Belmont, Calif.: Wadsworth, 1968.
Uses animals for experimentation to show the critical periods in development and especially early experience. Major emphasis is on the importance of socialization.

Sigel, Irving E., and F. H. Hooper: *Logical Thinking in Children,* New York: Holt, Rinehart and Winston, 1968.
A collection of studies and research reports on Piaget's theory of cognition: knowledge is not the description of reality, but the result of intervention between a child and his environment. Topics include child understanding of spatial concepts and number concepts, and the growth of logical structures.

Vygotsky, Lev S.: *Thought and Language,* edited and translated by Eugenia Hanfmann and Gertrude Vakar (1934), Cambridge, Mass.: The M.I.T. Press, 1962.
Reports on experimental studies of the interrelations of thought and language. Author reviews and analyzes Piaget's theory of language development and William Stern's theory in order to develop his own. Uses as a working hypothesis the relation between the education process and mental development. Finds that as the acquisition of language skills increases, so does the child's control of his own behavior. Comprehension of the physical and social environment increases as does the ability to make himself understood.

White, Robert W.: "Motivation Reconsidered: The Concept of Competence," *Psychological Review,* vol. 66, pp. 297–323, 1959.
"Effectance motivation" depends on the child confronting material that is congruent with his underlying skills so that he is able to succeed, and thus achieve the feeling of efficacy. The importance of a multitude of early experiences to provide the opportunity for skill development is stressed.

Yamamoto, Kaoru (ed.): *The Child and His Image: Self Concept in the Early Years,* Boston: Houghton Mifflin, 1972.
Seven specialists in early education and child psychology discuss the acquisition of feelings and attitudes about oneself, finding a place in the school setting as well as the home, and relationships with other people.

Zigler, Edward: "The Environmental Mystique: Training the Intellect as

the Development of the Child," *Childhood Education,* vol. 46, pp. 402–12, May 1970.
An analysis of selected research on emotional and motivational development indicating the need to attend to areas of affective behavior and the development of social competence.

PART IV. PRACTICES AND PROGRAMS

The state of the art of "research and development" in early childhood education is indicated in the titles listed below. Efforts to provide alternative educational programs, to evaluate large-scale projects, and to disseminate the most effective practices are described. It is evident that the new programs for 3- to 5-year-olds from low-income families must differ from traditional nursery school programs.

Appalachia Educational Laboratory, Inc.: *Appalachia Preschool Program: A Process,* First Year Report 1968–1969, Charleston, W. Va.: The Laboratory, 1970.
A home-oriented program which attempted to provide access to education for 3-, 4-, and 5-year-olds by means of television, radio, home visitation, mobile facilities, etc. Developed children's program, "Around the Bend."
————: *Evaluation Report: Early Childhood Education Program; 1969–1970 Field Test, Summary Report,* 1971.

Arizona Center for Early Childhood Education: *The Tucson Early Education Model,* Rev. Nov. 8, 1971. Tucson, Ariz.: The Center, University of Arizona, 1971.
A follow-up descriptive report for TEEM also described in the entry under Hughes, Marie M. Emphasizes the development of language competence, an intellectual base, a motivational base, and social skills. Uses a child-centered process curriculum.

Badger, Earladeen D.: *A Mothers' Training Program: Educational Intervention By Mothers of Disadvantaged Infants,* Urbana, Ill.: Institute for Research on Exceptional Children, 1969.
A program of instruction for poverty mothers in a parent and child center in Illinois devised to offer child-rearing practices and daily conduct of the household which would contribute to the intellectual growth of the child. See also E. Badger in *Children,* vol. 18, pp. 168–173, September–October 1971, a follow-up report indicating sucess in the above program.

Bereiter, Carl, and Siegfried Englemann: *Teaching the Disadvantaged Child in the Preschool,* Englewood Cliffs, N.J.: Prentice-Hall, 1966.
A structural pedagogy designed to accelerate children's rate of development (particularly language) with time the crucial element in the intervention process. Award highest priority to academic skill

development to eliminate language handicaps. Authors identify conceptual skills, arrange instructional materials and conditions to refine these skills in a compressed time period.

Bogatz, Gerry Ann, and Samuel Ball: *The Second Year of Sesame Street: a Continuing Evaluation,* 2 vols., Princeton, N.J.: Educational Testing Service, 1971.
A full descriptive report to the Children's Television Workshop which includes a summary of major findings in both first and second years.

Caldwell, Bettye M., and Julius B. Richmond: *The Children's Center—a Microcosmic Health, Education, and Welfare Unit,* Syracuse, N.Y.: State University of New York, 1967 (mimeographed).
A progress report submitted to The Children's Bureau, Department of Health, Education, and Welfare, chronicling the development of the Center. Gives operational details of the program and some evaluative data which relate to first-year results. Program for children 6 months to 5 years included: health program; educational program outlining useful assumptions about growth-fostering experiences; and the welfare program.

Cicirelli, Victor, et al.: *The Impact of Head Start: An Evaluation of the Effects of Head Start on Children's Cognitive and Affective Development,* vols. I and II, Bladensburg, Md.: Westinghouse Learning Corporation, 1969.

Cicirelli, Victor G., et al.: "The Impact of Head Start: a Reply to the Report Analysis," *Harvard Educational Review,* vol. 40, pp. 105–129, February 1970.
Reply to Smith and Bissell disputes both the criticisms of the Westinghouse methodology and the re-analysis of the data which authors say focuses only on the sub-samples and is based on very small numbers. Also, they say the re-analysis is based on a statistically erroneous procedure.

Datta, Lois-ellin: *A Report on Evaluation Studies of Project Head Start,* Washington, D.C.: Office of Child Development, Project Head Start, 1969.
Summaries of available data indicate the immediate impact of some Headstart programs, as well as the longer-range impact. References are good source of Headstart studies.

Demonstration and Research Center for Early Education (DARCEE): *A Manual for the Training of Family Day-Care Workers,* Paul R. Dokecki (Project Director), Nashville, Tenn.: John F. Kennedy Center for Research on Education and Human Development, George Peabody College for Teachers, 1971.
Presents a detailed sequence of actual training sessions along with rationale, objectives of the program; useful lists of references and materials; and a glossary.

Deutsch, Martin, and L. S. Goldstein: *An Evaluation of the Effectiveness of an Enriching Curriculum in Overcoming the Consequences of Environmental Deprivation,* New York: New York University, Institute for Developmental Studies, 1965–1968.

A series of reports of the Early Childhood Project, New York City. See also, New York University, Institute for Developmental Studies, *Progress Report, August 1967–February 1968: Research Program in Early Childhood Education,* and Deutsch and Associates, *The Disadvantaged Child,* New York: Basic Books, 1967.

Durham Education Improvement Program: *Educational Intervention in Early Childhood,* Final Report, Robert L. Spaulding, editor and director, 3 vols., Durham, N.C.: EIP, 1970.

"A report of a five-year longitudinal study of the effects of early educational intervention in the lives of disadvantaged children in Durham, N.C." A Ford Foundation project. "Vol. I describes the original proposal, the research strategies employed, the intervention rationale, the curricular programs developed, the characteristics of the children and their families, and the results of the overall program of educational intervention." Vol. II contains appendices. Vol. III consists of abstracts of special studies conducted by investigators in these areas: behavior modification, learning studies, classroom learning, parent-child studies, EIP youth program, infant development, test evaluation, social relations, cognitive characteristics.

Educational Testing Service: *Soviet Preschool Education, vol. II: Teacher's Commentary,* Henry Chauncey (ed.), New York: Holt, Rinehart and Winston, 1969.

Communicates in considerable detail the ways and means of education for children two months through seven years, including the guiding philosophies. Shows that the Soviets teach everything as early as they can, with an emphasis on precocity linked to "intentional environmentalism." This manual is used as the basic text for training of personnel. Spells out what is to be said and done from hour to hour with special emphasis on the development of morality and collectivism as well as subject matter and self-reliance. Much cross-age helping indicated.

vol. I: Program of Instruction. (not available for annotation)

Elkind, David: "Preschool Education: Enrichment or Instruction?" *Childhood Education,* vol. 45, pp. 321–328, 1969.

Clarifies the conflicting issues, sketching briefly the major components of the two value systems. Lists precautions needed, but does not have an answer to the question cited in title.

ERIC Clearinghouse on Early Childhood Education: *Head Start Curriculum Models: A Reference List,* Urbana, Ill.: ERIC, 1970 (Mimeographed).

A list of eleven different curriculum models citing many articles, curriculum aids, books, progress reports, and other writings relating to each model.

————: *Review of Research 1965 to 1969 of Project Head Start,* Urbana, Ill.: ERIC, 1971.
Categories discussed: sub-population characteristics, demonstration programs, teacher characteristics, parent participation, community relations.

Evans, Ellis D. *Contemporary Influences in Early Childhood Education.* New York: Holt, Rinehart and Winston, Inc., 1971.
Deals with broad educational strategies applicable to children ages three to six. Attempts to distill the conceptual bases of early education strategies in order to clarify their distinctive and common features. Limited to "formal" programs rather than "day care." Written from a research point of view. Comprehensive treatment, with extensive bibliographies following each section. The Montessori Method; Project Head Start and Follow Through; Structural Pedagogy for Language Development; Behavior Analysis Procedures; Piagetian Influences; the British Infant School Movement, and others are fully treated with research on each method cited if it is available.

Frost, Joe L. (ed.): *Early Childhood Education Rediscovered: Readings,* New York: Holt, Rinehart and Winston, 1968.
Puts issues in proper perspective:

Part 1   "Do Young Children Need Preschools?" And if so, what should they provide?
Part 2   "The Rediscovery of Montessori"
Part 3   "The Rediscovery of Piaget"
Part 4   "Cognitive Development in Young Children" with selections from J. McVicker Hunt, Lawrence Kohlberg, and others.
Part 5   "The Promise of Head Start"
Part 6   "Cognitive and Affective Bases for Learning to Learn"
Part 7   "Developing Literacy in Young Children"
Part 8   "What Should Be Taught in the Preschool?"
Part 9   "Planning for Early Childhood Education"

Gordon, Ira J.: *Early Child Stimulation Through Parent Education,* Final report to the Children's Bureau, U.S. HEW, Gainesville, Fla.: University of Florida, 1969 (Mimeographed).
Complete report covering project and findings.

Gray, Susan, and others: *Before First Grade: The Early Training Project for Culturally Disadvantaged Children,* New York: Teachers College Press, 1966.
The authors try to identify specific needs of the children and to develop lesson plans and teaching procedures to meet them. The book describes techniques, materials, and day-by-day activities adapted to abilities and interests of each child. A research-demonstration study.

Gray, Susan W., and R. A. Klaus: *The Early Training Project: A Seventh*

Year Report, Nashville, Tenn.: George Peabody College for Teachers, 1969.

Hawkins, Frances P.: *The Logic of Action, From a Teacher's Notebook,* Boulder, Colo.: Elementary Science Advisory Center, University of Colorado, 1969.
An illustrated record of the development of 4-year-old deaf children in the skillful hands of an experienced teacher who brought variety and enrichment to them with materials of early science. Shows that, given a rich environment, with open-ended "raw" materials, children can and do take part in choosing their own learning tasks, and learn well. A fascinating story, thoughtfully conceived, clearly told.

Head Start Test Collection: *Annotated Bibliographies on Language Development Tests, School Readiness Measures, Measures of Social Skills, Self-Concept Measures, and Tests for Spanish-Speaking Children,* Princeton, N.J.: Educational Testing Service, 1971.

High/Scope Educational Research Foundation, Ypsilanti, Mich.: The Foundation, 1970.
A brochure describing a newly formed foundation which evolved out of the Ypsilanti Perry Preschool Project. Established to study the effects and promote the development of a cognitively oriented curriculum and provide services for projects in infant education, Planned Variation Head Start, Follow Through, and parent-child center development.

Hoepfner, Ralph, Carolyn Stern, and Susan G. Nummedal (eds.): *CSE-ECRC Preschool/Kindergarten Test Evaluation.* Los Angeles: UCLA Center for the Study of Evaluation and the Early Childhood Research Center, 1971.
Evaluates about 120 preschool and kindergarten level tests, presenting the data in tables with ratings of "good," "fair," or "poor," based on the authors' "Taxonomy of Goals of Preschool-Kindergarten Education." The taxonomy covers affective, intellectual, psychomotor, and subject domains.

Hughes, Marie M., and others: *The Tucson Early Education Model,* 1968, Microfiche ED 033 753.
Uses a language-based curriculum, classroom techniques, and staffing patterns developed specifically for Mexican-American children.

Karnes, Merle B., et al.: "An Approach for Working with Mothers of Disadvantaged Preschool Children," *Merrill-Palmer Quarterly of Behavior and Development,* vol. 14, pp. 174–184, 1968.

———: *Research and Development Program on Preschool Disadvantaged Children,* 3 vols., final report, Washington, D.C.: USOE, 1969. ED 036663–ED 036665.

Kellogg, Elizabeth T., and D. M. Hill: *After Head Start . . . What Then? Following Through With Young Children,* Washington, D.C.: National Association for the Education of Young Children, 1969.

The pictorial story of Boulder, Colorado's Follow Through program which used the Bank Street College of Education approach for staff development and consultation. A two-week lesson is photographed in detail. The experiential approach to learning is portrayed by the camera moving back and forth among Headstarters and Follow Through kindergarteners and first-graders.

Kirschner Associates, Inc.: *A National Survey of the Impacts of Head Start Centers on Community Institutions,* Washington, D.C.: U.S. Project Head Start, 1970.
Found that Headstart did effect changes in local educational and health institutions in all the communities studied. (Comparison communities did not evidence such changes.) Changes: concern with the needs and problems of the poor and of minorities; revision of curricula, schedules, approaches, services, etc.; increased involvement of the public, including the poor, in positions of influence, changed employment criteria so that neighborhood people occupy important paraprofessional positions.

Lane, Mary B.: *Educational and Mental Health Consequences of a Nursery School Program in a Cross Cultural Setting,* San Francisco: San Francisco State College, n.d. (Mimeographed).
"The two- to five-year-old acquires his most significant learnings through the process of identification. . . . Emphasis will be consciously placed upon a kind of adult response that is consistently trustful and trusting" (p. 4).

Lane, Mary B., et al.: *Nurseries in Cross-Cultural Education,* San Francisco: San Francisco State College, School of Education, 1971.
Final report of a five-year project with an interdisciplinary approach to a family-oriented, cross-cultural nursery program. Theoretical orientation and practical steps taken in implementation are clearly spelled out. Appendix includes testing instruments and rating scales.

Levenstein, Phyllis: "Cognitive Growth in Preschoolers Through Verbal Interaction with Mothers," *American Journal of Orthopsychiatry,* vol. 40, pp. 426–432, April 1970.
Over a seven-month period of home sessions stimulating verbal interaction between mother and child with use of toys and books, a 17 point IQ gain in the child population (low-income preschoolers) was found.

Maccoby, Eleanor E., and Miriam Zellner: *Experiments in Primary Education: Aspects of Project Follow-Through,* New York: Harcourt Brace Jovanovich, 1970.
Compares alternative approaches to compensatory education, discussing concomitant issues when they are translated into everyday classroom practice. Analyzes psychological assumptions, educational philosophies, and teaching methods underlying the programs. Discusses problems arising from such experimental programs. Among programs mentioned are the EDC approach (David Armington); E-B

or Engelmann-Becker Program; Behavior Analysis Program (Donald Bushell); Bank Street Program (Gilkeson and Zimiles); the Florida Project (Ira Gordon); instructional games; Tucson Early Education Model (M. Hughes); The Responsive Model (Nimnicht); Resnick's Primary Education Project; and the cognitively oriented approach (David Weikart). Views about learning: what it is, how it occurs, and what should be learned, are analyzed in light of these programs.

Miller, Louise, et al.: *Experimental Variation of Head Start Curricula: A Comparison of Current Approaches,* Progress Report no. 5, Nov. 1, 1969–Jan. 31, 1970. Louisville, Ky.: University of Louisville, 1970.
Reports a two-year study in which four quite different programs were compared: Bereiter-Engelmann, DARCEE (structured cognitive), Montessori, and traditional. Found they differ with respect to behavior of both teachers and children and had significantly different effects on children with respect to variables measured.

New York University, Institute for Developmental Studies: *Interim Progress Report to Ford Foundation,* Part I, New York: The Institute, 1967.
A mimeographed report, the first part of which gives detailed description of curriculum, materials, activities, room arrangements, etc. for the pre-kindergarten and kindergarten program designed for environmentally disadvantaged children. See also, Deutsch, Martin and L. S. Goldstein listed above.

Nimnicht, Glen, et al.: *The New Nursery School, Greeley, Colorado.* Book and pamphlets for teachers, New York: General Learning Corporation, Early Learning Division, 1969.
Description of a cognitively oriented program using autotelic responsive environment with materials specifically developed for it.

Ostrovsky, Everett S.: *Father to the Child: Case Studies of the Experiences of a Male Teacher with Young Children,* New York: G. P. Putnam's Sons, 1959.
An early study demonstrating the need for the adult made presence in the classrooms of the young.

Prescott, Elizabeth, and others: *Group Day Care as a Child-Rearing Environment: An Observational Study of Day Care Program,* Pasadena, Calif.: Pacific Oaks College, 1967. (ERIC ED 024 453)
Describes fully day-care programs (for preschoolers) indicating factors predictive of differences in programs and evaluating the effectiveness of day care centers. Fifty Los Angeles day-care center teachers were observed for four 20-minute periods daily for ten days. Considers possibilities for interventions which might change certain aspects of the child-rearing environment for the better.

Resnick, Lauren B.: *Design of an Early Learning Curriculum,* Working Paper 16, Learning Research and Development Center, Pittsburgh: University of Pittsburgh, December 1969.

Presents a rationale for curriculum development in the preschool years and outlines a methodology for curriculum design in general. General Learning Corporation was earmarked to design a computer-based information management system to aid in individualization. Included (1) orienting and attending skills, (2) perceptual and motor skills, (3) conceptual and linguistic skills. Used component analyses to identify prerequisite behaviors and systematically build learning objectives. Appendix A: "Skills for Inclusion in an Early Learning Curriculum."

Shapiro, E., and Barbara Biber: *The Developmental-Interaction Approach to the Education of Young Children,* From Final Report of Follow Through Research Program, 1968–1969, New York: Bank Street College of Education, 1969.

Shaw, Jean W., and Maxine Schoggen: *Children Learning: Samples of Everyday Life of Children at Home,* Nashville, Tenn.: George Peabody College for Teachers, Demonstration and Research Center for Early Education, 1969.
A resource book to be used as supplementary material for training adults who work with children.

Sigel, Irving E.: "Developmental Considerations of the Nursery School Experience," in *Concepts of Development in Early Childhood Education,* Peter B. Neubauer (ed.) Springfield, Ill.: Charles C Thomas, 1965, pp. 84–111.

Smith, Marshall S., and J. S. Bissell: "Report Analysis: The Impact of Head Start," *Harvard Educational Review,* vol. 40, pp. 51–104, February 1970.
Present a history of Headstart and of the national evaluation by the Westinghouse Learning Corporation and Ohio University. The reanalysis suggests contrary findings: some full-year Headstart centers were effective, particularly with black children in urban areas. The authors raise serious questions about the Westinghouse sampling procedures and focus on the relationship between program evaluation and public policy. See Cicirelli et al. for a reply.

Southwest Educational Development Laboratory: *An Early Childhood Education Model—a Bilingual Approach,* by Shari Nedler, Austin, Tex.: The Laboratory, n.d., (Mimeographed).
Focuses on the special learning problems of Mexican-American children and emphasizes the development of bilingual competence. Intervention activities: all children receive instruction in Spanish, then English, in same lessons at child's own pace; time with a responsive adult; field trips; manipulative objects; play and exploratory activities. Introduces filmstrip: "Bridging the Gap."

————: *Parent Participation in Preschool Day Care,* by David B. Hoffman et al. Atlanta, Ga.: The Laboratory, 1971.

Overview of principles and methods for parent involvement, focused on the disadvantaged. Last section includes a review of successful programs followed by sample questionnaires, program abstracts, and names and addresses of parent participation programs.

Spaulding, Robert L.: See Durham Education Improvement Program.

U.S. Office of Child Development: *Review of Research 1965 to 1969 of Project Head Start,* Edith H. Grotberg, Coordinator of Research, Washington, D.C.: USOCD, 1969.
Considers sub-population characteristics in language: cognitive, intellectual, and achievement behavior; social-emotional behavior and self-concept. Demonstration programs, teacher characteristics, parent participation, community relations are included.

U.S. Office of Education: *Preschool Program in Compensatory Education,* Washington, D.C.: U.S. Government Printing Office, 1969. 6 vols., (It Works Series 1).
Six successful programs are described: Preschool Program, Fresno, Calif.; Infant Education Research Project, Washington, D.C.; Early Childhood Project, New York City; Perry Preschool Project, Ypsilanti, Mich.; Diagnostically Based Curriculum, Bloomington, Ind., and Academic Preschool, Champaign, Ill.

Weaver, Kitty: *Lenin's Grandchildren: Preschool Education in the Soviet Union,* New York: Simon and Schuster, 1971.
Describes current Russian preschool education, which the author feels is designed to meet the needs of the whole child. Based on 1967 and 1969 visits and interviews without interpreters. Emphasis seen as character development.

Weikart, David P., Constance K. Kamii, and Norma Radin: *Perry Preschool Project Progress Report,* Ypsilanti, Mich.: Ypsilanti Public Schools, 1964 (mimeographed).
Reports on a study designed to learn the potential of preschool intervention for overcoming the effects of poverty on later school achievement. Describes an offshoot, the Ypsilanti Home Teaching Project. For current information, see *High/Scope Educational Research Foundation.*

Weikart, David (ed.): *Preschool Intervention: Report on the Perry Preschool Project,* Ann Arbor, Mich.: Campus Publishers, 1967.
Describes a program which endeavors to build up in disadvantaged 4-year-olds competencies in physical knowledge, logical knowledge, and the ability to represent, á la Piaget.

Weikart, David P., et al.: *Ypsilanti-Carnegie Infant Education Project Progress Report,* Ypsilanti, Mich.: Department of Research and Development, Ypsilanti Public Schools, 1969.
Intensive nursery school program included work with parents to encourage them to support the child's education.

PART V. INFORMATIVE TEXTS AND
PRACTICAL PAMPHLETS

It is obvious that we are not going to "throw out the baby with the bath." Many of the texts listed below are the familiar "classic" helps to the professionals in the field of early childhood education. Some are new, with differing program priorities, gleaned from many of the research and development projects cited in previous pages. But all will prove useful to the practitioner seeking specific answers to specific problems arising in day-to-day contact with the very young child. Annotations have been omitted for the most part.

BOOKS

Allen of Hurtwood, Lady: *Planning for Play*, Cambridge, Mass.: The MIT Press, 1968.
Fully illustrated plans and projects with practical suggestions and even prices for developing adventure playgrounds, supervised play parks, play groups, clubs, spaces for children to use their imaginations and energies.

Baker, Katherine Read, and Xenia F. Fane: *Understanding and Guiding Young Children*, Englewood Cliffs, N.J.: Prentice-Hall, 1970.

Barnouw, Elsa, and Arthur Swan: *Adventures with Children in Nursery School and Kindergarten*, New York: Agathon Press, 1970.

Beyer, Evelyn: *Teaching Young Children*, New York: Pegasus, 1968.

Brearley, Molly, et al.: *The Teaching of Young Children: Some Applications of Piaget's Learning Theory*, New York: Schocken Books, 1970.

Christianson, Helen, and others: *The Nursery School: Adventure in Living and Learning*, Boston: Houghton Mifflin, 1961.

Dittman, Laura L. (ed.): *Early Child Care: The New Perspectives*, New York: Atherton Press, 1968.

Foster, Josephine, and Neith E. Headley: *Education in the Kindergarten*, 4th ed., New York: American Book, 1966.

Hess, Robert D., and Doreen J. Croft: *Teachers of Young Children*, Boston: Houghton Mifflin, 1972.

Hymes, James L., Jr.: *Teaching the Child Under Six*, Columbus, Ohio: Charles E. Merrill, 1968.

King, Edith W., and August Kerber: *The Sociology of Early Childhood Education*, New York: American Book, 1968.

Landreth, Catherine: *Early Childhood Behavior and Learning*, 2d ed., New York: Knopf, 1967.

Leeper, Sarah H., et al.: *Good Schools for Young Children: A Guide for Working with Three-, Four-, and Five-Year Old Children*, 2d edition, New York: Macmillan, 1968.

Montessori, Maria: *The Montessori Method* (1909), New York: Schocken Books, 1961.
> The basic text on the subject. Also see the following:

Montessori, Maria. *Education for a New World,* Wheaton, Ill.: Theo-sophical Press, 1959.

————: *Spontaneous Activity in Education,* New York: Schocken Books, 1965.

NAEYC. *Montessori in Perspective.* Washington, D.C.: The Association, 1966.

Rambusch, Nancy: *Learning How to Learn: An American Approach to Montessori,* Baltimore: Helicon Press, 1962.

Standing, E. M.: *The Montessori Revolution in Education* (1962), New York: Schocken Books, 1966.

Painter, Genevieve: *Teach Your Baby,* New York: Simon & Schuster, 1970.
> An adaptation made for parents who serve as teachers in a tutorial language program. Mothers are also trained to lead other mothers in study-group discussions on child-rearing practices.

Pitcher, Evelyn, and others: *Helping Young Children Learn,* Columbus, Ohio: Charles E. Merrill, 1966.

Read, Katherine H.: *The Nursery School, A Human Relations Laboratory,* 5th ed., Philadelphia: W. B. Saunders, 1971.

Sharp, Evelyn: *Thinking Is Child's Play,* New York: E. P. Dutton, 1969.
> Describes the way preschool children acquire the ability to reason, and lists forty mind-sharpening games, patterned after Piaget, which parents can play with their youngsters to speed along the process.

Taylor, Katherine W.: *Parents and Children Learn Together,* New York: Teachers College Press, 1968.

Todd, Vivian E., and Helen Hefferman: *The Years Before School: Guiding Pre-School Children,* New York: Macmillan, 1964.

PAMPHLETS

Association for Childhood Education International: *Kindergarten Portfolio,* Washington, D.C.: The Association, 1970.
> Fourteen leaflets to answer issues and questions raised by kindergarten teachers, administrators, parents, and concerned adults—by experts in the field.

————: *A Lap to Sit On ... And Much More,* Reprints from *Childhood Education,* Washington, D.C.: The Association, 1971.
> First of a series, "Helps for Day Care Workers," designed to guide adults who work with children at preschool and elementary level.

————: *Nursery School Portfolio,* Washington, D.C.: The Association, 1969.
> A packet of sixteen brief but practical leaflets.

Bacmeister, Rhoda W.: *Teachers for Young Children—The Person and the*

Skills, New York: Early Childhood Education Council of New York, 1970.
Outlines briefly basic personal qualities needed as well as teaching skills and competencies.

Bouchard, R. A., and B. Mackler: *A Prekindergarten Program for Four-Year-Olds, with a Review of Literature on Preschool Education,* New York: The Center for Urban Education, 1967.

California, State Department of Education: *Curriculum Guide for Compensatory Preschool Educational Programs,* Sacramento: The Department, 1970.

Haase, R. W.: *Designing the Child Development Center,* Washington, D.C.: U.S. Government Printing Office, 1968.

Haberman, Martin, and Blanche Persky (eds.): *Preliminary Report of the Ad Hoc Joint Committee on the Preparation of Nursery and Kindergarten Teachers,* Washington, D.C.: NEA, National Commission on Teacher Education and Professional Standards, 1970.
Addresses itself to the following: Why do we need personnel for early childhood education programs? How can we insure program quality and still meet the shortage of personnel? What are the alternative approaches for evaluating competence?

Heath, D. H.: "The Education of Young Children: At the Crossroads?" *Young Children,* vol. 25, pp. 75–84, December 1969.

Howard, Norma K. (comp.): *Day Care: an Annotated Bibliography,* Urbana, Ill.: Educational Resources Information Center, Clearinghouse on Early Childhood Education, 1971.

Leeper, Sarah H.: *Nursery School and Kindergarten,* Washington, D.C.: National Education Association, 1968.
(What Research Says to the Teacher, no. 22)

Murphy, Lois B., and Ethel M. Leeper: *Caring for Children,* Washington, D.C.: U.S. Office of Child Development, 1970, 5 vols.
A series of brief, illustrated pamphlets offering guidelines for child care center personnel from the Bureau of Headstart and Early Childhood: No. 1, The Ways Children Learn; No. 2, More Than a Teacher; No. 3, Preparing for Change; No. 4, Away from Bedlam; and No. 5, The Vulnerable Child.

National Association for the Education of Young Children: *The Cognitively Oriented Curriculum, A Framework for Preschool Teachers,* Washington, D.C.: The Association, 1970.
The Association has also issued: *Curriculum Is What Happens: Planning is the Key,* 1970; *Play and Playgrounds,* 1970; *Some Ways of Distinguishing a Good Nursery School or Center for Young Children,* 1965; and *What Does the Nursery School Teacher Teach?* 1965.

Newman, Sylvia: *Guidelines to Parent-Teacher Cooperation in Early Childhood Education,* Brooklyn, N.Y.: Book-Lab, Inc., 1971.

A practical "how-to" booklet with suggestions for a workshop program for parents of preschoolers.

Saylor, Mary Lou: *Parents: Active Partners in Education,* Washington, D.C.: American Association of Elementary-Kindergarten-Nursery Educators, NEA, 1971.
Offers specific guidelines for implementing a program in home-school cooperation, dealing with both parent and teacher anxieties. Shows the need for teachers to set the stage and follow through.

Scottish Department of Health and Social Security: *Our Young Children,* London: Her Majesty's Stationery Office, 1969.
Profusely illustrated brochure describes the child's basic needs which are normally satisfied in the home and how these may be met when children of several families are brought together in private homes or nursery groups.

Spodek, Bernard (ed.): *Preparing Teachers of Disadvantaged Young Children,* Washington, D.C.: National Association for the Education of Young Children, 1966.

U.S. Office of Education: *Educating Children in Nursery Schools and Kindergartens,* Washington, D.C.: U.S. Government Printing Office, 1964.

Weikart, David P., et al.: *The Cognitively Oriented Curriculum: a Framework for Preschool Teachers,* Urbana, Illinois: University of Illinois Press, 1971.
Same as National Association for the Education of Young Children publication.

Wylie, Joanne (ed.): *A Creative Guide for Preschool Teachers,* Wayne, N.J.: Western Publishing Company, 1966.
"Goals, activities, and suggested materials for an organized program" (subtitle).

PERIODICALS

Childhood Education, Washington, D.C. Association for Childhood Education International, Annual Membership $12 includes *Childhood Education.*
Published monthly October through May, official journal of ACEI.

Children Today, Washington, D.C.: Office of Child Development, Children's Bureau. $2.
Published six times annually, an interdisciplinary journal of the professions serving children.

ERIC/ECE Newsletter, Urbana, Ill.: ERIC Clearinghouse on Early Childhood Education. Free.
Monthly, September through June.

Head Start Newsletter, Washington, D.C.: Project Head Start, Office of Child Development. Free.
Published monthly.

International Journal of Early Childhood, Oslo, Norway: Organisation Mondiale pour L'education Presecolier, $3.50/yr.
Published semi-annually.

PEN, the Preschool Education Newsletter, New York: Multi Media Education, Inc., $6/yr.
Monthly, seven times/yr., reports of innovation and experimentation from university laboratory schools, private preschools, and public preschool/day care centers.

Report on Preschool Education, Washington, D.C.: Capitol Publications, Inc., $40/yr.
A biweekly news service on federal programs for early childhood development.

ORGANIZATIONS SERVING YOUNG CHILDREN

American Association of Elementary-Kindergarten-Nursery Education, NEA
1201 – 16th Street, N.W.
Washington, D.C. 20036

Association for Childhood Education International
3615 Wisconsin Avenue, N.W.
Washington, D.C. 20016

Association for Supervision and Curriculum Development, NEA
1201 – 16th Street, N.W.
Washington, D.C. 20036

Child Study Association of America
9 East 89th Street
New York, N.Y. 10028

Day Care and Child Development Council of America, Inc.
1426 H Street, N.W.
Washington, D.C. 20005

Demonstration and Research Center for Early Education (DARCEE)
Peabody College, Box 151
Nashville, Tenn. 37203

National Association for the Education of Young Children
1834 Connecticut Avenue, N.W.
Washington, D.C. 20009

National Laboratory on Early Childhood Education
805 West Pennsylvania Avenue
Urbana, Ill. 61801

INDEX